THE MANAGERIAL REVOLUTION

"I come now to the last branch of my charge: that I teach princes villainy, and how to enslave. If any man will read over my book...with impartiality and ordinary charity, he will easily perceive that it is not my intention to recommend that government or those men there described to the world, much less to teach men how to trample upon good men, and all that is sacred and venerable upon earth, laws, religion, honesty, and what not. If I have been a little too punctual in describing these monsters in all their lineaments and colours, I hope mankind will know them, the better to avoid them, my treatise being both a *satire* against them, and a true *character* of them..."

NICCOLO MACHIAVELLI,
from a Letter to a Friend.

THE MANAGERIAL REVOLUTION

WHAT IS HAPPENING IN THE WORLD

JAMES BURNHAM

GREENWOOD PRESS, PUBLISHERS
WESTPORT, CONNECTICUT

The Library of Congress has catalogued this publication as follows:

Library of Congress Cataloging in Publication Data

Burnham, James, 1905–
   The managerial revolution.

   1. World politics--20th century. 2. Social
problems. 3. Capitalism. 4. Socialism. I. Title.
[JC252.B8 1972]   330.15   71-138102
ISBN 0-8371-5678-5

Originally published in 1941 by the John Day Company, Inc., New York

Reprinted with the permission of the John Day Company, Inc.

Reprinted in 1972 by Greenwood Press
A division of Congressional Information Service
88 Post Road West, Westport, Connecticut 06881

Library of Congress Catalog Card Number 71-138102

ISBN 0-8371-5678-5

Printed in the United States of America

P

CONTENTS

THE MANAGERIAL REVOLUTION

I

THE PROBLEM

DURING THE course of the second world war, which began on September 1, 1939, growing numbers of persons came to the conclusion that this war could not be adequately understood in the usual military and diplomatic terms. Of course, each participant in every big war is careful to explain that it fights, not for any vulgar purpose of mere conquest, but for liberty, justice, God, and the future of mankind. The second world war is no exception to this general rule which seems to express a deep need of men's moral nature when confronted with the task of mutual slaughter. Nevertheless, with all allowances for the general rule, there still remains, on the part of trained and intelligent as well as casual observers, the conviction that this war is not an ordinary war.

The difference has been stated by some in calling the war a "revolution"; more particularly, a "social revolution." For example, the well-known writer, Quincy Howe, in his radio commentaries insisted time after time on such an interpretation. Germany, he kept repeating, is not merely sending a remarkably organized military machine across its borders. Her military machine is the carrier of a social revolution which is transforming the social system on the European continent. The same point was made in numerous dispatches from Otto Tolischus after his expulsion from Germany, where he had been stationed for many years as chief correspondent of the New York *Times*. I mention these two men not because their opinion was exceptional but rather because they conspicuously and consistently upheld a view which has come to be shared by so many others.

However, when we examine what such observers have said and written, we discover that, though they have been firm in their insistence that the second world war is a social revolution, they have been by no means clear in describing what kind of revolution it is, what it consists of, where it is leading, what type of society will emerge from it.

We must be careful not to permit historical judgment to be distorted by the staggering emotional impact of the war itself. If a major social revolution is now in fact occurring, the war is subordinate to the revolution, not the other way around. The war in the final analysis—and future wars—is an episode in the revolution. We cannot understand the revolution by restricting our analysis to the war; we must understand the war as a phase in the development of the revolution.

Moreover, the role of Germany in the revolution, if it is a revolution, should not be exaggerated. The modern world is interlocked by myriad technological, economic, and cultural chains. The social forces which have been dramatically operative within Germany have not stopped at the Reich's national boundaries. If they came to so startling a head in Germany, this does not mean that they have not been driving steadily beneath the surface—and not so far beneath—in other nations, in all other nations for that matter. For us who live in the United States, it is the United States that is our most natural first interest. The outworn fallacies of the belief in the military isolation of the United States from the rest of the world are not one tenth so grave as the fallacies of the belief in our social isolation.

*   *
*

It is by no means obvious what we mean when we speak of a "social revolution," especially when we try to distinguish a social revolution from a merely "military" or "political" revolution. Several conflicting definitions have been attempted, as a rule accompanying special and conflicting theories of history, of which the definitions are a part. It seems, however, possible to describe the chief constituents of what can intelligibly be meant by a "social revolution" without committing ourselves in advance to any special theory. These chief constituents seem to be three:

1. There takes place a drastic change in the most important social (economic and political) institutions. The system of property relations, the forms under which economic production is carried on, the legal structure, the type of political organization and regime, are all so sharply altered that we feel compelled to call them different in kind, not merely modified in degree. Medieval (feudal) property relations, modes of economic production, law, political organization are all replaced by modern (bourgeois or capitalist) property relations, modes of production, law, and political organization. During the course of the revolution it often happens that the old institutions are quite literally smashed to pieces, with new institutions developing to perform analogous functions in the new society.

2. Along with the changes in social institutions there go more or less parallel changes in cultural institutions and in the dominant beliefs which men hold about man's place in the world and the universe. This cultural shift is plainly seen in the transition from feudal to modern capitalist society, both in the reorganization of the form and place of such institutions as the Church and the schools, and in the complete alteration of the general view of the world, of life, and of man which took place during the Renaissance.

3. Finally, we observe a change in the group of men which holds the top positions, which controls the greater part of power and privilege in society. To the social dominance of feudal

lords, with their vassals and fiefs, succeeds the social dominance of industrialists and bankers, with their monetary wealth, their factories and wage-workers.

In this conception there is a certain arbitrariness. The fact is that social and cultural institutions, beliefs, and relationships of social power always change, are subject to a continuous modification. It is impossible to draw an exact temporal line dividing one type of society from another. What is important is not so much the fact of change, which is always present in history, as the *rate* of change. In some periods the rate of social change is far more rapid than in others. Whatever one's professed theory of history, it can hardly be denied that the rate of change of social institutions, beliefs, and relative power of various social groups was incomparably higher in, say, the two centuries from 1400 to 1600 than in the six centuries preceding 1400; that, indeed, there was a much greater total change in those two centuries than there had been during the six centuries from 800 to 1400. What we seem to mean by a social revolution is identical with such a period of maximum rate of change. We all recognize the society that prevailed before such a period as a different type from that which is consolidated after it. Historians differ widely about when the "modern era" began, but they all unite in making a sharp distinction between medieval and modern society.

To say that a social revolution is occurring at the present time is, then, equivalent to saying that the present is a period characterized by a very rapid rate of social change, that it is a period of *transition* from one type of society—that type which has prevailed from, roughly, the fifteenth century to the early part of the twentieth—to a new and different type of society. For centuries, men's activities are worked out within a given, more or less stable, framework of social and cultural institutions; changes take place, but not to such an extent as to alter the basic framework. Occasionally, in human history, the changes take place so rapidly and are so drastic in extent that the framework itself is shattered and a new one takes its place.

The problem of this book is as follows: I am going to assume the general conception of a social revolution which I have just briefly stated. I am going to assume further (though not without evidence to back up this assumption) that the present is in fact a period of social revolution, of transition from one type of society to another. With the help of these assumptions, I shall present a theory—which I call "the theory of the managerial revolution"—which is able to explain this transition and to predict the type of society in which the transition will eventuate. To present this theory is the problem, and the *only* problem, of this book.

I do not wish to pretend that this theory is a startling and personal innovation. On the contrary. When, during the past years, I have presented it in lectures or conversation, I am generally told, "Why, that is just what I have been thinking lately," or, "That is what I was telling so-and-so only a few days ago." This reaction has seemed to me a reason not for dropping the theory as trivial or banal but rather for bringing it as fully and explicitly as possible into the light, so that it may be examined publicly and critically, to be rejected, accepted, or suitably modified as the evidence for and against it may demand.

During the past twenty years many elements of the theory have been included in various articles and books, to which I must acknowledge a general indebtedness without being able to name any particular one by which I have been specially influenced. What is new in the outline—it is hardly more than that—which will follow is the name given to the theory, which is not unimportant; the number of diverse historical factors which are synthesized under it; the elimination of assumptions which have heretofore obscured its significance; and the manner of presentation.

With reference to the last, another word is necessary. I am not writing a *program* of social reform, nor am I making any *moral* judgment whatever on the subject with which I am dealing. As I have stated, I am concerned exclusively with the attempt to elaborate a *descriptive* theory able to explain the character of the present period of social transition and to predict, at least in general, its outcome. I am not concerned, in this book at any rate, with whether the facts indicated by this theory are "good" or "bad," just or unjust, desirable or undesirable—but simply with whether the theory is true or false on the basis of the evidence now at our disposal.

This warning, I know, will not be enough to prevent many who read this book from attributing to it a program and a morality. The elimination of such considerations is extremely rare in what is written about history, society, and politics. In these fields we are, perhaps understandably, more anxious for salvation than for knowledge; but experience ought to teach us that genuine salvation is possible only on the foundation of knowledge. And, though this book contains no program and no morality, if the theory which it puts forward is true, or partly true, no intelligent program or social morality is possible without an understanding of the theory.

II

THE WORLD WE LIVED IN

WE LIVE, then, in a period of rapid transition from one type or structure of society to another type. But, before answering our central problem of the world tomorrow, we must have a coherent idea of the world yesterday. We cannot really understand where we are going unless we have at least some notion of where we start from. What were the chief characteristics of the "modern world," the type of society usually referred to as "capitalist" or "bourgeois," which was dominant from the end of the Middle Ages until, let us say in order to fix a date, 1914, the beginning of the first world war?

In the attempt to describe the chief characteristics of capitalist society (or any society) we are met at once with certain difficulties. What shall we describe? We cannot describe everything: all the books ever written are not long enough for that. Whatever facts we select may seem arbitrarily selected. Nevertheless, we have already a guide to the particular kind of arbitrariness that is relevant to our purpose. Our problem is concerned with social revolution; and social revolution, according to the conception which has been outlined, is a matter of the most important economic and political institutions, widespread cultural institutions and beliefs, and ruling groups or classes. When these change drastically, the type of society has changed, and a revolution has occurred. It is modern or capitalist society in terms of these, then, that must be described. We do not have to include an account of the thousands of other features of modern society which might be relevant to some different purpose.

There is a second arbitrariness as well. In describing capitalist society, not only do we select out only a few institutional features, but we limit our survey to only a certain (minor) percentage of the earth's surface and a certain (minor) percentage of the earth's population. It might seem rather narrowly conceited for us to draw our conception of what the modern world has been like almost exclusively from a few European nations and the United States. There are more territory and more people, after all, in Asia, Africa, and South America. However, this arbitrariness, too, can be motivated. It is, indeed, a sufficient motivation to point out that our special problem is to discover what is happening, and is going to happen, to the kind of society that has prevailed during modern times in such nations as England, the United States, France, and Germany, not the kind of society that may have existed in central India or China or Africa.

Even apart from this, however, it is not unreasonable to define modern society in terms of the institutions of these nations. It is they that have been the most powerful influences in post-medieval times, not only within their own boundaries, but on a world scale. Their institutions have profoundly affected those of Asia, Africa, and South America; whereas the reverse is not true—the institutions indigenous to those vast continents have had no comparable effect on the great modern powers.

It is fairly clear what nations and peoples we must pay most attention to when trying to sum up the nature of modern capitalist society. England with its empire comes first on all counts. Prior to the rise of England, France deserves special notice for an earlier approximation to certain key modern political forms; and the Italian city states, the cities of the Germanic Hansa (Leagues), and later the cities of the Lowlands for crucial economic developments. France gets renewed importance in the late eighteenth century; and, in the nineteenth, France and England are joined by the United States and Germany, and, in lesser roles, Russia, Italy, and Japan. The modern world has been the world of these nations, not of Afghanistan or Nicaragua or Mongolia.

1

Modern capitalist society has been characterized by a typical mode of economy. The mode of economy has gone through a number of major phases and transformations, has been more fluid and changing than any other economy known to history; but throughout these transformations certain decisive features have persisted. All of these features are sharply different from the outstanding features of feudal economy, which preceded capitalist economy and out of which capitalist economy evolved. Among the most important and typical of them may be listed the following:

1. Production in capitalist economy is *commodity production.* Thousands of diverse goods are turned out by the processes of production, diverse in their nature and suited to the fulfillment of thousands of different human needs. Some can warm us, some decorate us, some feed us, some amuse us, and so on. But in capitalist economy all of these diverse goods can be directly compared with each other in terms of an abstract property—sometimes called their "exchange value"—represented either exactly or approximately (depending upon the economic theory which analyzes the phenomenon) by their monetary *price.* Products looked at from the point of view, not of those qualities whereby they can satisfy specific needs, but of exchange value, in which respect all products are the same in kind and differ only in quantity, are what is meant by "commodities." All things appear on the capitalist market as commodities; everything, thus, shoes and statues and labor and houses and brains and gold, there receives a monetary value and can, through monetary

symbols, go through the multitudinous operations of which money is capable.

All societies, except the most primitive, have produced *some* of their goods as commodities. But in every society except the capitalist, and very notably in the feudal society which preceded capitalism, commodities have made up a very small segment of total production. In the first place, in other societies by far the greater proportion of goods was produced for use by the immediate producers, did not enter into exchange at all, and therefore had no occasion for functioning as commodities. You cannot eat or wear exchange value or money; not the price of goods but the qualities that enable them to satisfy specific needs are all that enters into subsistence production. But even where goods entered into exchange in other societies, again notably in feudal society, they ordinarily did not do so as commodities. Exchange for the most part in the Middle Ages was not for money or through the intermediary of money but *in kind;* and there, too, what interested the buying or selling peasant was not the price he could get or would have to pay but whether he had a surplus of one kind of goods capable of satisfying one kind of need that he could trade for something else satisfying some other need.

2. The all-important, all-pervasive role of *money* is an equally obvious feature of capitalist economy, is indeed a necessary consequence of commodity production. Money is not an invention of capitalism; it has been present in most other societies, but in none has it played a part in any way comparable to what capitalism assigns it. The difference is readily enough shown by the fact that almost all of the complex banking, credit, currency, and accounting devices whereby money in its various forms is handled have their origin in modern times; and even more strikingly shown by the fact that the great majority of people in the Middle Ages never saw any money at all during their entire lives. No one, on the other hand, will have to be persuaded how important

money has been in the modern world, whether he thinks of it in terms of personal life or government debts.

A certain belief in connection with money is worth mentioning, though it is not peculiar to capitalist society: the belief, namely, that all forms of money, such as paper money, drafts, credits, etc., have an ultimate dependence upon metallic money, especially silver and gold, and, in developed capitalism, above all on gold. Until recently this was more or less a dogma of most economists, as it still is of some; and various laws, not without some justification in fact, were worked out to relate prices and values, or even the movement of production as a whole, to the amount of metallic money present.

3. In capitalist society, money has not one but two entirely different major economic functions. In the mighty development of the second of these lies another of the distinguishing features of capitalist economy. On the one hand, money is used as a medium of exchange; this is the use which is found in other types of society, and with respect to this use capitalism differs from them only, as we have seen, in the far greater extent, coming close to totality in developed capitalism, to which exchange is carried out through the intermediary of money.

On the other hand, money is used as *capital;* "money makes money"; and this function was developed little, often not at all, in other types of society. Under capitalism, money can be transformed into raw materials, machines, and labor; products turned out and retranslated into money; and the resultant amount of money can exceed the initial amount—a profit, that is to say, can be made. This process can be carried out, moreover, without cheating anyone, without violating any accepted legal or moral law; but, quite the contrary, fully in accordance with accepted rules of justice and morality.

It is true that the difference between money functioning as capital and thereby making more money and money functioning as a loan and thereby making interest is somewhat abstruse when once we get beneath the accountants' figures where the difference is usually clear enough. It is also true that money was, though much less extensively, loaned out at interest in other societies—though not in all of them by any means—before capitalism. However, if we note what actually happened, the decisive practical distinction re-emerges.

During the Middle Ages, money was loaned on a considerable scale for two primary purposes: for making war; and for what Veblen called "conspicuous waste" in such projects as building great castles, memorials, and churches. When it was repaid with interest (as it often was not, hence the extremely high nominal rates of interest, often well over 100%), the funds for repayment had been obtained by levying tribute of one sort or another, or by outright pillage of conquered peoples, not, as in the case of money used as capital, from what is regarded as normal productive economic processes. The principal exception to these limitations was long-distance trading, where the merchant (who was in the Middle Ages proper often also the caravan leader or ship's captain) had a chance to make a good deal of money which was perhaps halfway between capital profit and interest on the money he and his friends had put into the venture. Where, in some of the Italian and Germanic towns, additional capital functions of money were to be found, we are meeting the first stages of capitalist economy, not typical feudal economic institutions.

This medieval situation is clearly reflected in the writings of the philosophers and theologians on economic subjects. No conception of money functioning as capital can be found in them. Even exacting interest on money loaned (permitting money, even in that sense, to make money)—since they realized what uses loans were ordinarily put to—was unequivocally condemned as the grave sin of usury. In designating it a sin, the philosophers were astute: they rightly grasped that the practice was subversive and that if it spread it would work to the destruction of the fabric of *their* society. Interestingly enough, a moral exception was sometimes made to money loaned at interest for merchant-shipping, which, as it was the one important productive use for such funds, was found to be less sinful or even virtuous.

4. Under capitalism, production is carried on *for profit.* Some writers, more interested in apologizing for capitalism than in understanding it, seem to resent this commonplace observation as a slur. This is perhaps because they understand it in the psychological sense that is often attributed to it—namely, that individual capitalists are psychologically always motivated by a personal desire for profit, which is sometimes, though certainly not invariably, the case. The observation is not, however, psychological, but economic. Normal capitalist production is carried on for profit in the sense that a capitalist enterprise must operate, over a period, at a profit or else close down. What decides whether a shoe factory can keep going is not whether the owner likes to make shoes or whether people are going barefoot or badly shod or whether workers need wages but whether the product can be sold on the market at a profit, however modest. If, over a period of time, there continues to be a loss instead of a profit, then the business folds up. Everybody knows that this is the case.

Moreover, this was *not* the case in medieval economy. In agriculture, by far the chief industry, production was carried on not for a profit but to feed the growers and to allow for the exactions (in kind, for the most part) of feudal suzerains and the Church. In other industries (amounting in all to only a minute percentage of the economy) the medieval artisan usually made goods (clothes, say, or furniture or cloth or shoes) only on order from a specific person because that person wanted them; and he usually made the goods out of raw materials supplied by the customer.

5. Capitalist economy is strikingly characterized by a special kind of periodic economic *crisis,* not met with or occurring only very rarely and on limited scales in other types of society. These capitalist crises of production have no relation either to "natural catastrophes" (drought, famine, plague, etc.) or to people's biological and psychological needs for the goods that might be

turned out, one or the other of which determined most crises in other types of society. The capitalist crises are determined by economic relations and forces. It is not necessary for our purpose to enter into the disputed question of the exact causes of the crises; whatever account is given, no one denies their reality, their periodic occurrence, and their basic difference from dislocations of production and consumption in other types of society.

6. In capitalist economy, production as a whole is regulated, so far as it is regulated, primarily by "the market," both the internal and the international market. There is no person or group of persons who consciously and deliberately regulates production as a whole. The market decides, independently of the wills of human beings. In the earliest (mercantile) and again in the late stages of capitalist development, monopoly devices and state intervention try to gain some control over production. But they operate only in restricted fields, not in the total productive process, and even in narrow fields they never succeed in emancipating production altogether from the market. This is not surprising, for deliberate regulation of production as a whole (a "plan," as it is called nowadays) would be incompatible with the nature of capitalism. It would destroy the commodity basis of the economy, the profit motivation, and the rights of individual ownership.

7. The institutional relations peculiar to capitalist economy serve, finally, to stratify large sections of the population roughly into two special classes. These two classes are not to be found in other types of society for the evident reason that the classes are defined by relations peculiar to capitalism; and neither class can exist without the other, again because they are defined partly in terms of each other.

The boundary line between the two classes is by no means exact, and it is possible for given individuals to pass from one of the classes into the other. The general division is nevertheless sufficiently clear. One of these classes is comprised of those who *as individuals* own, or have an ownership interest in, the instruments of production (factories, mines, land, railroads, machines, whatever they may be); and who hire the labor of others to operate these instruments, retaining the ownership rights in the products of that labor. This class is usually called the *bourgeoisie* or the capitalists.

The second class, usually called the proletariat or the workers, consists of those who are, in a technical sense, "free" laborers. They are the ones who work for the owners. They are "free" in that they are "freed from," that is, have no ownership interest in, the instruments of production; and in the further sense that they are free to sell their labor to those who do hold such ownership, renouncing, however, ownership rights in the product of their labor. They are, in short, wage-workers.

It must be emphasized that these two classes did not exist, or existed only to a trivial extent, in other types of society. In many societies, for example, there were slaves and slave-holders. In feudal society the majority of the people were serfs or villeins. These engaged in agriculture and were "attached to" the land—they were not "free from" the instrument of production, namely, the land; they could not be ousted from the land, which it was their right, not to own in a legal sense, but to use; and, with certain exceptions, they could not leave the land. The industrial crafts were carried on, not by employers and wage-workers, but by artisans, who owned their own tools and what machines were used, and worked "for themselves."

There are, of course, many other features of capitalist economy which I have not mentioned. If our purpose were to analyze capitalism itself, several of these, such as capitalism's dynamic expansionism at certain stages, its technological advances, and others, would be as important as some that I have listed. But our purpose is to analyze not capitalism but the type of society which is succeeding it and in particular to clarify how that type of society *differs* from capitalism. The review of capitalist society in this chapter, and what it stresses, is wholly subordinate to our central problem.

The seven features of capitalist economy which I have summarized are none of them, however, minor. So important and pervasive are they that they seemed to many people, seem to many even today, a necessary and permanent part of the structure of social life. People thought, and still think, so automatically in these terms that they do not realize they are doing anything more than recording unchangeable fact. That the owner of a factory should own also its products; that we need money to buy things; that most people should work for wages for others; that a business has to lower production or cut wages or even stop when it can't make a profit—all this seems as natural to many as the need to breathe or eat. Yet history tells flatly that all of these institutions are so far from being inevitably "natural" to man that they have been present in only a small fraction, the last few hundred years, of the lengthy history of mankind.

2

It is not easy to generalize about the chief characteristics of the political institutions of capitalist society. They show a greater diversity, both at different periods of time and in different nations, than the economic institutions. We can, however, select out some, which are either common to capitalist society throughout its history or typical of the chief capitalist powers.

1. The political division of capitalist society has been into a comparatively large number of comparatively large *national states*. These states have no necessary correspondence with biological groupings or with any personal relations among the citizens of the states. They are fixed by definite though changing geographical boundaries, and claim political jurisdiction over human beings within those boundaries (with the exception of certain privileged foreigners, who are granted "extra-territorial"

rights). The habits of some map makers in school texts make us liable to forget that nations in the modern sense are not at all a universal form of human political organization.

The political authority of the national states is embodied in a variety of institutions, the final authority exercised by some man or group of men, usually a parliament. Each nation claims absolute political autonomy or sovereignty: that is, it recognizes no jurisdiction superior to itself (in practice, naturally, it was only the great nations that could uphold such claims). The central and controlling political relation for each individual person is that of being the *citizen* of a nation.

Such a system and conception are in the widest contrast to the medieval system and conception. The central and controlling political relation for each individual person under feudalism (with the exception of the inhabitants of a few towns) was not to be the citizen of the abstracted institution, the nation, but to be "so-and-so's man," the vassal or serf of such and such a suzerain. His political loyalty and duty were owed to a *person,* and, moreover, to the person who was his immediate superior in the feudal hierarchy. Dante's Satan occupies the lowest point in Hell for the gravest of all feudal sins: "treachery to his lord and benefactor."

There was, in medieval Europe, at the same time more unity and greater diversity than in the modern system of national states. The political unity was no doubt far more real in theory than in fact, but through the Church, the most powerful of all social institutions (controlling for a while from a third to a half of Europe's arable land) and everywhere present, some genuine unity in law and the conception of political rights and duties did exist. The Church itself claimed, as delegated from God, not only spiritual but political sovereignty over all mankind, and at the height of its power (around the year 1200) came close to making its claim good. Within this partial unity, a kind of political atomism, even chaos, was usual. Hundreds, even thousands, of local feudal lords—counts, barons, dukes, earls, including many bishops and abbots of the Church who were feudal lords on their own account—held political power over constantly changing groups of people and territories. The limits of their political sovereignty were never clearly defined and depended ordinarily on their military power of the moment; a vassal lord obeyed his suzerain about as much as his weakness or his schemes made necessary, and little more. The great vassals made no bones about disobeying those who called themselves kings whenever they could get away with it; indeed, vassals were not seldom more powerful than the nominal kings whom, in words, they might acknowledge. There was nothing even approximating the centralized fundamental authority of the modern national state.

2. Capitalist society was the first which had, in some measure, a world extent. From one point of view, the world ramifications were a result of economic developments: the search for markets, sources of raw materials, and investment outlets was extended everywhere. But along with this most of the earth was brought in one way or another within the orbit of capitalist political institutions. The great powers, including within their own immediate borders only a small fraction of the territory and population of the world, reduced most of the rest of the world to either colonies or dominions or spheres of influence or, in many cases, to weak nations dependent for their continued existence upon the sufferance of the powers.

The world extension of capitalism did not mean the development everywhere in the world of nations comparable to the few dominating capitalist powers or the full sharing of the social and cultural institutions of capitalist society. Most of Asia, Africa, and the Americas, even southeastern Europe—the greater part of the land and peoples of the earth, that is to say—remained poor and backward relations in the capitalist family. They were parts of capitalist society primarily in the sense of being controlled by, subject to (and indeed, as such, necessary to the existence of) the great capitalist nations. The typical institutions of capitalist culture of the advanced variety, its way of life, made only small dents in their cultural mass. Generalizing the facts, we are entitled to conclude that this division on the world arena between the great advanced powers and the subject backward territories and peoples was an integral part of the structural arrangements of capitalist society.

3. By the term, "the state," we are referring to the actual central political institutions of society—to the governmental administration, the civil bureaucracy, the army, courts, police, prisons, and so on. The role of the state in capitalist society has varied greatly from time to time and nation to nation, but some traits have remained fairly constant.

As compared, for example, with the central political institutions of feudalism, the capitalist state has been very firm and well organized in asserting its authority over certain fields of human activity which have been generally recognized as falling within the state's peculiar jurisdiction. Within its national boundaries, for instance, it has enforced a uniform set of laws, exacted general taxation, controlled the major armed forces, kept lines of communication open, and so on.

But, though the state's authority was so firm in some fields, there have been others where it did not penetrate, or penetrated only very lightly. *The scope of the activities of the state, that is to say, has been limited.*

This limitation of the range of the state's activities was a cardinal point in the most famous of all capitalist theories of the state, the liberal theory. The prime interest of liberalism was the promotion of the capitalist economic process. According to the liberal theory of the state, the business of the state was to guarantee civil peace ("domestic tranquillity"), handle foreign wars and relations, and with that to stand aside and let the economic process take care of itself, intervening in the economic process only in a negative way to correct injustices or obstacles and to keep the market "free."

The "state" of liberal theory was an unattainable and, in reality, unwished-for ideal. Actual states always did intervene in the economic process more actively than the theory called for: with subsidies, tariffs, troops to put down internal disturbances or follow investments to foreign parts, or regulations benefiting one or another group of capitalists. In the early days of capitalism, intervention by the "mercantilist" state was even more widespread. But in spite of this gap between theory and fact, there was a large kernel of truth in the liberal theory and a decisive, if only partial, correspondence with capitalist reality. The capitalist state intervened in the economic process, but the interventions, in extent and depth, never went beyond what was after all a fairly narrow limit. In the economic field, we might say, the state always appeared as subordinate to, as the handmaiden of, the capitalists, of "business," not as their master.

There is a simple reason for this relation: capitalist economy is the field of "private enterprise," based upon private property rights vested in individuals as individuals; an invasion by the state beyond a certain point into the economic process could only mean the destruction of those individual property rights—in fact even if not in legal theory—and therefore the end of capitalist economic relationships.

In many nations there were also other important fields besides the economic which the state's activities touched very little, such as the Church, whose separation from the state has been such a cherished doctrine in the political history of the United States.

4. Political authority, sovereignty, cannot remain up in the clouds. It has to be concretized in some man or group of men. We say that the "state" or "nation" makes the laws that have to be obeyed; but actually, of course, the laws have to be drawn up and proclaimed by some man or group of men. This task is carried out by different persons and different sorts of institutions in different types of society. The shift in what might be called the institutional "locus" of sovereignty is always an extremely significant aspect of a general change in the character of society.

From this point of view, the history of the political development of capitalism is the history of the shift in the locus of sovereignty to *parliament* (using the word in its general sense) and more particularly to the *lower house* of parliament. In almost all capitalist nations, the authority to make laws was vested in a parliament, and the laws were in fact made by the parliament. Moreover, the political shift to parliament as central authority coincided historically, on the whole, with the general development of capitalist society.

The lower house of the English Parliament (it should be noted that both houses together of the U. S. Congress correspond to the single House of Commons in England) or the "Third Estate" of the French National Assembly was the recognized representative of the "burgess," the *bourgeoisie*—the merchants, bankers, and industrialists, in short, the capitalist class (together, in the English Commons, with the nonfeudal squirearchy). The growing institutional supremacy of the lower house of parliament, therefore, over the feudal lords and later over the king (who co-operated with the capitalists in the early stages of the modern era) was the parallel in the political field to the supplanting of feudal relations by capitalist relations in the economic field—and, it may be added, of feudal ideologies by capitalist ideologies in the cultural field.

5. The restriction of range of the state's activities, noted in 3 above, must not be thought to have any necessary connection with political democracy; nor, in general, is there any necessary connection between democracy and capitalism. The "limited state" of capitalism may—and there have been many examples in modern history—be an extreme dictatorship in its own political sphere: consider the absolute monarchies of the sixteenth and seventeenth centuries, the theocratic state of Oliver Cromwell, the Napoleonic state. Even the supremacy of parliament need not imply any considerable democracy.

There may be some grounds for believing that a regime of partial democracy was most natural for consolidated capitalist society. At the least, the most powerful and fully developed capitalist nations have tended toward such a regime. The democracy of the capitalist state was never complete. It did not extend to economic and social relations, for that was excluded by the character of those relations. Even in the political field, it was restricted, in one way or another, to only a portion of the adult population. At all times it was intolerant of any serious opposition opinion that went beyond the general structure of capitalist institutions. Nevertheless, except for some primitive groups, it probably went further than any democracy known in human history before capitalism.

In spite of this, we must, particularly today, stress the point that political democracy and capitalism are not the same thing. There have been many politically democratic states in societies which were not capitalist; and there have been many nondemocratic states in capitalist society. Political orators, war-propagandists, and others who use words emotively rather than scientifically confuse these facts of history. They speak of "democracy" when they mean "capitalism" or of "capitalism" when they mean "democracy," or they lump the two together in such phrases as "our way of life." If the fate of democracy is in truth bound up with the fate of capitalism, that is something to be independently proved, not to be taken for granted by using language loosely.

6. The legal system of capitalist society, enforced by the state, was, of course, such as to uphold the general structure of capitalist society and to set up and enforce rules for acting within that structure.

3

It is even harder than in the case of political institutions to generalize about the belief patterns of capitalist society. For our purpose, however, it is not necessary to be at all complete. It is enough if we choose a few prominent beliefs—the prominence can be tested by their appearance in great public documents such as constitutions, or declarations of independence or of the rights of man—which nearly everyone will recognize as typical of capitalist society and which both differ from typical feudal beliefs and are sharply at issue in the present period of social transition.

The beliefs with which we are concerned are often called "ideologies," and we should be clear what we mean by "ideology." An "ideology" is similar in the social sphere to what is sometimes called "rationalization" in the sphere of individual psychology. An ideology is *not* a scientific theory, but is nonscientific and often antiscientific. It is the expression of hopes, wishes, fears, ideals, not a hypothesis about events—though ideologies are often thought by those who hold them to be scientific theories. Thus the theory of evolution or of relativity or of the electronic composition of matter are scientific theories; whereas the doctrines of the preambles to the Declaration of Independence or the Constitution of the United States, the Nazi racial doctrines, Marxian dialectical materialism, St. Anselm's doctrine of the meaning of world history, are ideologies.

Ideologies capable of influencing and winning the acceptance of great masses of people are an indispensable verbal cement holding the fabric of any given type of society together. Analysis of ideologies in terms of their practical effects shows us that they ordinarily work to serve and advance the interests of some particular social group or class, and we may therefore speak of a given ideology as being that *of* the group or class in question. However, it is even more important to observe that no major ideology is content to profess openly that it speaks only for the group whose interests it in fact expresses. Each group insists that its ideologies are universal in validity and express the interests of humanity as a whole; and each group tries to win universal acceptance for its ideologies. This is true of all the ideologies mentioned in the preceding paragraph.

The significance of ideologies will be further elaborated in connection with the managerial revolution.

1. Among the elements entering into the ideologies typical of capitalist society, there must be prominently included, though it is not so easy to define what we mean by it, *individualism*. Capi-

talist thought, whether reflected in theology or art or legal, economic, and political theory, or philosophy or morality, has exhibited a steady concentration on the idea of the "individual." We find the "individual" wherever we turn: in Luther's appeal to "private interpretation" of the Bible as the test of religious truth; in the exaggerated place of "conscience" in Puritanism; in the economic notion of the economic process's consisting of millions of separated individuals each pursuing his own highest profit, or the correlated moral notion of morality's consisting in each individual's pursuing his own greatest personal pleasure; in the individualistic geniuses of Renaissance and modern art or the individualistic heroes of modern literature (the fascination that Hamlet has had for capitalist society is well deserved); in the very conception of the heart of democracy's lying in the private individual's privately setting forth his will by marking a private ballot....

Now the individualist idea of the individual is not an ultimate any more than any other idea. It has its special and distinguishing features, differing from those possessed by the idea of the individual found in other types of society. According to the prevailing capitalist idea, the fundamental unit of politics, psychology, sociology, morality, theology, economics was thought of as the single human individual. This individual was understood as complete "in himself," in his own nature, and as having only *external* relations to other persons and things. Though Hegel and his followers notoriously reject this conception, it is unquestionably typical, and is implicit where not explicit in most of the influential doctrines and public documents of the fields just mentioned. The Church, the state, the ideal utopia, are not realities in themselves but only numerical sums of the individuals who compose them.

2. In keeping with the general ideology of individualism was the stress placed by capitalist society on the notion of "private initiative." Private initiative, supposed, in the chief instance, to

provide the mainspring of the economic process, was discovered also at the root of psychological motivation and moral activity.

3. The status of the capitalist individual was further defined with the help of doctrines of "natural rights" ("free contract," the standard civil rights, "life, liberty, and the pursuit of happiness," etc.) which are held to belong in some necessary and eternal sense to each individual. There is no complete agreement on just what these rights are, but lists of them are given in such documents as the Declaration of Independence, the preamble and Bill of Rights of the Constitution of the United States, or the French Declaration of the Rights of Man.

4. Finally, in capitalist society, the theological and supernatural interpretation of the meaning of world history was replaced by the idea of progress, first appearing in the writers of the Renaissance and being given definite formulation during the eighteenth century. There were two factors in the idea of progress: first, that mankind was advancing steadily and inevitably to better and better things; and, second, the definition of the goal toward which the advance is taking place in naturalistic terms, in terms we might say of an earthly instead of a heavenly paradise.

It should not be supposed that there was any systematically worked out ideology which can be considered *the* ideology of capitalism. Many variants are possible. Dozens of differing ideologies were elaborated by philosophers, political theorists, and other intellectuals. Their concepts, slogans, and phrases, filtered down, became the commonplaces of mass thinking. But all, or almost all, the ideologies, and the mass thinking, were, we might say, variations on related themes. They had a common focus in a commonly held set of words and ideas and assumptions, among which were prominently to be found those that I have listed.

4

In developed capitalist society it is evident that the position of greatest social power and privilege was occupied by the capitalists, the *bourgeoisie*. The instruments of economic production are, simply, the means whereby men live. In any society, the group of persons controlling these means is by that very fact socially dominant. The *bourgeoisie*, therefore, may be called in capitalist society the *ruling class*. However, the idea of a "ruling class," as well as the notion of a "struggle for power" among classes, raise issues so closely related to the central problem of this book that I propose to return to them in greater detail in Chapter V.

Probably no one would agree throughout with the selection and emphasis I have made in this outline of major features of capitalist society. However, few would, I think, deny that these *are* among the major features; or, more important, that the disappearance of any considerable percentage of them would make it hard to regard the consequent structure of society as any longer "capitalist."

That all of these features, and many others along with them, will disappear—and disappear in a matter of years, or decades at the most, not generations—is the negative half of the theory of the managerial revolution.

III

THE THEORY OF THE
PERMANENCE OF CAPITALISM

DURING THE past century, dozens, perhaps even hundreds, of "theories of history" have been elaborated. These differ endlessly among themselves in the words they use, the causal explanations they offer for the historical process, the alleged "laws" of history which they seem to discover. But most of these differences are irrelevant to the central problem with which this book is concerned. That problem is to discover, if possible, what type (if indeed it is to be a different type) of social organization is on the immediate historical horizon. With reference to this specific problem, all of the theories, with the exception of those few which approximate to the theory of the managerial revolution, boil down to two and only two.

The first of these predicts that capitalism will continue for an indefinite, but long, time, if not forever: that is, that the major institutions of capitalist society, or at least most of them, will not be radically changed.

The second predicts that capitalist society will be replaced by socialist society.

The theory of the managerial revolution predicts that capitalist society will be replaced by "managerial society" (the nature of which will be later explained), that, in fact, the transition from capitalist society to managerial society is already well under way.

It is clear that, although all three of these theories might be false, only one of them can be true; the answer that each of them gives to the question of what will actually happen in the future plainly denies the answers given by the other two.

If, then, the theory of the managerial revolution is true, it must be possible to present considerations sufficient to justify us in regarding the other two theories as false. Such demonstration would, by itself, make the theory of the managerial revolution very probable, since, apart from these three, there are at present no other serious theoretical contenders.

I propose, therefore, in this and the following chapter to review briefly the evidence for rejecting the theory of the permanence of capitalism and the theory of the socialist revolution.

*   *
  *

Oddly enough, the belief that capitalist society will continue is seldom put in theoretical form. It is rather left implicit in what people say and do, and in the writings and sayings of most historians, sociologists, and politicians. Nevertheless, there is little doubt that the majority of people in the United States hold this belief, though it has been somewhat shaken in recent years.

When examined, this belief is seen to be based not on any evidence in its favor but primarily on two assumptions. Both of these assumptions are flatly and entirely false.

The first is the assumption that society has always been capitalist in structure—and, therefore, presumably always will be. In actual fact, society has been capitalist for a minute fragment of total human history. Any exact date chosen as the beginning of capitalism would be arbitrary. But the start of capitalist social organization on any wide scale can scarcely be put earlier than the fourteenth century, A.D.; and capitalist domination must be placed much later than that.

The second assumption is that capitalism has some necessary

kind of correlation with "human nature." This, as a matter of fact, is the same assumption as the first but expressed differently. To see that it is false, it is not required to be sure just what "human nature" may be. It is enough to observe that human nature has been able to adapt itself to dozens of types of society, many of which have been studied by anthropologists and historians and a number of which have lasted far longer than capitalism.

With these assumptions dropped, the positive case for the view that capitalism will continue doesn't amount to much, in fact has hardly even been stated coherently by anyone.

But, apart from this lack of positive defense, we can, I think, list certain sets of facts which give all the grounds that a reasonable man should need for believing that capitalism is not going to continue; that it will disappear in a couple of decades at most and perhaps in a couple of years (which is as exact as one should pretend to be in these matters). These facts do not demonstrate this in the way that a mathematical or logical theorem is demonstrated; no belief about future events can be so demonstrated. They simply make the belief more probable than any alternative belief, which is as much as can be done. (In what follows, for reasons which will become evident later, I do not include reference to Germany, Italy, or Russia.)

1. The first, and perhaps crucial, evidence for the view that capitalism is not going to continue much longer is the continuous presence within the capitalist nations of *mass unemployment* and the failure of all means tried for getting rid of mass unemployment. The unemployed, it is especially significant to note, include large percentages of the youth just entering working age.

Continuous mass unemployment is not new in history. It is, in fact, a symptom that a given type of social organization is just about finished. It was found among the poorer citizens during the last years of Athens, among the urban "proletariat" (as they were called) in the Roman Empire, and very notably, at the end of the

Middle Ages, among the dispossessed serfs and villeins who had been thrown off the land in order to make way for capitalist use of the land.

Mass unemployment means that the given type of social organization has broken down, that it cannot any longer provide its members with socially useful functions even according to its own ideas of what is socially useful. It cannot support these masses for any length of time in idleness, for its resources are not sufficient. The unemployed hover on the fringe of society, on the one hand like a terrible weight dragging it down and bleeding it to death, on the other a constant irritant and reservoir of forces directed against the society.

Experience has already shown that there is not the slightest prospect of ridding capitalism of mass unemployment. This is indeed becoming widely admitted among the defenders of capitalism, as well as many spokesmen of the New Deal. Even total war, the most drastic conceivable "solution," could not end mass unemployment in England and France, nor will it do so in this country. Every solution that has any possibility of succeeding leads, directly or indirectly, outside the framework of capitalism.

2. Capitalism has always been characterized by recurring economic crises, by periods of boom followed by periods of depression. Until a dozen years ago, however, the curve of total production always went higher in one major boom period than in the boom preceding. It did so not only in terms of the actual quantity of goods produced but in the relative quantity of the volume of goods compared to the increased population and plant capacity. Thus, in spite of the crises, there was a general over-all increase in capitalist production which was simply the measure of the ability of capitalist social organization to handle its own resources. Since the world crisis of 1927-29, this over-all curve has reversed; the height of a boom period, relative to population and potential capacity, is lower than that of the preceding boom. This new direction of the curve is, in its turn, simply the expres-

sion of the fact that capitalism can no longer handle its own resources.

3. The volume of public and private debt has reached a point where it cannot be managed much longer. The debt, like the unemployed, sucks away the diminishing blood stream of capitalism. And it cannot be shaken off. Bankruptcies, which formerly readjusted the debt position of capitalism, hardly make a dent in it. The scale of bankruptcy or inflation which could reduce the debt to manageable size would at the same time—as all economists recognize—utterly dislocate all capitalist institutions.

4. The maintenance of the capitalist market depended on at least comparatively free monetary exchange transactions. The area of these, especially on a world scale, is diminishing toward a vanishing point. This is well indicated by the useless gold hoard at Fort Knox and the barter methods of Russia, Germany, and Italy.

5. Since shortly after the first world war, there has been in all major capitalist nations a permanent agricultural depression. Agriculture is obviously an indispensable part of the total economy, and the breakdown in this essential sector is another mark of the incurable disease afflicting capitalism. No remedies—and how many they are that have been tried!—produce any sign of cure. The farming populations sink in debt and poverty, and not enough food is produced and distributed, while agriculture is kept barely going through huge state subsidies.

6. Capitalism is no longer able to find uses for the available investment funds, which waste in idleness in the account books of the banks. This mass unemployment of private money is scarcely less indicative of the death of capitalism than the mass unemployment of human beings. Both show the inability of the capitalist institutions any longer to organize human activities. During the past decade in the United States, as in other capitalist nations, new capital investment has come almost entirely from state, not from private, funds.

7. The continuance of capitalism was, we saw, dependent upon a certain relationship between the great powers and the backward sections and peoples of the earth. One of the most striking developments of the past fifteen years, which has been little noticed, is the inability of the great capitalist nations any longer to manage the exploitation and development of these backward sections. This is nowhere better illustrated than in the relations between the United States and South America. The United States, in spite of its imperious necessity for the nation's very survival, has not and cannot devise a scheme for handling the economic phase of its "hemisphere policy." Though during the past few years and above all during the war the road has been wide open, nothing gets done. Here again, the only workable schemes are compelled to leave the basis of capitalism.

8. Capitalism is no longer able to use its own technological possibilities. One side of this is shown by such facts as the inability of the United States to carry out a housing program, when the houses are needed and wanted and the technical means to produce them in abundance are on hand. (This is the case with almost all goods.) But an equally symptomatic side is seen in the inability to make use of many inventions and new technical methods. Hundreds of these, though they could reduce immeasurably the number of man-hours needed to turn out goods, and increase greatly the convenience of life, nonetheless sit on the shelf. In many entire economic sectors—such as agriculture, building, coal mining—the technical methods today available make the usual present methods seem stone age; and nearly every economic field is to some degree affected. Using the inventions and methods available would, it is correctly understood, smash up the capitalist structure. "Technological unemployment" is present in recent capitalism; but it is hardly anything compared to what technological unemployment would be if capitalism made use of its available technology.

These facts, also, show that capitalism and its rulers can no longer use their own resources. And the point is that, if they won't, someone else will.

9. As symptomatic and decisive as these economic and technical developments is the fact that the ideologies of capitalism, the bourgeois ideologies, have become impotent. Ideologies, we have seen, are the cement that binds together the social fabric; when the cement loosens, the fabric is about to disintegrate. And no one who has watched the world during the past twenty years can doubt the ever-increasing impotence of the bourgeois ideologies.

On the one hand, the scientific pretensions of these ideologies have been exploded. History, sociology, and anthropology are not yet much as sciences; but they are enough to show every serious person that the concepts of the bourgeois ideologies are not written in the stars, are not universal laws of nature, but are at best just temporary expressions of the interests and ideals of a particular class of men at a particular historical time.

But the scientific inadequacy of the ideologies would not by itself be decisive. It does not matter how nonscientific or antiscientific an ideology may be; it can do its work so long as it possesses the power to move great masses of men to action. This the bourgeois ideologies once could do, as the great revolutions and the imperial and economic conquests prove. And this they can no longer do.

When the bourgeois ideologies were challenged in the Saar and the Sudetenland by the ideology of Nazism, it was Nazism that won the sentiment of the overwhelming majority of the people. All possible discounts for the effects of Nazi terrorism must not delude us into misreading this brute fact.

Only the hopelessly naïve can imagine that France fell so swiftly because of the mere mechanical strength of the Nazi war machine—that might have been sufficient in a longer run, but not to destroy a great nation with a colossal military establishment in a few weeks. France collapsed so swiftly because its people had no heart for the war—as every observer had remarked, even through the censorship, from the beginning of the war. And they had no .heart for the war because the bourgeois ideologies by which they were appealed to no longer had power to move their hearts. Men are prepared to be heroes for very foolish and unworthy ideals; but they must at least believe in those ideals.

Nowhere is the impotence of bourgeois ideologies more apparent than among the youth, and the coming world, after all, will be the youth's world. The abject failure of voluntary military enlistment in Britain and this country tells its own story to all who wish to listen. It is underlined in reverse by the hundreds of distinguished adult voices which during 1940 began reproaching the American youth for "indifference," "unwillingness to sacrifice," "lack of ideals." How right these reproaches are! And how little effect they have!

In truth, the *bourgeoisie* itself has in large measure lost confidence in its own ideologies. The words begin to have a hollow sound in the most sympathetic capitalist ears. This, too, is unmistakably revealed in the policy and attitude of England's rulers during the past years. What was Munich and the whole policy of appeasement but a recognition of bourgeois impotence? The head of the British government's traveling to the feet of the Austrian housepainter was the fitting symbol of the capitalists' loss of faith in themselves. Every authentic report during the autumn of 1939 from Britain told of the discouragement and fear of the leaders in government and business. And no one who has listened to American leaders off the record or who has followed the less public organs of business opinion will suppose that such attitudes are confined to Britain.

All history makes clear that an indispensable quality of any man or class that wishes to lead, to hold power and privilege in society, is boundless self-confidence.

*   *
*

Other sets of facts could easily be added to this list, but these are perhaps the most plainly symptomatic. Their effect, moreover, is cumulative; the attempted remedies for them, experience shows, only aggravate them. They permit no other conclusion than that the capitalist organization of society has entered its final years.

IV

THE THEORY OF THE PROLETARIAN SOCIALIST REVOLUTION

THE SECOND and only other serious alternative to the theory of the managerial revolution is the theory that capitalist society is to be replaced by socialist society. This belief is held by socialists, communists, in general by all who call themselves Marxists; and, in slightly different words, by anarchists and anarcho-syndicalists. Interestingly enough, it is also held by many others who do not at all consider themselves to be Marxists, by not a few, even, who are *against* socialism. Many "liberals" believe that socialism is going to come. And there are staunch capitalists and defenders of capitalism, who, though the prospect is not at all to their taste, believe likewise.

First, we must be clear about what is meant by "socialist society."

It is worth emphasizing that with respect to the central and only problem of this book—the problem of what type of society is to prevail in the immediate future and for the next period of human history—the theories of anarchists, socialists, communists, and their subvarieties are the same. They all agree, in general, as to what they mean by "socialist society" (even though they may *call* it something else—"communism" or "anarchist society"), and they all agree *that* it is going to come. Their differences are on *how* it is going to come and on what ought to be done to help it along, not on the prediction that it *will* come.

The determining characteristics of what they mean by socialist society are that it is *classless,* fully *democratic,* and *international.*

By "classless" is meant that in socialist society no person or group of persons has, directly or indirectly, any property rights in the instruments of production different from those possessed by every other person and group; it amounts to the same thing to say that in socialist society there are *no* property rights in the instruments of production, since a property right has meaning only if it differentiates the status of those who have it from that of those who do not. The democracy of the hypothetical socialist society is to extend, and completely, to all social spheres—political, economic, and social. And socialist society is to be organized on an international scale; if this cannot be done completely in the first stages, at least this is to be the *tendency* of socialism. If not at once international, it is to be always internationalist—as indeed it would have to be if it is ever to become actually international.

There is another important point of agreement, at least since Marx himself, among all the serious organized groups which have held the theory we are now analyzing. This is the belief that the working class, the proletariat, has a special and decisive role to play in the transformation of society along socialist lines. The main strength of the social movement that will establish socialism is to be drawn from the working class. This belief can readily be granted, for, if the main strength did not come from the working class, where indeed could it come from?

Put very simply, the Marxist movement understands the process as follows: the working class will take over state power (by insurrectionary means according to the Leninist wing of Marxism; by parliamentary means according to the reformist wing); the state will then abolish private property, either all at once or over a short period of time; and, after a certain period of adjustment (called by the Leninist wing the "dictatorship of the proletariat"), socialism will be ushered in. Under socialism itself, in keeping with its fully democratic, classless structure, state power in the sense of the coercive institutions of government .(police, army, prisons) will disappear altogether.

(Anarchism differs from Marxism in believing that the state cannot be used for ushering in the free classless society, but must be abolished at once, with the job of socialization to be carried out by the workers' organizations—unions, co-operatives, etc. The net result, however, is the same.)

Those who believe that capitalist society is to be replaced by socialist society, in particular Marxists, to whom we are justified in devoting primary attention, also, of course, believe that capitalist society is not going to last, which is implied by their more general belief. This second belief, that capitalism is not going to last, is identical with the conclusion of Chapter III, and I naturally have no quarrel with it, though I do not agree with all of the reasons which Marxists advance for holding the belief. But the proposition that capitalism is not going to last much longer is not at all the same as the proposition that socialism is going to replace it. There is no necessary connection between the two. And our primary concern is with the second.

A survey of Marxist literature quickly reveals that it is far, far weightier in the analysis of capitalism by which it reaches the conclusion that capitalism will not last (though Marx himself gravely underestimated the time-span allotted to capitalism) than in the analysis by which it motivates the all-important positive belief that socialism will replace capitalism. Yet the fullest agreement with the first, and I agree with very much of it, does not in any way compel us to accept the second. In fact, careful study will show that Marxists offer scarcely any *evidence* for the second belief. They base it almost entirely upon one argument and two assumptions. The argument is meaningless with respect to the problem; one assumption is either meaningless or false; and the second is simply false.

The argument is a deduction from the metaphysical theory of "dialectical materialism." It is held that Hegel's metaphysical logic of thesis, antithesis, and synthesis somehow guarantees that out of the clash of the two antithetical classes, *bourgeoisie* and proletariat, socialism will issue. The deduction may be all right, but no deduction from any metaphysical theory can ever tell us what is going to happen in the actual world of space and time; this we can predict, with some measure of probability, only from experience and the inferences which we make from experience. This argument, therefore, need concern us no further.

The first assumption is put by Marxists (and others) in this way: that socialism is the "only alternative" to capitalism. They then assert, in effect, the following syllogism: since capitalism is not going to last (which we have granted) and since socialism is the only alternative to capitalism, therefore socialism is going to come. The syllogism is perfectly valid, but its conclusion is not necessarily true unless the second premise is true: and that is just the problem in dispute.

It is hard to know just what is meant by the statement that socialism is the "only alternative" to capitalism. If this is another deduction from the metaphysics, it is meaningless so far as predicting the future goes. Logically, there are any number, a theoretically infinite number, of alternatives to capitalism, including all the types of society there ever have been and all that anyone can imagine. Practically, no doubt, most of these can be disregarded, since they are fantastic in relation to the actual situation in the world. But at least a few can surely not be ruled out in advance without examining the actual evidence. And the evidence will show that another type of society, managerial society, is not merely a *possible* alternative to both socialism and capitalism (which is enough to upset the assumption) but a more probable alternative than either.

The second assumption is, in effect, the following: that the abolition of capitalist private property rights in the instruments of production is a sufficient condition, a sufficient guarantee, of the establishment of socialism—that is, of a free, classless society. Now we already have available historical evidence, both from ancient and modern times, to show that this assumption is not correct. Effective class domination and privilege does, it is true, require control over the instruments of production; but this need not be exercised through individual private property rights. It can be done through what might be called corporate rights, possessed not by individuals as such but by institutions: as was the case conspicuously with many societies in which a priestly class was dominant—in numerous primitive cultures, in Egypt, to some degree in the Middle Ages. In such societies there can be and have been a few rich and many poor, a few powerful and many oppressed, just as in societies (like the capitalist) where property rights are vested in private individuals as such.

Russia, as we shall repeatedly see, has already *proved* that such phenomena are not confined to former ages. The assumption that the abolition of capitalist private property guarantees socialism must be entirely rejected. It has simply no justification on the facts. It is a hope, that is all; and, like so many hopes, one scheduled for disappointment.

With the collapse of this argument and these assumptions, the case for the belief that socialism is coming is very slight. Of course, many people would like it to come, and regard socialism as the noblest and best form of society that could be sought as an ideal. But we must not permit our wishes to interfere with a reasoned estimate of the facts. The prediction that socialism is coming could correctly rest only upon a demonstration drawn from contemporary events themselves, upon showing that there are present today in society powerful tendencies, more powerful than any other, toward socialism, that socialism is the most probable outcome of what is happening. And contemporary events show nothing of the kind; they *seem* to some to do so only because they accept these unjustified assumptions or because they confuse their wishes with reality.

Moreover, there is ample evidence from actual events that socialism is *not* coming, and we must now turn to a brief survey of some of this evidence. Among the evidence, the facts about the

Marxist movement itself are especially significant, since the Marxist movement is the chief organized social force, if there is any, through which the establishment of socialism could take place. And here a word of methodological warning is in order.

The Marxist movement is subdivided into many groups. The two chief of these, in numbers and influence, are the reformist (socialist, or social-democratic) wing, consisting primarily of those parties loosely affiliated with the Second International, together with a number of unaffiliated parties in various countries having similar programs; and the Stalinist wing, consisting of those parties which are sections of the Communist or Third International. In addition to these, there are the opposition branches sprung, like Stalinism, from the Leninist adaptation of Marxism, chief among which are the small Trotskyist parties joined in what they call the Fourth International; and countless additional parties, groups, and sects, each claiming descent in its own way from Marx.

When I speak of the "Marxist movement" or of "Marxists," I mean all of these groups and individuals, all those, that is to say, identified in common speech as Marxist and who, historically and theoretically, have a plausible connection with Marx and Marx's theories. This must be made clear because of a habit which Marxists have taken over, perhaps, from the Church. Whenever an analysis is made of actions of members of the Church or institutions of the Church which might seem to be detrimental to the good name of the Church and its divine claims, the reply is always given that these actions are not "really" those of the Church, which is a mystic and supernatural body, but only of some erring human acting not for the Church but in keeping with his sinful human nature. By this argumentative method, the record of the Church is, of course, perfect.

Similarly, each variety of Marxist denies responsibility for the actions of all other varieties, and indeed for all actions of his own group which have not worked out well or which have seemed to move away from instead of toward socialism. Just as with the

Church, the case for Marxism is irreproachable by this method. We can, however, permit neither of them this comforting luxury. When we deal the cards, we will make sure that they are not stacked.

* * *

1. The Russian events, since 1917, will occupy us in other connections. Here I wish to observe that, taken at their face value, they are powerful evidence against the theory that socialism is coming. Of course I refer to the actual events, not the fairy stories spun by the official and unofficial Soviet apologists. The main pattern of these events is plain enough for anyone who *wants* to know it, and there is no way to make anyone see who has decided in advance to keep his eyes shut.

In November, 1917, the Bolshevik party, professing a program of the transformation of society to a socialist structure and supported by a large proportion, probably a majority, of the Russian workers and poorer peasants, took over state power in Russia. A few months later, private property rights in the chief instruments of production were abolished, and property rights were vested in the state. During the first years of the revolution, the regime successfully defended itself in a series of civil wars and wars of intervention by hostile powers. The regime has kept in power ever since and is now in its twenty-fourth year.

Socialist society means, we have seen, a society which is classless, democratic, and international. If socialism is in truth realizable, if it is scheduled to be the type of society for the next period of human history, we would not, perhaps, necessarily have expected that Russia should already have achieved socialism. We would rightly take into account the special difficulties resulting from the fact that the revolution occurred not in an advanced nation but in Russia, in 1917: that is, in a nation very backward both economically and culturally, devastated by the results of the war, and surrounded by enemies both external and internal (though at the same time we would wonder why, contrary to the opinion of all socialist theoreticians prior to 1917, the revolution *did* occur in a backward instead of an advanced country).

Nevertheless, we should correctly expect, on the basis of the theory that socialism is on its way, to find, without difficulty and prominently to be noticed, unmistakable *tendencies toward* socialism. This would mean that, though Russia today would not necessarily be socialist—that is, free, classless, and international—yet it would be closer than it was at the beginning of the revolution: more free, nearer to the elimination of classes and class distinctions, and, if not international, then internationalist.

Such expectations were in fact held by the leaders of the revolution itself and by most others who believed in socialist theory, even those unsympathetic to Russia. Indeed, these expectations were so strong among Marxists that they acted as effective dark glasses, preventing Marxists from seeing, or admitting if they saw, what was actually going on in Russia. Today they still continue to blind the Stalinist dupes to be found in all countries.

Reality, however, as is so often the case, was rude to the optimistic expectations. Far from showing tendencies toward socialism, far from taking steps in the direction of socialism, the Russian revolutionary society developed in a plainly contrary direction. With respect to the three decisive characteristics of socialist society—classlessness, freedom, and internationalism—Russia is immeasurably further away today than during the first years of the revolution; nor has this direction been episodic but rather a continuous development since those early years. This has occurred in direct contradiction to Marxist theory: in Russia the key conditions, as it was thought, for the advance, if not to socialism at least well into its direction, were present—the assumption of state power by a Marxist party "of the workers," and above all the supposedly crucial abolition of private property rights in the chief instruments of production.

The capitalists were, with trivial exceptions, eliminated from Russian society and have not returned. In spite of this, a new class stratification, along economic lines, has proceeded to such a point that it equals or exceeds in sharpness that found in capitalist nations. This is shown on the one hand in the absolute elimination of the great masses of the people from any shred of control (the crux of property right) over the instruments of production. It is shown equally well in the income stratification. According to Leon Trotsky, in an article published in late 1939, and to my personal knowledge based on a careful collation and analysis of statistics published in the Soviet press, the upper 11% or 12% of the Soviet population now receives approximately 50% of the national income. This differentiation is sharper than in the United States, where the upper 10% of the population receives approximately 35% of the national income.

(If it is objected that Trotsky, as an enemy of Stalin, would have been "prejudiced" in giving this figure, it may be remarked that this article was written when Trotsky was in the midst of a bitter polemical struggle against views held primarily by myself in which he defended his unshaken belief that Russia remained still a workers' socialized state; the normal bias, if there were any, would under the circumstances have veered toward a playing down rather than up of the degree of class stratification as shown by income figures. The percentages, moreover, correspond well enough with those given by other competent observers— the Stalinist apologists, who are not competent, have not even pretended to give figures on so delicate a question; and allowance for a very wide margin of error would not alter the significance.)

Though freedom and democracy were never very extensive in revolutionary Russia, there was a considerable measure during the first years of the revolution—the years, that is to say, of greatest tribulation, of famine and civil war and wars of intervention, when any type of society and regime might well have been expected to lessen or suspend freedom. The democracy was represented by the existence of legal opposition parties, public factions of the Bolshevik party itself, important rights possessed by local soviets, workers' committees in factories, trade unions, etc., and by such factors as the elimination of titles, special modes of addressing "superiors," fancy uniforms, educational discrimination, and the other outward marks of social class distinctions.

Every shred of freedom and democracy has by now been purged from Russian life. No opposition of any kind (the lifeblood of any freedom) is permitted, no independent rights are possessed by any organization or institution, and the outward marks of class differences and despotism have one by one returned. All the evidence indicates that the tyranny of the Russian regime is the most extreme that has ever existed in human history, not excepting the regime of Hitler.

In keeping with socialist theories of internationalism, the leaders of the Russian Revolution expected their spark to touch off the world revolution. This did not happen, but for the early years the leaders remained internationalist in outlook and practice, theoretically indifferent to national boundaries, and looking upon the Russian state itself as merely a fort of the international socialist masses, to be used or sacrificed if need be to the higher interests of the world revolution. After the first years, for this internationalism there was substituted an ever-growing nationalism which has in recent times come to exceed anything ever present under the Czars themselves. The pseudo-internationalism, still occasionally manifested and allegedly represented by the existence of the Communist International and its parties, is simply the extension of Russian nationalism on the world arena and internationalist only in the sense that Hitler's fifth columns or the British or United States intelligence services are internationalist.

If we review honestly the developments in Russia, it is clear that in no important respect has the theory that socialism is coming been justified; every Russian development runs counter to what that theory leads us, and did lead those who believed it, to expect. Naturally, "dialecticians" can explain away what has happened in Russia. They can say that it was all because Stalin got into power instead of Trotsky or because of the failure of other nations to revolt or because of Russia's backwardness. Next time...things will be different. But the fact remains that Stalin did get into power, that the other nations did not ' successfully revolt, and that the revolution did take place in a backward country; and that the Russian revolution led not toward socialism but toward something most unlike socialism. Russia was, and this is admitted by all parties, the "first experiment in socialism." The results of *this* experiment are evidence for the view that socialism is not possible of achievement or even of approximation in the present period of history. Such an experiment, or even several of them, are not by themselves conclusive and final demonstration—no experiments are ever conclusive and final. But we must draw the lessons of the facts we have until, perhaps, different facts are placed at our disposal.

But to anticipate briefly: Though Russia did not move toward socialism, at the same time it did not move back to capitalism. This is a point which is of key significance for the problem of this book. All of those who predicted what would happen in Russia, friends and enemies, shared the assumption which I have already discussed in this chapter: that socialism is the "only alternative" to capitalism; from which it followed that Russia— since presumably it could not stay still—would either move toward socialism or back to the restoration of capitalism. *Neither of these anticipated developments has taken place.* All of the attempts to explain the present Russian setup as capitalist—of which there have recently been a number—or about to become capitalist have broken down miserably (no *capitalist* has any illusions on that score). Trotsky, otherwise the most brilliant of all analysts of Russia, to his death clung desperately to this "either...or" assumption, and in late years consequently became less and less able to explain sensibly or predict what happened. The only way out of the theoretical jam is to recognize that the assumption must be dropped, that socialism and capitalism are not the sole alternatives, that Russia's motion has been toward neither capitalism nor socialism, but toward *managerial society,* the type of society now in the process of replacing capitalist society on a world scale.

2. The second set of facts, constituting evidence that socialism is not coming, has already been mentioned: the expected socialist revolution, even the *nominally* socialist revolution such as took place in Russia, did not take place elsewhere, or, if attempted as in Germany, several Balkan nations, and in China, did not succeed. Yet socialist theory gave every reason to expect that it would come and would succeed, and socialist theoreticians did expect it. All important conditions supposed to be necessary for the transition to socialism were present in the immediate postwar era. The working class, presumed carrier of the socialist revolution, proved unable to take power, much less to inaugurate socialism. Yet most of the capitalist world was in shambles; the workers, as the principal part of the mass armies, had arms in their hands, and the example of Russia was before them.

3. One point of great importance has been proved conclusively by the Russian events: namely, that the second assumption we have discussed—the assumption that the abolition of capitalist private property rights in the instruments of production is a sufficient condition, a sufficient guarantee, of the establishment of socialism—is false. These rights were abolished in Russia, in 1918. Socialism has not come about, nor even been approached. In fact, the abolition of these rights not merely did not guarantee socialism, but did not even keep power in the hands of the workers—who, today, have no power at all. The presumed necessary connection between doing away with capitalist private property rights, on the one hand, and classlessness and freedom, on the other, does not exist. This the facts have *proved,* and theory, if theory is to make the slightest pretense to representing the facts, will have to adjust itself accordingly.

This, in turn, is close to decisive for the belief that socialism is about to come. For this belief was really based, more than on anything else, on the conviction that this necessary connection did exist. The problem of bringing socialism—the free, classless, international society of Marx's ideal and Marx's predictions—has always been thought, by all varieties of Marxists, to be, in final analysis, that of doing away with bourgeois private property rights. Now we know that this is not enough to bring socialism. If we still believe that socialism is possible, we will have to believe it on other grounds than those which were felt in the past to be sufficient.

4. *If* socialism is to come, the working class, as we have seen, has always, and rightly, been held to be the primary social group which will have a hand in its coming. According to Marx himself, the inherent development of capitalist society as it tended toward centralization and monopoly was such that there would take place the "proletarianization" of the overwhelming bulk of the population; that is, almost everyone would become workers. This made socialism easy, because the workers would have almost no one except a handful of finance-capitalists to oppose their course.

As is well known, this development did not take place as predicted by Marx. Sectors of the economy even of advanced nations, in particular agriculture, resisted the process of reduction to full capitalist social relations; most persons engaging in agriculture are neither capitalists nor workers (in the technical sense) but small independent producers. Small independent proprietors remain in many lines of endeavor; and the last seventy-five years have seen the growth of the so-called "new middle class," the salaried executives and engineers and managers and accountants and bureaucrats and the rest, who do not fit without distortion into either the "capitalist" or "worker" category.

This was already evident before 1914. Since the first world war, however, the social position of the working class has gravely deteriorated. This deterioration may be seen in a number of related developments:

(a) The rate of increase in the number of workers—especially the decisive industrial workers—compared to the total population has slowed down, and in the last decade, in many nations, has changed to a decrease.

(b) The bulk of the unemployed come from the working class.

(c) Changes in the technique of industry have, on the one hand, reduced more and more workers to an unskilled, or close to unskilled, category; but, on the other, have tied the process of production more and more critically to certain highly specialized skills, of engineering, production planning, and the like, requiring elaborate training not possessed by, or available to, many workers. With the methods of production used in Marx's own day, there was a higher percentage of skilled workers to unskilled. The gap in training between an average worker and the average engineer or production manager was not so large—indeed, in most plants and enterprises there was no need to recognize a separate category of engineers and scientists and production managers, since their work was either not needed or could be performed by any skilled worker.

Today, however, without the highly trained technical workers the production machine would quickly run down; as soon as serious trouble arose, or change or replacement was needed, or plans for a new production run were to be made, there would be no way of handling the difficulties. This alters gravely the relative position of the workers in the productive process. In Marx's time one could think without too much strain of the workers' taking over the factories and mines and railroads and shipyards, and running them for themselves; at least, on the side of the actual running of the productive machine, there was no reason to suppose that the workers could not handle it. Such a possibility is today excluded on purely technical grounds if on no others. The workers, the proletarians, could not, by themselves, run the productive machine of contemporary society.

(d) There has been a corresponding change in the technique of making war, which, since social relations are ultimately a question of relative power, is equally decisive as a mark of the deterioration in the social position of the working class.

Capitalist society was the first advanced culture to introduce mass militias, or armies of the citizenry. The mass armies were proved to be necessary to capitalism, as Machiavelli had foretold, by the unfortunate experiences with mercenary armies and then, later, small standing armies, the characteristic troops of the first centuries of capitalist society. But mass armies were at the same time potentially dangerous to the rulers of capitalist society, since, when they were formed, arms and training were given to the workers, who might decide to use them not against the foreign enemy but against the domestic rulers. Marxist theory, especially the Leninist branch of Marxism, naturally made a crucial point of this capitalist phenomenon, and in reality based revolutionary strategy upon it: the workers, armed in the mass by their rulers, were to turn their guns in the other direction.

In modern times, up to the first world war, the infantry was the decisive branch of the armed forces. The weapons and maneuvers used by the infantry were comparatively simple: it took little skill or training to be able to learn them. Anybody can take his place in a mass infantry attack. Thus if the ordinary soldiers of the line (the armed workers) revolted, they could be expected to put up a perfectly adequate fight against the elements of the armed forces which failed to revolt.

Beginning with the first world war, and carried vastly farther in the second, this military situation has been radically altered. Mass infantry is not eliminated, yet at any rate. But victory is today seen to depend upon complicated mechanical devices—airplanes, tanks, and the rest—to produce and handle which requires, once more, considerable skill and training. The industrial worker cannot learn these overnight; and it is noteworthy that the members of the air corps and other highly mechanized branches of the armed forces are drawn scarcely at all from the ranks of the industrial workers. Just as the new techniques of industry weaken the general position of the workers in the productive process as a whole, so do the new techniques of warfare weaken the potential position of the workers in a revolutionary crisis. Street barricades and pikestaffs, even plus muskets, are not enough against tanks and bombers.

5. The important social groups having as their professed aim the transition to socialism are the various Marxist political parties. Practical *success* for such parties does not at all guarantee the victory of socialism as the Russian experience shows: in general, there is no necessary correspondence between the professed aims of a political party and what happens when it takes power. But practical *failure* of these parties is additional, and strong, evidence against the prediction that socialism will come, since it removes one of the chief social forces which have been pointed to as motivation for the prediction. And the fact is that during the past two decades Marxist parties have collapsed on a world scale. Their fate can be pretty well summed up as follows: they have all either failed socialism or abandoned it, in most cases both.

These parties, it should be recalled, comprised in their ranks and sympathizing circles, tens of millions of persons throughout the world. During the past twenty years, they have simply disappeared from existence in nation after nation. Wherever fascism has risen (and even, as in several Balkan nations, where fascism has not been conspicuously present), the Marxist parties have gone under, usually without even a fight for survival. The greatest of all Marxist movements, that of Germany, bowed to Hitler without raising a hand. Nor should we permit ourselves to be deluded by refugee Marxists who, whether to give themselves prestige (and an audience) or out of sincere self-deception, tell us about the "vast underground movements." There is not the slightest real indication of the persistence of large organized underground movements. What has happened to the members of the Marxist parties is that many of them, particularly including many of the most vigorous, have been absorbed into the fascist movements; others have abandoned their hopes and become wholly passive; and, in any case, the new political techniques serve to atomize the remainder—as they do all opposition—so that they cannot exist as an organized force and therefore cannot function seriously in the political arena, since only organized groups are of importance politically.

But the physical elimination of many Marxist parties is not the only form of their collapse. Some apologists try to excuse Marxism by saying that it has "never had a chance." This is far from the truth. Marxism and the Marxist parties have had dozens of chances. In Russia a Marxist party took power. Within a short time it abandoned socialism, if not in words at any rate in the effect of its actions. In most European nations there were, during the last months of the first world war and the years immediately thereafter, social crises which left a wide-open door for the Marxist parties: without exception they proved unable to take and hold power. In a large number of countries—Germany, Denmark, Norway, Sweden, Austria, England, Australia, New Zealand, Spain, France—the reformist Marxist parties have administered the governments, and have uniformly failed to introduce socialism or make any genuine step toward socialism; in fact, have acted in a manner scarcely distinguishable from ordinary liberal capitalist parties administering the government. The Trotskyist and other dissident opposition wings of Marxism have remained minute and ineffectual sects without any influence upon general political developments. The last distorted partial upsurge of the Marxist parties, in connection with the Popular Front movement (which was, in origin, simply a device of the Communist International for implementing one side of the Kremlin's foreign policy of the moment), shows a record of utter incompetence and weakness (France) and disastrous, no matter how heroic, defeat (Spain); and ended with a whimper at Munich.

A detailed record of the Marxist parties since 1914 would only emphasize and re-emphasize the impression that is obtained from the briefest of surveys. The general summary is, once again, that these parties have, in practice, at every crucial historical test—and there have been many—either failed socialism or abandoned it. This is the fact which neither the bitterest foe nor the most ardent friend of socialism can erase. This fact does not, as some think, prove anything about the moral quality of the socialist ideal. But it does constitute unblinkable evidence that, whatever its moral quality, socialism is not going to come.

6. The practical collapse of the Marxist parties has paralleled the collapse of the Marxist ideology.

In the first place, the grander scientific pretensions of Marxism have been exploded by this century's increases in historical and anthropological knowledge and by the clearer contemporary understanding of the nature of scientific method. The Marxian philosophy of dialectical materialism takes its place with the other outmoded speculative metaphysics of the nineteenth century. The Marxian theory of universal history makes way for more painstaking, if less soul-satisfying, procedures in anthropological research. The laws of Marxian economics prove unable to deal concretely with contemporary economic phenomena. It would be wrong, of course, to deny all scientific value to Marx's own writings; on the contrary, we must continue to regard him as one of the most important figures in the historical development of the historical sciences—which sciences, even today however, are only in their infancy. But to suppose, as Marxists do, that Marx succeeded in stating the general laws of the world, of man and his history and ways, is today just ludicrous.

The situation with Marxist ideology is the same as that with the leading capitalist ideologies. As we saw in connection with the latter, however, the scientific inadequacy of an ideology is not necessarily important. What is decisive is whether an ideology is still able to sway the hearts and minds of masses of men, and we know that this result does not have to have any particular relation to scientific adequacy. Nevertheless, in the case of Marxism more than in that of most other ideologies (though to some extent with all), the exposure of scientific inadequacy is itself a factor tending·to decrease the mass appeal. (Perhaps it is rather that scientific criticism doesn't really get to work until mass appeal begins to decline.) For one of the big selling points of Marxism has been that it is the "only scientific doctrine" of society, and this has undoubtedly been a powerful emotional stimulant to its adherents.

The power of an ideology has several dimensions: it is shown both by the number of men that it sways and also by the extent to which it sways them—that is, whether they are moved only to verbal protestations of loyalty, or to a will to sacrifice and die under its slogans. This power is tested particularly when an ideology, in reasonably equal combat, comes up against a rival. From all of these points of view the power of Marxist ideology, or rather of the strictly *socialist* aspects of Marxist ideology, has gravely declined. This is especially noticeable among that so-decisive section of the population, the youth, who are no longer willing to die for the words of socialist ideology any more than for those of capitalist ideologies. The only branch of the Marxist ideology which still retains considerable attractive power is the Stalinist variant of Leninism, but Stalinism is no longer genuinely socialist. Just as in the case of the Stalinist party, the Marxist ideology has kept power only by ceasing to be socialist.

An ideology, of course, does not gain great attractive power merely because of the words that are in it or the skill of those who propagate it. These factors cannot be disregarded, but an ideology is not able to make a widespread way among the masses unless, in however distorted and deceptive a form, it expresses actual needs and interests and hopes of the masses, and corresponds, at least in some measure, with the actual state of social conditions and possible directions of their development. The weakening of the attractive force of both capitalist and socialist ideologies is a result primarily of the fact that they no longer express convincingly those needs and interests and hopes, no longer correspond at all adequately to actual social conditions and the actual direction of social development.

7. The falsity of the belief that socialism is about to arrive has been shown by an analysis of the unjustified assumptions upon which that belief is usually based and by a review of specific evidence countering that belief. To these must be added, what

has so far been only hinted at but what will occupy us largely in pages to come, the positive indications, already compelling, that not capitalism and not socialism but a quite different type of society is to be the outcome of the present period of social transition.

V

THE STRUGGLE FOR POWER

THE GENERAL field of the science of politics is the struggle for social power among organized groups of men. It is advisable, before proceeding with the positive elaboration of the theory of the managerial revolution, to try to reach a certain clarity about the meaning of "the struggle for power."

The words which we use in talking about social groups are, many of them, taken over directly from use in connection with the activities of individuals. We speak of a group "mind" or group "will" or "decision"; of a war "of defense"; and similarly of a "struggle" among groups. We know, roughly at least, what we mean when we apply these words to individuals and their actions; but a moment's reflection should convince us that groups do not have minds or wills or make decisions in the same sense that applies to individuals. "Defense" for an individual usually means preventing some other individual from hitting him; "struggle" means literal and direct physical encounter, and we can easily observe who wins such a struggle. But "defense" and "struggle" in the case of social groups—classes or nations or races or whatever the groups may be—are far more complicated matters.

Such words are, when applied to groups, *metaphors*. This does not mean, as we are told by our popularizing semanticists who do not understand what semantics teaches, that we ought not use such words. It means only that we must be careful, that we must not take the metaphor as expressing a full identity, that we must relate our words to what actually happens.

In all but the most primitive types of organized society, the instruments by which many of the goods (almost all of them nowadays) which are necessary for the maintenance and adornment of life are produced are *technically* social in character. That is, no individual produces, by himself, everything that he uses; in our society most people produce, by themselves, hardly anything. The production is a social process.

In most types of society that we know about, and in all complex societies so far, there is a particular, and relatively small, group of men that *controls* the chief instruments of production (a control which is summed up legally in the concept of "property right," though it is not the legal concept but the *fact* of control which concerns us). This control (property right) is never absolute; it is always subject to certain limitations or restrictions (as, for instance, against using the objects controlled to murder others at will) which vary in kind and degree. The crucial phases of this control seem to be two: first, the ability, either through personal strength, or, as in complex societies, with the backing— threatened or actual—of the state power acting through the police, courts, and armed forces to prevent access by others to the object controlled (owned); and, second, a preferential treatment in the distribution of the products of the objects controlled (owned).

Where there is such a controlling group in society, a group which, as against the rest of society, has a greater measure of control over the access to the instruments of production and a preferential treatment in the distribution of the products of those instruments, we may speak of this group as the socially dominant or ruling class in that society. It is hard, indeed, to see what else could be meant by "dominant" or "ruling" class. Such a group has the power and privilege and wealth in the society, as against the remainder of society. It will be noted that this definition of a ruling class does not presuppose any particular kind of government or any particular legal form of property right; it rests upon the facts of control of access and preferential treatment, and can be investigated empirically.

It may also be observed that the two chief factors in control (control of access and preferential treatment in distribution) are closely related in practice. Over any period of time, those who control access not unnaturally grant themselves preferential treatment in distribution; and contending groups trying to alter the relations of distribution can accomplish this only by getting control of access. In fact, since differences in distribution (income) are much easier to study than relations of control, those differences are usually the plainest evidence we have for discovering the relations of control. Put more simply: the easiest way to discover what the ruling group is in any society is usually to see what group gets the biggest incomes. Everyone knows this, but it is still necessary to make the analysis because of the fact that control of access is not *the same thing* as preferential treatment in income distribution. The group that has one also, normally, has the other: that is the general historical law. But for brief periods this need not invariably be the case, and we shall see later how significant the distinction is at the present time.

In feudal society by far the major instrument of production was the land—feudal economy was overwhelmingly agricultural. *De facto* control of the land (with important restrictions) and preferential treatment in the distribution of its products were in the hands of the feudal lords (including the lords of the Church), not of course as capitalist landlords but through the peculiar institutions of feudal property rights. These lords therefore constituted the ruling class in feudal society. So long as agriculture remained the chief sector of economy and so long as society upheld the feudal property rights, the lords remained the ruling class. The ruling class remained the same in structure, even though the individuals composing it might, and necessarily did, (through death, marriage, ennoblement, and so on) change.

Since the coercive institutions of the state (armed forces, courts, etc.) in feudal society enforced these rights, we may properly speak of the medieval state as a *feudal* state.

To an ever-increasing extent in post-medieval society, the decisive sectors of economy are not agricultural but mercantile, industrial, and financial. In modern society, the persons who control access to, and receive preferential treatment in, the distribution of the products of the instruments of production in these fields—and to a varying extent in the land also—are those whom we call "capitalists"; they constitute the class of the "*bourgeoisie.*" Their control is exercised in terms of the typical property rights recognized by modern society, with which we are all familiar. By our definition, the *bourgeoisie* or capitalists are the ruling class in modern society. Since the society recognizes these rights, we may properly speak of it as bourgeois or capitalist society. Since these rights have been enforced by the political institutions of modern society, by the state, we may speak similarly of the bourgeois or capitalist state.

Once again, the existence of the bourgeois *class* does not depend upon the existence of any particular individuals; the individual members change. The existence of the class means only that there is in society a group exercising, in terms of these recognized bourgeois property institutions, a special degree of control over the access to the instruments of production, and receiving as a group preferential treatment in the distribution of the products of these instruments.

What, let us ask, would be the situation in a *classless* society, a society organized along socialist lines? For society to be "classless" would mean that within society there would be no group (with the exception, perhaps, of temporary delegate bodies, freely elected by the community and subject always to recall) which would exercise, as a group, any special degree of control over access to the instruments of production; and no group receiving, as a group, preferential treatment in distribution. Somewhat more strictly on the latter point: there would be no group receiving by virtue of special economic or social relations preferential treatment in distribution; preferential treatment might be given to certain individuals on the basis of some noneconomic factor—for example, ill persons might receive more medical aid than healthy persons, men doing heavy physical work more food than children or those with sedentary occupations—without violating economic classlessness.

A new class rule in society would, in contrast, mean that society would become organized in such a way that a new group, defined in terms of economic or social relations differing from both feudal relations and bourgeois relations, would, as a group, in relation to the rest of the community, exercise a special degree of control over access to the instruments of production and receive preferential treatment in the distribution of the products of those instruments.

What, then, is meant by the "class struggle," the "struggle for power?" We say, often, that the *bourgeoisie* entered into a struggle for power with the feudal lords and, after a period, were victorious in that struggle. This is another of the metaphors drawn from personal combat and applied to group conflict. We must examine in what sense the metaphor can be legitimately used. The inquiry, of course, is important for us, not in connection with the struggle for power of the past, but with the struggle today and tomorrow.

It is certainly *not* the case that the capitalists of the world at some point got together, held a series of meetings, and came to the decision that they would embark upon a struggle for power against the feudal lords in order to organize society in such a manner as to be most beneficial to themselves; then went out and did battle against the assembled feudal lords, defeated them, and took over in person control of all the key institutions of society. Such behavior would presuppose a degree of consistency and scientific clarity that has been possessed by no class in history.

In the first and most fundamental place, the successful "struggle for power" of the *bourgeoisie* against the feudal lords can be interpreted as simply a picturesque way of expressing the result of what did, in fact, actually happen: namely, in the Middle Ages society was organized in a way that made the feudal lords the ruling class, possessed of chief power and privilege; later on society was organized differently, in a way that made the *bourgeoisie* the ruling class. Under this interpretation, to say that today a certain social class, other than the *bourgeoisie,* is struggling for power and will win that struggle need mean no more than the prediction that in a comparatively short time society will be organized in a new and different manner which will place the class in question in the position of the ruling class, with chief power and privilege. This is *part* of what is meant hereafter in this book when I speak, in connection with the managerial revolution, of the managers' "struggle for power."

However, more than this is meant. Though the *bourgeoisie* did not act in the conscious and critical manner that is suggested by a too-literal reading of the phrase, "struggle for power," they certainly did do something, and not a little, to extend and consolidate their social domination. Though they were often far from clear about what they wanted out of history, they did not just sit back and let history take its own course.

Two factors were of decisive importance in transforming society to a bourgeois structure: a great deal of fighting and wars to break the physical power of the feudal lords, and the propagation on a mass scale of new ideologies suited to break the moral power of feudalism and to establish social attitudes favorable to the bourgeois structure of society. Now, the capitalists did not, in any considerable measure, do the actual fighting in the wars, nor themselves elaborate the new ideologies; but the capitalists financed those who did the fighting and the thinking. The actual fighting was done in the early centuries for the most part by armies of mercenary soldiers who, after the introduction of gunpowder, were more than a match for the feudal knights and their retainers; and, later on, especially in the great revolutions, by the non-bourgeois masses, the workers and poor peasants. The ideologies were for the most part worked out by intellectuals—writers and political theorists and philosophers—and by lawyers.

Let us note: the hundreds of wars and civil wars fought from the fifteenth to the eighteenth century (by which time the social dominance of the *bourgeoisie* was assured in the major nations) were extremely various in character and motivation; from the point of view of the participants they were fought for religious, dynastic, territorial, commercial, imperial, and any number of other purposes. It is a gross perversion of history to hold that in them the *bourgeoisie* lined up on one side to fight feudal armies on the other. Indeed, even so far as more or less open class conflicts were concerned, the capitalists from the beginning were fighting each other as well as fighting against the feudal lords.

But two facts about these wars are of special significance for us. First, that the net result in terms of alterations of the structure of society was to benefit, above all, the *bourgeoisie,* as against all other sections of society, and to leave the *bourgeoisie* ever more securely the ruling class in society. Second, the bulk of the actual fighters were not themselves capitalists. Presumably, at least where it was not a matter of direct compulsion, most of those who fought believed that they did so for ends which were beneficial to themselves; but, at least so far as economic and social benefit went, this turned out, for the non-bourgeois bulk of the fighters, either not to be the case at all or at least far secondary to the benefit resulting to the capitalists.

Similar remarks apply to the development of the new ideologies. From the time of the Renaissance a number of more or less related new ideologies—religions, philosophies, moralities, theories of law and politics and society—were developed, and some of them became widely believed. None of these ideologies spoke openly in the name of the *bourgeoisie;* none of them said that the best kind of society and politics and morality and religion and universe was one in which the capitalists were the ruling class; they spoke, as all important ideologies do, in the name of "truth" and for the ostensible welfare of all mankind.

But, as in the case of the wars, two facts are of special significance for us. First, that the net result of the widespread acceptance of some of these new ideologies was to promote patterns of attitude and feeling in society which benefited, above all, the social position of the *bourgeoisie* and the institutions favorable to the *bourgeoisie*. Second, belief in, and advocacy of, these ideologies were not at all confined to the *bourgeoisie* but spread to all sections of the population. Presumably, the non-bourgeois sections of the population believed because they thought that these ideologies expressed their interests and hopes and ideals. Judged in terms of economic and social results, this was either not the case at all or true for the non-bourgeois groups only to a very minor degree as compared with the capitalists.

There was a general and a special phase in the development of bourgeois dominance. In general, the capitalists, starting from the small medieval towns and trading centers where primitive capitalist relations were already present at the height of the Middle Ages, gradually extended their dominance by reducing a greater and greater percentage of the widening economy to their control: that is, by bringing an ever-greater percentage of trade and production within the structure of the capitalist form of economic relations, by making an ever-greater percentage of the instruments of production the property of capitalists. This process continued an almost unbroken expansion until the first world war. Not only were already existing sectors of the economy shifted to a capitalist basis, as when an individual master craftsman with an apprentice or two changed himself into an employer by hiring employees for wages to work with his tools and materials at his workshop and for his profit; even more spectacularly did the capitalists expand the total area of the economy, the total of production, an expansion for which the capitalist economic relations were far better suited than the feudal.

It must be stressed that the building of bourgeois dominance began and was carried far within feudalism, while the structure of society was predominantly feudal in character, while, in particular, the political, religious, and educational institutions were still controlled in the primary interests of the feudal lords. This was possible because society accorded the capitalists, at least to a sufficient extent, those "rights" necessary for carrying on capitalist enterprise—of contract, of taking interest, hiring free workers for wages, etc.—in spite of the fact that most of these rights were directly forbidden by feudal law, custom, and philosophy (often, as in the case of taking interest, pious formulas were used to get around the prohibitions), and in spite of the fact that the wide extension of capitalist relations meant necessarily the destruction of the social dominance of the feudal lords. By the time the feudal lords, or some of them, woke up to what was happening and the threat to themselves, and tried to fight back, the battle was already just about over: for the *bourgeoisie* already controlled effectively the key bastions of society. If feudal society had refused from the beginning to recognize the bourgeois rights, the outcome might have been very different; but this is a useless speculation, since, in practice and in fact, these rights were, sufficiently, recognized.

The fact that the *bourgeoisie* did build up their social dominance, did reduce ever-widening sectors of the economy to their control, within the still-persisting framework of feudal society was, it would seem, a necessary condition for their appearing as the ruling class of the succeeding type of society. This point, in reverse, can reveal to us a decisive but neglected reason why socialism is not going to come. We have granted that, if socialism were going to come, the proletariat would have to be the social class chiefly concerned in its arrival. But the position of the proletariat in capitalist society is not at all the same as that of the *bourgeoisie* in late feudal society. The proletariat does not have a long period to build up gradually its social dominance, which means, above all, to extend control over greater and greater percentages of the instruments of production, a control expressed usually in the language of property rights. On the contrary, it does not have any such control, nor can it have in bourgeois society, or virtually none.

Marxists have sometimes thought that the development of trade-unions can make up for this deficiency. This is completely an illusion. Experience has proved that trade-unions are not an anticapitalist institution, not subversive of capitalist control over the instruments of production to any important or long-term extent, but are precisely capitalist institutions organized on the basis of, and presupposing, capitalist economic relations, a fact which is well known to most leading trade-unionists.

The proletariat, thus, has no established base, such as was possessed by the *bourgeoisie,* from which to go on to full social domination. It does not have the social equipment for the fight.

To return, however, to the *bourgeoisie.* I have spoken of this gradual extension of bourgeois control as the general phase of the development of bourgeois dominance. This was not enough to revolutionize the structure of society and to consolidate the position of the capitalists as the ruling class. So long as important institutions of society were dominated by the feudal lords and feudal ideas, the position of the capitalists was insecure, and the possibilities of capitalist expansion were severely restricted. In particular was this true in the case of the political institutions of society, of the state, since the state comprises the coercive instrumentalities of society, charged with enforcing rights and obligations. A feudal state, to take obvious examples, might at any time, and often did, back the cancellation of debts with an appeal to the violated Church doctrines against taking interest, might prevent serfs from leaving the land to seek work as free laborers, might permit the exaction of feudal dues on capitalist enterprises, and so on.

Capitalism and the capitalists confronted the problem of state power. To assure their dominance and advance, the *bourgeoisie* had to "take over state power." Here again we deal in a metaphor. What was needed for the development of capitalism and the dominance of the capitalists, and what in time, in fact, resulted, was a transformation in state institutions such that, instead of enforcing the rights and obligations of feudal society adjusted to the dominance of the feudal lords, they enforced the rights and obligations of capitalist society, adjusted to the dominance of the capitalists. In saying that the *bourgeoisie* took over state power and held it in England, France, the United States, or wherever it may have been, we do not necessarily mean that capitalists walked in physically or even that many government officials were drawn from the ranks of the capitalists. A bourgeois state, a state "controlled" by the *bourgeoisie,* means fundamentally a state which, by and large, most of the time and on the most important occasions, upholds those rights, those ways of acting and thinking, which are such as to permit the continued social dominance of the *bourgeoisie.*

As a matter of fact, the transformation of the state institutions into integral parts of a capitalist society was a lengthy and complicated process, sometimes, but not always, including bitter civil wars as decisive steps.

In the fifteenth and sixteenth and even the seventeenth centuries, the early capitalists, we know from the records of those times, worked closely with the princes or kings. The king in feudal society had been relatively unimportant, one feudal lord among others, often with less actual power than his chief vassals. When the kings began to strengthen their central authority and to try to build nations in the modern sense, their most obvious enemies were the feudal lords, including feudal lords who were supposed to be their own vassals. The kings sought support from the capitalists. The capitalists gave support to the kings because they, too, wanted stronger nations with national armies and navies to protect trade routes, and uniform laws, currencies, and taxes, so that trade could be carried on without constant interruption from a hundred feudal barons who considered themselves independent lords; because they made huge sums of money from dealings with the princes; and because they exacted protection and privileges in return for the aid they gave. In the wars and peace treaties, the elections of popes or emperors, the voyages of explorers and conquering armies during the sixteenth century, we always find a most prominent part played by the money of the Fugger or Medici or Welser or the other great merchant-bankers of Augsburg or Antwerp or Lyons or Genoa.

But the princes, too, could not be trusted in business matters, as many of these same great sixteenth-century capitalists found to their bankruptcy and ruin. The *de facto* alliance between prince and capitalists was dissolved, and the prince was ousted, made a figurehead, or at the least restricted in the area of society over which his power extended. There were more wars and revolutions, and the "ideal" bourgeois state of the late eighteenth and nineteenth centuries emerged: political power vested in the lower house of a parliament with full assurance that the parliament was, by constitution, law, habit, custom, and belief, dedicated to the upholding of the structure of rights and obligations in terms of which society is organized as capitalist.

One last observation in connection with the "struggle for power" of the *bourgeoisie*. Where did the early capitalists come from? They came from several sections of society: adventurers and brigands turned easily into capitalists after success in some escapade; artisans or master craftsmen became capitalists when they began to hire workers for wages; the biggest capitalists of the early period came from the ranks of the merchant-shippers, who were, as we saw, a special group even in the Middle Ages proper. The point I wish to note is that in some, not a few, cases the capitalists came from the ranks of the old ruling class, from among the feudal lords themselves. Many of the feudal lords were killed off in the various wars; the family lines of many others died out or sank into impoverished obscurity. But some of them turned themselves into capitalists: by driving the serfs off their land and engaging in agriculture as capitalist landlords; by undertaking the capitalist exploitation of mines on their land; or by using for capitalist ventures gold or jewels or money that they had acquired. We must remember, for the future also, that for a ruling class to be eliminated from society in favor of another ruling class does not mean that all of its individual members and their families disappear. Some of them may be found, perhaps prominently found, economically and socially metamorphosed, in the ranks of the new ruling class.

In describing the character of the present social transition and of the new type of society which is now developing, I shall continue to use the language of the "struggle for power." I shall speak of the class of managers as fighting for power, in particular for state power, as "having" and propagating typical ideologies, and I shall speak of the "managerial state" and "managerial society." I shall use this language because it is easy, well known, and picturesque; but its metaphorical significance must not be overlooked. It covers social processes of the greatest complexity which I shall assume, as we always assume when we try to learn from experience, are not too dissimilar in general form to those of the struggle for power "conducted" by the *bourgeoisie,* which I have sketchily touched on in this chapter.

VI

THE THEORY OF THE
MANAGERIAL REVOLUTION

WE ARE NOW in a position to state in a preliminary way the theory of the managerial revolution, the theory which provides the answer to our central problem.

The theory holds, to begin with, that we are now in a period of social transition in the sense which has been explained, a period characterized, that is, by an unusually rapid rate of change of the most important economic, social, political, and cultural institutions of society. This transition is *from* the type of society which we have called capitalist or bourgeois *to* a type of society which we shall call *managerial*.

This transition period may be expected to be short compared with the transition from feudal to capitalist society. It may be dated, somewhat arbitrarily, from the first world war, and may be expected to close, with the consolidation of the new type of society, by approximately fifty years from then, perhaps sooner.

I shall now use the language of the "struggle for power" to outline the remaining key assertions of the theory:

What is occurring in this transition is a drive for social dominance, for power and privilege, for the position of ruling class, by the social group or class of the *managers* (as I shall call them, reserving for the moment an explanation of whom this class includes). This drive will be successful. At the conclusion of the transition period the managers will, in fact, have achieved social dominance, will be the ruling class in society. This drive, moreover, is world-wide in extent, already well advanced in all nations, though at different levels of development in different nations.

The economic framework in which this social dominance of the managers will be assured is based upon the state ownership of the major instruments of production. Within this framework there will be no direct property rights in the major instruments of production vested in individuals as individuals.

How, then, it will be at once asked (and this is the key to the whole problem), if that is the economic framework, will the existence of a ruling class be possible? A ruling class, we have seen, means a group of persons who, by virtue of special social-economic relations, exercises a special degree of control over access to the instruments of production and receives preferential treatment in the distribution of the product of these instruments. Capitalists were such a group precisely because they, as individuals, held property rights in the instruments of production. If, in managerial society, no individuals are to hold comparable property rights, how can any group of individuals constitute a ruling class?

The answer is comparatively simple and, as already noted, not without historical analogues. The managers will exercise their control over the instruments of production and gain preference in the distribution of the products, not directly, through property rights vested in them as individuals, but indirectly, through their control of the state which in turn will own and control the instruments of production. The state—that is, the institutions which comprise the state—will, if we wish to put it that way, be the "property" of the managers. And that will be quite enough to place them in the position of ruling class.

The control of the state by the managers will be suitably guaranteed by appropriate political institutions, analogous to the guarantee of bourgeois dominance under capitalism by the bourgeois political institutions.

The ideologies expressing the social role and interests and aspirations of the managers (like the great ideologies of the past an indispensable part of the struggle for power) have not yet been fully worked out, any more than were the bourgeois ideologies in the period of transition to capitalism. They are already approximated, however, from several different but similar directions, by, for example: Leninism-Stalinism; fascism-nazism; and, at a more primitive level, by New Dealism and such less influential American ideologies as "technocracy."

This, then, is the skeleton of the theory, expressed in the language of the struggle for power. It will be observed that the separate assertions are designed to cover the central phases involved in a social "transition" and in the characterization of a "type of society" which were discussed in Chapters I and II.

But we must remember that the language of the struggle for power in metaphorical. No more than in the case of the capitalists, have the "managers" or their representatives ever got together to decide, deliberately and explicitly, that they were going to make a bid for world power. Nor will the bulk of those who have done, and will do, the fighting in the struggle be recruited from the ranks of the managers themselves; most of the fighters will be workers and youths who will doubtless, many of them, believe that they are fighting for ends of their own. Nor have the managers themselves been constructing and propagating their own ideologies; this has been, and is being, done for the most part by intellectuals, writers, philosophers. Most of these intellectuals are not in the least aware that the net social effect of the ideologies which they elaborate contributes to the power and privilege of the managers and to the building of a new structure of class rule in society. As in the past, the intellectuals believe that they are speaking in the name of truth and for the interests of all humanity.

In short, the question whether the managers are conscious and critical, whether they, or some of them, set before themselves the goal of social dominance and take deliberate steps to reach that goal, this question, in spite of what seems to be implied by the language of the "struggle for power," is not really at issue.

In simplest terms, the theory of the managerial revolution asserts merely the following: Modern society has been organized through a certain set of major economic, social, and political institutions which we call capitalist, and has exhibited certain major social beliefs or ideologies. Within this social structure we find that a particular group or class of persons—the capitalists or *bourgeoisie*—is the dominant or ruling class in the sense which has been defined. At the present time, these institutions and beliefs are undergoing a process of rapid transformation. The conclusion of this period of transformation, to be expected in the comparatively near future, will find society organized through a quite different set of major economic, social, ad political institutions and exhibiting quite different major social beliefs or ideologies. Within the new social structure a different social group or class—the managers—will be the dominant or ruling class.

If we put the theory in this latter way, we avoid the possible ambiguities of the overly picturesque language of the "struggle for power" metaphor. Nevertheless, just as in the case of the bourgeois revolution against feudalism, human beings are concerned in the social transformation; and, in particular, the role of the ruling class-to-be is by no means passive. Just what part, and how deliberate a part, they play, as well as the part of other persons and classes (bourgeois, proletarian, farmer, and the like), is a matter for specific inquiry. What they *intend* and *want* to do does not necessarily correspond with the actual effects of what they *do* say and do; though we are primarily concerned with the actual effects—which will constitute the transformation of society to a managerial structure—we are also interested in what the various groups say and do.

These remarks are necessary if we are to avoid common misunderstandings. Human beings, as individuals and in groups, try to achieve various goals—food, power, comfort, peace, privilege, security, freedom, and so on. They take steps which, as they see them, will aid in reaching the goal in question. Experience teaches us not merely that the goals are often not reached but that the effect of the steps taken is frequently toward a very different result from the goal which was originally held in mind and which motivated the taking of the steps in the first place. As Machiavelli pointed out in his *History of Florence,* the poor, enduring oppressive conditions, were always ready to answer the call for a fight for freedom; but the net result of each revolt was merely to establish a new tyranny.

Many of the early capitalists sincerely fought for the freedom of individual conscience in relation to God; what they got as a result of the fighting was often a harsh and barren fundamentalism in theology but at the same time political power and economic privilege for themselves. So, today: we want to know what various persons and groups are thinking and doing; what they are thinking and doing has its effects on historical processes; but there is no obvious correspondence between the thoughts and the effects; and our central problem is to discover what the effects, in terms of social structure, will be.

It should be noted, and it will be seen in some detail, that the theory of the managerial revolution is not merely predicting what may happen in a hypothetical future. The theory is, to begin with, an interpretation of what *already* has happened and is now happening. Its prediction is simply that the process which has started and which has already gone a very great distance will continue and reach completion. The managerial revolution is not just around the corner, that corner which seems never quite to be reached. The corner of the managerial revolution was turned some while ago. The revolution itself is not something we or our children have to wait for; we may, if we wish, observe its stages before our eyes. Just as we seldom realize that we are growing old until we are already old, so do the contemporary actors in a major social change seldom realize that society is changing until the change has already come. The old words and beliefs persist long after the social reality that gave them life has dried up. Our wisdom in social questions is almost always retrospective only. This is, or ought to be, a humiliating experience for human beings: if justice is beyond us, we would like at least to claim knowledge.

VII

WHO ARE THE MANAGERS?

WE MUST NOW clear up a question the answer to which has so far been postponed. Who are these managers, the class which is in the process of becoming the ruling class of society? The answer which interests us will not be given in terms of individuals: that is, we do not want to know that Mr. X, Miss Y, and other separate persons are managers. The answer that we need will be, first of all, in terms of *function:* by virtue of what function is it that we shall designate an individual as a manager? Whoever the individual may be, now or in the future, how are we to decide whether or not he is a manager? The functions that are of initial and prime importance to us are, of course, those functions in relation to the major instruments of production, since it is the relation to the instruments of production which decides the issue of class dominance, of power and privilege, in society.

The first part of the answer might seem to be only a verbal juggle and of no more value than any other verbal juggle: the managers are simply those who are, in fact, managing the instruments of production nowadays. Certainly, saying this does not appreciably advance our understanding. We must, therefore, investigate more carefully to see just who is doing the managing; and, in the investigation, we shall have to analyze out several ideas which are confusedly grouped together under the concept of "management."

It would seem obvious that in capitalist society it would be the capitalists who, in decisive respects at least, do the managing. If they do not manage the instruments of production, how could they maintain their position as ruling class, which depends upon control over the instruments of production? This is obvious, and the answer to this question is that they could not. It is the fact that during the past several decades the *de facto* management of the instruments of production has to a constantly increasing extent got out of the hands of the capitalists that so plainly proves society to be shifting away from capitalism and the capitalists losing their status as the ruling class. In ever-widening sectors of world economy, the actual managers are not the capitalists, the *bourgeoisie;* or, at the very least, the managerial prerogatives of the capitalists are being progressively whittled down. The completion of this process means the elimination of the capitalists from control over the economy; that is, their disappearance as a ruling class.

Let us make some distinctions: It is unnecessary to stress that the most important branches of modern industry are highly complex in technical organization. The tools, machines, and procedures involved are the results of highly developed scientific and technical operations. The division of labor is minute and myriad; and the turning out of the final product is possible only through the technical co-ordination of a vast number of separate tasks, not only within the individual factory, but in mines, farms, railroads, steamships, affiliated processors, and the like.

If we continue to look purely at the technical side of the process, we may observe the following: In comparison with the organization of industry in the period prior to modern mass production, the individual tasks, with the notable exception of a comparatively small percentage, require relatively less skill and training on the part of the individual worker. A century ago it took many years and considerable native aptitude to make a skilled general mechanic of the kind who then made engines or buildings or carriages or tools or machines. Today it takes a couple of weeks to make a worker ready to take his full place on a production or assembly line. Even so-called skilled work today usually needs no more than a few months' training. But, conversely, at the same time today a small percentage of tasks requires very great training and skill. Or let me put it in this way: within the process of production, the gap, estimated both in amount of skill and training and in difference of type of function, between the average worker and those who are in charge, on the technical side, of the process of production is far greater today than in the past.

From among those tasks which, today, require lengthy training and considerable skill, three may be separated out.

One type is found widely in those industries which, like the building industry, have not yet been organized in accordance with modern methods. There is, however, no technical reason why this has not been done in such industries. If it were done, the relative number of highly skilled workers in, for example, building would at once enormously decrease.

Another type consists of those tasks which need elaborate training in the physical sciences and in engineering. These have greatly increased in recent decades. A century ago, there were scarcely any highly trained chemists, physicists, biochemists, or even engineers functioning directly in industry, a fact which is plainly witnessed by the almost complete lack of educational facilities for training such industrial scientists and engineers. The comparatively primitive techniques of those days did not require such persons; today few branches of industry could operate without their constant services.

The third type consists of the tasks of the technical direction and co-ordination of the process of production. All the necessary workers, skilled and unskilled, and all the industrial scientists will not turn out automobiles. The diverse tasks must be organized, co-ordinated, so that the different materials, tools, machines, plants, workers are all available at the proper place and moment and in the proper numbers. This task of direction and co-ordination is itself a highly specialized function. Often it, also, requires acquaintance with the physical sciences (or the psychological and social sciences, since human beings are not the least among the instruments of production) and with engineering. But it is a mistake (which was made by Veblen, among others) to confuse this directing and co-ordinating function with the scientific and engineering work which I have listed under the second type of task. After all, the engineers and scientists of the second type are merely highly skilled workers, no different in kind from the worker whose developed skill enables him to make a precision tool or operate an ingenious lathe. They have no functions of guiding, administering, managing, organizing the process of production, which tasks are the distinctive mark of the third type. For these tasks, engineering and scientific knowledge may be, though it is not always, or necessarily, a qualification, but the tasks themselves are not engineering or science in the usual sense.

It is this third type of function which, in the fullest and clearest meaning, I call "managing"; and those who carry out this type of function are they whom I call the "managers." Many different names are given them. We may often recognize them as "production managers," operating executives, superintendents, administrative engineers, supervisory technicians; or, in government (for they are to be found in governmental enterprise just as in private enterprise) as administrators, commissioners, bureau heads, and so on. I mean by managers, in short, those who already for the most part in contemporary society are actually managing, on its technical side, the actual process of production, no matter what the legal and financial form—individual, corporate, governmental—of the process. There are, to be sure, gradations among the managers. Under the chief operating executives of a corporation like General Motors or U. S. Steel or a state enterprise like the TVA there are dozens and hundreds of lesser managers, a whole hierarchy of them. In its broader sense the class of managers includes them all; within the class there are the lesser and the greater.

But, it may well be commented, there is nothing new in the existence of managers. Industry has always had to have managers. Why do they suddenly assume this peculiar importance? Let us examine this comment.

In the first place, industry did not always require managers, at the very least not at all in the sense that we find them today. In feudal times the individual serf and his family tilled the small plot of soil to which he was attached; the individual artisan with his own tools turned out his finished product. No manager intervened to regulate and organize the process of production. Managers entered in only to the negligible sector of economy where larger-scale enterprise was employed.

Even in earlier capitalist times, the function of technical management was not crucial. The process of production was so simple, the division of labor so little developed compared to today, that hardly any special skill and training were necessary to carry out the functions of management. Nearly anyone who had any reasonable acquaintance with the industry in question could handle them.

Equally decisive for our purpose is the differentiation in *who* does the managing, what prerogatives attach to management, and how the functions of management are related to other economic and social functions.

In the earlier days of capitalism, the typical capitalist, the ideal of the ideologists before and after Adam Smith, was himself his own manager so far as there were managerial functions other than those assigned to some reliable skilled worker in the shop. He was the individual entrepreneur, who owned the whole or the greater share of a factory or mine or shop or steamship company or whatever it might be, and actively managed his own enterprise; perhaps to retire in old age in favor of management by his heirs. But, as is well known, the growth of large-scale public corporations along with the technological development of modern industry have virtually wiped such types of enterprise out of the important sections of the economy; with a few exceptions, they remain only among the "small businesses" which are trivial in their historical influence.

These changes have meant that to an ever-growing extent the managers are no longer, either as individuals or legally or historically, the same as the capitalists. There is a combined shift: through changes in the technique of production, the functions of management become more distinctive, more complex, more specialized, and more crucial to the whole process of production, thus serving to set off those who perform these functions as a separate group or class in society; and at the same time those who formerly carried out what functions there were of management, the *bourgeoisie,* themselves withdraw from management, so that the difference in function becomes also a difference in the individuals who carry out the function.

Let us take a hypothetical and over-simplified example in order to make more precise what is meant by "management" and to separate this off from other ideas which are often grouped with it. We will let our example be an imaginary automobile company. In connection with the ownership, control, and management situation in relation to this company, we may distinguish the following four groups:

1. Certain individuals—the operating executives, production managers, plant superintendents, and their associates—have charge of the actual technical process of producing. It is their job to organize the materials, tools, machines, plant facilities, equipment, and labor in such a way as to turn out the automobiles. These are the individuals whom I call "the managers."

It should be observed that the area of production which any

group of them manages is most variable. It may be a single small factory or mine or a single department within a factory. Or it may be a large number of factories, mines, railroads, and so on, as in the case of the chief managers of the great United States corporations. In theory the area could be extended to cover an entire interrelated branch of industry (automobiles, mines, utilities, railroads, whatever it might be) or most, or even all, of the entire mechanism of production. In practice in the United States at present, however, there do not exist managers *in this sense* for whole branches of industry (with possibly one or two exceptions), much less for a major portion or all of industry as a whole. The organization and co-ordination of industry as a whole is carried on through the instrumentality of "the market," without deliberate and explicit management exercised by specific managers, or indeed, by anyone else.

2. Certain individuals (among whom, in the United States at present, would ordinarily be found the highest ranked and best paid of the company officials) have the functions of guiding the company toward a *profit;* of selling the automobiles at a price and in the most suitable numbers for yielding a profit; of bargaining over prices paid for raw materials and labor; of arranging the terms of the financing of the company; and so on. These functions are often also called those of "management" and those who fulfill them, "managers." However, there is clearly no necessary connection between them and the first type of function. From the point of view of the technical process of production, a car would be neither worse nor better because of what it sold for (it could be given away and still be the same car, technically speaking) or what the materials which went into it cost; nor, so far as technical problems go, does the difference between bank loans at 4% or 5% show up in the power of the motor, or a change in dividend rate alter the strength of the frame.

In order to distinguish this group from the first, I shall call the individuals who make it up "finance-executives" or simply "executives," reserving the terms "management" and "managers" for the first group only.

3. Certain individuals (among whom in the United States at present would be many of the directors of the company and more particularly the bankers and big financiers who actually appoint the directors) have problems different from either of the first types. Their direct concern is not, or need not be, either the technical process of production or even the profit of the particular company. Through holding companies, interlocking directorates, banks, and other devices, they are interested in the financial aspects not merely of this automobile company but of many other companies and many market operations. They may wish to unite this company with others, in order perhaps to sell a stock or bond issue to the public, independently of the effect of the merger on the technical process of production or on the profits of our original company. They may want, for tax or speculative or other reasons, to lower the profit of this company, and could do so by, for example, raising prices charged by supply companies which they also were interested in. They may want to put some competitors out of business or influence politics or inflate prices; and any of such aims might be altogether independent of the requirements of production or profit in the particular automobile company. Any number of variants is possible. I shall call this third group the "finance-capitalists."

4. Finally there are certain individuals (a comparatively large number as a rule in the United States at present) who own in their names stock certificates in the automobile company and who are formally and legally the "owners" of our company. In fact, however, the great bulk of them, comprising in sum the legal "owners" of the substantial majority of the stock of the company, have an entirely passive relation to the company. The only right they possess with reference to the company is to receive, as against those who do not have stock certificates regis-

tered in their names, money in the form of dividends when on occasion dividends are declared by the directors.

This four-fold separation into "managers," "executives," "finance-capitalists," and "stockholders" is, in reality, a separation of *function,* of four of the types of relation in which it is possible to stand toward a certain section of the instruments of production. It is theoretically possible, therefore, that one and the same individual, or one and the same group of individuals, should perform all four of these functions, should stand in all four of these relations to the instruments of production in question (in our hypothetical case, the tangible assets of the automobile company). That is, one and the same individual (Henry Ford, as of some years ago, was a late and favorite example) or group of individuals could manage the production of the company, direct its policy so as to make a profit, integrate its activities in relation to banks and to other companies (if such were in question), and be the sole stockholder of the company. Not only is such an identity possible: until comparatively recently, it was normally the case.

Today, however, it is very seldom the case, especially in the more important sections of industry. The four functions are much more sharply differentiated than in the past; and they are, as a rule, performed by different sets of persons. It is not always so, of course; but it tends to become more and more so. Even where there is overlapping, where the same individual performs several of these functions, his activities in pursuit of each are easily separable.

Two further facts about these groups may be noted: In most large corporations, which together are decisive in the economy, the bulk of the stockholders, holding in their names the majority of the shares of stock, have, as everyone knows, the passive relation to the company which has been referred to. With only the rarest exceptions, they exercise no real control over the company except for the minor element of control involved in their preferential sharing (as against nonstockholders) in the profits, or rather the declared dividends, of the company. But the third group in our list (the finance-capitalists) are also, some of them at any rate, stockholders. Together they usually do not own in the legal sense a majority of the shares, but they ordinarily own a substantial block of the shares, and have at their disposal liquid funds and other resources whereby they can, when need arises, obtain from the small stockholders enough "proxies" on stock shares to be able to vote a majority.

Thus this third group is in a legal position of ownership toward· the company and the instruments of production included among the company's assets: if not with the unambiguous title of an earlier capitalist, who in his own name owned all, or a majority of, the shares of a company, at least to a sufficient degree to preserve the meaning of the legal relationship.

Sometimes the executives of Group 2 are also included in Group 4 and have substantial legal interests of ownership in the company (that is, have registered in their own or their families' names substantial blocks of the company's stock). But this is very seldom the case with the managers proper, with the members of Group 1; these ordinarily have no legal ownership interest in the company, or at most a very small interest: that is, they are not usually large stockholders in the company.

Second, there is a complete difference among these groups with respect to the *technical* role of their respective functions in relation to the process of production. The process of production is technically and literally impossible unless someone is carrying out the functions of management, of Group 1—not necessarily the same individuals who carry them out today, but, at any rate, someone.

Some of the finance-executive functions comprised in Group 2 are also technically necessary to the process of production, though not necessarily in the same sense as today: that is, not necessarily (from a technical point of view) for the sake of profit as understood by capitalism. There must be some regulation of the quality, kinds, numbers, and distribution of products apart from the theoretic abilities of the instruments of production to turn products out. This regulation would not have to be achieved, however, as it is through the finance-executives, in terms of capitalist profits for the company. It could be done in subordination to some political or social or psychological aim—war or a higher standard of mass living or prestige and glory or the maintenance of some particular power relationship. In fact, with profit in the capitalist sense eliminated, the *technically necessary* functions of the finance-executives of Group 2 become part of the management functions of Group 1, if management is extended over all or most of industry. Management could, that is to say, absorb all of the technically necessary functions of the non-managing executives.

But, still from a strictly technical viewpoint, the remaining functions—the "profit-making" functions—of Group 2 and all the functions of Groups 3 and 4—finance-capitalist and stockholder—are altogether unnecessary (whether or not desirable from some other point of view) to the process of production. So far as the technical process of production goes, there need not be finance-capitalists or stockholders, and the executives of Group 2, stripped of many of their present functions, can be merged in the management Group 1.[1]

Not only is this development conceivable: it has already been almost entirely achieved in Russia, is approached more and more nearly in Germany, and has gone a considerable distance in all other nations. In the United States, as everywhere, it is precisely the situation to be found throughout *state enterprise.*

[1] I must warn that this fourfold division which I have made bears no relation to the usual division between "industrial capitalists" and "finance-capitalists." This latter distinction is of great importance in studying the historical development of capitalism, but seems to me of little value in the analysis of the structure of present-day capitalism. In particular, it is of no value in connection with the central problem of this book.

This development is a decisive phase of the managerial revolution.

*   *

    *

The so-called "separation of ownership and control," paralleling the growth of the great public corporations of modern times, has, of course, been a widely recognized phenomenon. A decade ago it was the principal subject of the widely read book, *The Modern Corporation and Private Property,* by Berle and Means. In this book, the authors showed that the economy of the United States was dominated by the two hundred largest nonbanking corporations (they did not discuss the relations of these to financial houses); and, second, that the majority of these corporations were no longer, in practice, controlled by their nominal legal owners (that is, stockholders holding in their names a majority of the shares of stock).

They divided these corporations according to "types of control." In a few, control was exercised by a single individual (more often, single family) who was legal owner of all or a majority of the stock; in others, by individuals or groups which owned not a majority but a substantial percentage of the stock. Most, however (in 1929, 65% of these 200 corporations with 80% of the total assets), they decided were what they called, significantly enough, "management-controlled." By "management-controlled," as they explained, they meant that the management (executives) of these companies, though owning only minor percentages of the shares of their corporations, were in actuality self-perpetuating, in control of the policies and the boards of directors of the companies and able to manipulate at will, through proxies, majority votes of the nominal owners, the shareholders. The American Telephone and Telegraph Corporation is the classic example of "management-control."

Though briefly, Berle and Means also took up the extremely important point that in the nature of the case there were sources of frequent conflict between the interests of the "control group" (most often, the management) and the legal owners. This is apparent enough to anyone who recalls the economic events of the past generation. Many books have been written about the difficulties of the run-of-the-mine common stockholders, often as a result of the policies of the "control group" of "their own" company. Wealth, power, and even other possible interests (such as maximum industrial efficiency) of the control group quite naturally do not often coincide with maximum dividends and security for the common stockholders.

The analysis by Berle and Means is most suggestive and indirectly a powerful confirmation of the theory of the managerial revolution, but as it stands it is not carried far enough for our purposes. In their concept of "management-control" they do not distinguish between management in the sense of actual direction of the process of production (the sense of our Group 1 and the only sense in which we refer to "management") and management in terms of profit, selling, financing, and so on (our Group 2, the finance-executives). Indeed, their use of "management," as is usually the case, is closer to the latter than the former, which results really from the fact that in most big corporations today the chief and best-known officials are of the second or executive, not of the first or manager, type. Moreover, Berle and Means do not include any study of the way in which their supposedly self-perpetuating and autonomous managements are in actuality often controlled by big banks or groups of financiers (our Group 3).

One result of such a refinement and amplification of the Berle and Means analysis would be to show that the sources of possible and actual conflict among the groups are far more numerous and more acute than they indicate. Among these sources, three should be stressed:

1. It is a historical law, with no apparent exceptions so far known, that all social or economic groups of any size strive to improve their relative position with respect to power and privilege in society. This law certainly applies to the four groups

into which we have divided those who stand in some sort of relation of ownership, management, or control toward the instruments of production. Each of these groups seeks to improve its position of power and privilege. But, in practice, an improvement in the position of one of them is not only not necessarily an improvement for the others; often it means a worsening of the position of one or all of the others.

In periods of great prosperity and expansion, this is not very irritating, since all four can advance relatively as against the rest of society; but, as we have already seen, such periods have ended for capitalism. In conditions which are now normal, an increase in income for the managers or even the executives of Group 2 means so much the less for Group 3 (the financiers) and Group 4 (the stockholders.)

Even more apparently, the relations of control over the operations of the instruments of production raise conflicts, since the sort of operation most favorable to one group (expanding or contracting production, for example) very often is not that most favorable to another. And, in general, there is a source of permanent conflict: the managers proper receive far less reward (money) than the executives and especially the finance-capitalists, who get by far the greatest benefits. From the point of view of the manager group, especially as economic conditions progressively decay, the reward allotted to the finance-capitalists seems inordinate and unjustified, all the more so because, as the managers see it more and more clearly, the finance-capitalists are not performing any function necessary to the process of production.

2. All four of these groups, to one or another degree, are powerful and privileged as against the great masses of the population, who have no interest of ownership, management, or control in the instruments of production and no special preferential treatment in the distribution of their products. Consequently, the masses have a tendency to strive for a greater share of power and privilege as against all four of these groups. The result of

this situation might be expected to be a merging of the conflicts among the four groups and a common front against the pressure of the masses. This has indeed been often the case. Nevertheless, the conflicts among the groups are real and cannot be eliminated even in the face of a common danger. In fact, the presence of the common danger is itself a source of new conflicts. This follows because the groups, from the very status they occupy and functions they fulfill, favor different methods of meeting the danger and of maintaining privilege as against the masses. The differences become sharpened under the crisis conditions of contemporary capitalism. This can be made clear by a single example:

The position, role, and function of the managers are in no way dependent upon the maintenance of capitalist property and economic relations (even if many of the managers themselves think so); they depend upon the technical nature of the process of modern production. Consequently the preservation of the capitalist relations is not an absolutely decisive question for the managers. The position, role, and function of the most privileged of all the groups, the finance-capitalists, are, however, *entirely* bound up with capitalist property and economic relations, and their preservation is decisive for even the continued existence of this group. This holds in general and cannot help affecting the situation with respect to more specific problems.

For instance, from the point of view of the technical position of the managers, the problem of unemployment is perfectly easy to solve: if the technical co-ordination and integration of industry were extended, unemployment could be wiped out in a month. Moreover, the managers, or many of them, are aware that unless mass unemployment is wiped out, all privileges, including their own, will be wiped out, either through national defeat by a nation which has wiped it out or by internal chaos. But mass unemployment cannot be eliminated without invading and finally abolishing capitalist property and economic relations. The position of the managers thus forces them toward solutions which would have such an effect. But the finance-capitalists (and even the executives, for that matter) are differently situated. Their position, depending on the capitalist relations, thereby depends also on the continuance of mass unemployment; they cannot entertain any solution that has a chance of eliminating unemployment without involving at the same time their own elimination. (If they think they can, they are simply mistaken, as they are beginning to find out in Germany and will before long find out elsewhere.)

3. A third source of conflict is found in what we might call "occupational bias," a point to which we shall return later. The different things which these different groups do promote in their respective members different attitudes, habits of thought, ideals, ways and methods of solving problems. To put it crudely: the managers tend to think of solving social and political problems as they co-ordinate and organize the actual process of production; the nonmanagerial executives think of society as a price-governed profit-making animal; the finance-capitalists think of problems in terms of what happens in banks and stock exchanges and security flotations; the little stockholders think of the economy as a mysterious god who, if placated properly, will hand out free gifts to the deserving.

But there is a more basic deficiency in the analysis of Berle and Means or any similar analysis. The truth is that, whatever its legal merits, the concept of "the separation of ownership and control" has no sociological or historical meaning. Ownership *means* control; if there is no control, then there is no ownership. The central aspects of the control which is ownership, are, as we have seen, control over access to the object in question and preferential treatment in the distribution of its products. If ownership and control are in reality separated, then ownership has changed hands to the "control," and the separated owner-ship is a meaningless fiction.

This is perfectly obvious as soon as we think about it. If I own a house, let us say, that means that—at least under normal circumstances—I can prevent others from entering it. In de-veloped societies with political institutions, it means also that the state (the police in this instance, backed by the courts) will if necessary enforce this control of mine over access to the house. If I cannot, when I wish to, prevent others from entering the house, if anyone else or everyone has the same rights of entry as I, then neither I nor anyone would say that I am the "owner" of the house. (I can, of course, alienate my control, either temporarily—through a lease—or permanently—through sale or gift—but these and similar acts do not alter the fundamental point.) Moreover, insofar as there are products of the house (warmth, shelter, privacy might be so considered, as well as rent) I, as owner, am, by the very fact of control over access in this case, entitled to preferential treatment in receiving these products.

Where the object owned takes the form of instruments of production (factories, machines, mines, railroads....) the situa-tion is the same, only more complicated. For sociological and practical purposes, the owner (or owners) of the instruments of production is the one (or group) that in *fact*—whether or not in theory and words—controls access to those instruments and controls preferential treatment in the distribution of their products.

These two rights (control of access and preferential treatment in distribution) are fundamental in ownership and, as we have noted, determine the dominant or ruling class in society—which consists simply of the group that has those rights, or has them, at least, in greater measure than the rest of society, with respect to the chief instruments of production.

Moreover, historical experience shows (as would be obvious without much experience) that these two rights are interrelated and that the first (control of access) is determinative of the second. That is to say: the group or groups which have control over access to the instruments of production will, as a matter of experienced fact, also receive preference in the distribution of the products of those instruments. Or in other words: the most powerful (in terms of economic relations) will also be the wealthiest. This does not apply to every separate individual concerned; and there may be a temporary dislocation in the relationship; but to groups, and over any period of time beyond a comparatively few years, it seems to apply always. Social groups and classes are, we might say, "selfish": they use their control to benefit primarily (not necessarily exclusively) themselves.

Berle and Means are therefore inconsistent, or at least incomplete, when they speak of "the separation of ownership and control." Those who control *are* the owners. The fact is that all four groups we have dealt with share at least to some degree in *control:* at the least they all control preferential treatment in the distribution of the products of the instruments of production, which is enough to constitute them owners; though in the case of the bulk of the stockholders, who have this control to a minor extent and none of the more decisive control over access, the ownership is of a very subordinate kind.

But if we reinterpret the phrase "separation of ownership and control" to mean "separation of control over access from control over preferential treatment in distribution"—and this is partly what lies back of the Berle and Means analysis—then we are confronted with a fact of primary importance. It is true that a partial separation of this kind has been taking place during recent decades. Income and power have become unbalanced. Those who receive the most preferential treatment in distribution (get the biggest relative share of the national income) have, in differing degrees in different nations and different sections of the economy, been losing control over access. Others, who do not receive such a measure in preferential treatment in distribution, have been gaining in the measure of control over access which they exercise. Historical experience tells us that such a lack of correlation between the two kinds of control (the two basic rights of property) cannot long endure. Control over access is decisive, and, when consolidated, will carry control over preferential treatment in distribution with it: that is, will shift ownership unambiguously to the new controlling, a new dominant, class. Here we see, from a new viewpoint, the mechanism of the managerial revolution.

VIII

THE MANAGERS MOVE TOWARD
SOCIAL DOMINANCE

THE CONTENTION of the last chapter that control over the instruments of production is everywhere undergoing a shift, away from the capitalists proper and toward the managers, will seem to many fantastic and naïve, especially if we are thinking in the first instance of the United States. Consider, it will be argued, the growth of monopoly in our time. Think of the Sixty Families, with their billions upon billions of wealth, their millions of shares of stock in the greatest corporations, and their lives which exceed in luxury and display anything even dreamed of by the rulers of past ages. The managers, even the chief of them, are only the servants, the bailiffs of the Sixty Families. How absurd to call the servant, master!

Such would have been the comment—except, perhaps, of a few in a few small towns—Florence, Genoa, Venice, Bruges, Augsburg—if anyone had in the early fifteenth century been so much a dreamer as to suggest that control was then shifting from the feudal lords toward the small, dull, vulgar group of merchants and traders and moneylenders. Consider, it would have been argued, the splendid, insolent dukes and barons and princes, with their shining armor and their castles and clouds of retainers, and the land, all the land, in their grasp. Merchants, moneylenders! they are only purveyors to the mighty, fit to provide them with the luxuries required by their station and occasionally to lend them a few despised ducats for provisioning an army or building a new fortress.

Yet, only a century thereafter (and change is more rapid now) the social heirs of those merchants and traders and moneylenders were, with their ducats, deciding the succession to thrones, the elections of emperors and popes, the winning of wars, the signing of peace. Within a century their social domination, though not yet consolidated, was assured. Yes, even the broad lands of the barons were passing into their hands as mortgages were foreclosed or as desperate lords strove hopelessly for the money they did not have and without which in the new age they could not even feed their children.

We must not anticipate. A process which is in midcourse is not finished. The big *bourgeoisie,* the finance-capitalists, are still the ruling class in the United States; the final control is still in their hands. But we must not view the world too narrowly nor limit our eyes to the surface. For it is a world process with which we are dealing, since capitalism is a world system: the United States is linked economically, socially, culturally, and, most dramatically of all (how well we know this today!), strategically with all the world. And the process goes all the way to the roots of society; it does not remain merely on the outer layers. If we lift our eyes to the world arena and sink them to the roots, we will see what is there: that the capitalists, the ruling class of modern society, are losing control, that the social structure which placed them in the position of ruling class is being transformed, not tomorrow, but now, as we watch. In the new structure, when its foundations are completed, there will be no capitalists.

We have seen that the rise to power and domination of the *bourgeoisie* meant, first of all, the progressive reduction of greater and greater percentages of the instruments of production to capitalist economic relations—that is, control by and in the primary interests of the capitalists instead of the feudal ruling class. This increase of percentage meant either putting on a capitalist basis areas of production which had been on a feudal basis, or, equally well, opening up, along capitalist lines, areas of production which had not existed under feudalism. (Either development was an increase in the total percentage of production under capitalist control.)

There was still another variable (though more difficult to measure) in this process of the extension of capitalist control: namely, the degree to which a given section of production was subject to capitalist relations. For example, so long as feudal lords, making use of the Church doctrine against usury, could repudiate loans and refuse to honor pledges they had made on loans, and get away with it, the business of loaning was not fully capitalist in character; or, similarly, with guild and serf restrictions interfering with the wage-relation between capitalist and worker; or feudal "just price" conceptions blocking free exchange of commodities on the market; etc. The extension of capitalist control was also indicated by the progressive overcoming of all such restrictions on the capitalist mode of economy.

We have also seen that, from one point of view, within the economic sphere the extension of capitalist control went on steadily and continuously, with scarcely an interruption. From the latter part of the Middle Ages on, virtually every decade found a higher percentage of the economy capitalist than had been the case during the preceding decade. Individual capitalists were wiped out, true enough, either by other capitalists, or often by feudal lords—nearly every great financier was ruined in the state bankruptcies of the latter part of the sixteenth century, for example. We are not, however, concerned with the fate of individual members of a class. The capitalists who were wiped out were not replaced by feudal lords or officials but by other capitalists.

At certain times, moreover, the extension of capitalist control was not slow and steady but sudden and large-scale. These times were in conjunction with wars, international, colonial, and civil. As the economic historian of the Renaissance, Richard Ehrenberg, puts it: "Political effects tend to be catastrophic, as opposed to the slow, almost imperceptible action of economic forces and interests."

The turning point in capitalist control over the economy was reached during the first world war (this is why I selected the date, 1914, as that of the beginning of the social transition from capitalist to managerial society). The curve of the extension of capitalist control, which had risen without interruption from the fourteenth century, abruptly broke downward and has sunk continuously ever since, heading swiftly toward zero. When once it is brought to our attention and when we think of it in terms of the world arena, this shift in control over the instruments of production away from the big capitalists, which has gone on since the beginning of the first world war, cannot possibly be denied, even from the most obvious point of view. All of Russia, one-sixth of the earth's land surface, was taken out of capitalist hands during the course of the war. In Italy and especially in Germany (because of its advanced technology and equipment far more decisive than Russia) and in what Germany conquers, capitalist control is plainly headed toward extinction. Russia and Germany will, however, occupy us in some detail later. In the present chapter, let us consider the situation in the United States itself, where the process with which we are dealing has gone a shorter distance than in any other major nation.

Insofar as the United States is capitalist, this means that control over the instruments of production is held by those who have capitalist property rights in those instruments. Historically and legally in the United States, this, in turn, means, above all, the few hundred great families ("the Sixty Families," as Ferdinand Lundberg called the chief of them in his book which took its title from that phrase) who, in point of fact, have in the form of stock and other ownership certificates much greater legal capitalist ownership rights than any other group.

There can be no question today about the control over preferential treatment in distribution which is possessed by these families. The funds available to them are colossal in relation to their small numbers. In spite of much that is written and said on the subject, probably few outside their ranks really comprehend the scale of luxury on which many of them live, a scale exceeding anything known before in history.

Nevertheless, we have seen that of the two decisive elements in actual ownership, control over preferential treatment in distribution is subordinate to control over access. With respect to the latter, though it is by no means yet out of the hands of the big *bourgeoisie,* though it can still be exercised by them on crucial occasions, it has on the whole been diminishing during the past generation.

This is indicated in one very interesting and important way by a phenomenon which might be called the withdrawal of the big *bourgeoisie* from production. The big capitalists, legally the chief owners of the instruments of production, have in actual life been getting further and further away from those instruments, which are the final source and base of social dominance. This began some time ago, when most of the big capitalists withdrew from industrial production to finance. At first this shift to finance (which was well under way by the turn of this century) did not mean any lessening of control over the instruments of production: rather the contrary, for through finance-capitalist methods a wider area than ever of the economy was brought, and was brought more stringently, under the control of the big capitalists. Nevertheless, the control necessarily became more indirect, exercised at second or third or fourth hand through financial devices. Direct supervision of the productive process was delegated to others, who, particularly with the parallel development of modern mass-production methods, had to assume more and more of the prerogatives of control—for example, the all-important prerogative of hiring and firing (the very heart of "control over access to the instruments of production") as well as organization of the technical process of production.

But the big capitalists did not stop their withdrawal at the level of finance. We find that they have more and more withdrawn, not merely from production proper, but from active and direct participation of any sort in the economic process. They spend their time, not in industry or even in finance, but on yachts and beaches, in casinos and traveling among their many estates; or, others of them, in charitable, educational, or even artistic activities. Statistics on such a point are difficult to get; but it is safe to say that a substantial majority of the members of the first Sixty Families listed by Lundberg has withdrawn from any serious direct active contact with the economic process. To rule society, let it be remembered, is a full-time job.

The point is emphasized by reflecting how much (it is often estimated at more than a half) of the wealth and legal ownership possessed by the big capitalists is now registered in the name of women. Such registration is often a legal device to aid in the preservation of the wealth, but it marks again the gap between the legal owners (in the capitalist sense) and the instruments of production: whatever the biological merits, it is a fact that women do not play a serious leading role in the actual economic process.

We are not interested in the moral side of this "withdrawal" of the big capitalist families. Differing moral criteria can be found to label their lives today as either more wasteful and parasitic or more enlightened than those of their predecessors. What interests us are the social implications, now and for the future, of this withdrawal. One consequence of the withdrawal is necessarily the assumption of more and more power over the actual processes of production, more and more of the time, by others than the chief legal owners of the instruments of production, in many instances by those whom we call the managers.

It could not be otherwise. Somebody is going to do the actual managing; and, the way things have happened, as the big capitalists do less of it, the managers have been doing more. Of course, as the situation still is in the United States, the power of the managers is still far from absolute, is still in the last analysis subordinate to that of the big capitalists. The big capitalists and the institutional relations of capitalism continue to provide a framework within which the managers must work: for example, in determining the raising or lowering of production output, the large-scale financial operations, the connections between different units of industry, and so on. The big capitalists intervene at occasional key moments that affect the broad directions of major policies. They keep, as a rule, a kind of veto right which can be enforced when necessary by, for example, getting rid of any rebellious managers. The managers remain in considerable measure delegates ("servants") of the big capitalists.

Such a delegation of power and control is, however, highly unstable. It has always happened that servants who discover themselves to be solidly enough established gradually turn on their masters, especially if they wake up to the fact that their masters are no longer necessary to them. Under the Merovingian kings of France in the Dark Ages, the Mayor of the Palace was originally the mere vulgar chief of the court servants. Gradually the actual control of administration got into the hands of the Mayors of the Palace. But, for several generations thereafter, the Merovingians, becoming more and more mere puppets, were kept as kings and lived with all the outward signs of kingship. The final act of doing away with them, which took place when the Mayor who was the father of Charlemagne proclaimed himself king, simply put in a formal way what had already happened in sociological reality.

The instruments of production are the seat of social domination; who controls them, in fact not in name, controls society, for they are the means whereby society lives. The fact today is that the control of the big capitalists, the control based upon capitalist private property rights, over the instruments of production and their operation is, though still real, growingly tenuous, indirect, intermittent. More and more of the time, over more and more phases of the productive process, no capitalist intervention appears. In another transition age, feudal lords, on harsh enough terms, leased out towns or lands to capitalists, who conducted capitalist operations with them in place of the feudal operations which the lords had before then directed. The lords remained lords and lived like lords; they had, seemingly, controlling rights, could throw out the capitalists at will and bleed them for even more returns than the contracts called for. But, somehow, after a while, it was the capitalists who had the town and the land and the industry, and the lord who was left with a long ancestry and noble titles—and an empty purse and vanished power.

Throughout industry, *de facto* control by the managers over the actual processes of production is rapidly growing in terms both of the aspects of production to which it extends and the times in which it is exercised. In some sections of the economy, the managerial control is already fairly thorough, even though always limited indirectly by big capitalist control of the banks and finance. Though the Berle and Means conception of "management-controlled" corporations fails, as we have seen, to clarify what is meant by management and how management is related to finance, yet there are many corporations, and these from among the greatest, not the secondary, where the managers in our sense are quite firmly entrenched, where owners, in the legal and historical capitalist meaning, have scarcely anything to do with the corporations beyond drawing dividends when the managers grant them.

But it might be asked: assuming that this development is taking place, does it not mean simply that the old big bourgeois families are on their way out of the front rank and new persons are about to take their places? This has happened many times before during the history of capitalism. The survival of capitalism, as we have seen, does not depend upon the survival of any given individual capitalists but of a ruling capitalist class, upon the fact that the social place of any individual capitalists who are eliminated is taken by other capitalists. This was what happened before, and outstandingly in the United States. If the old and wealthiest capitalists are slipping, then, it would seem, the newer managers will utilize their growing power to become the new members of the big *bourgeoisie*.

However, in spite of the fact that many of the managers doubtless have such an aim as their personal motivation, it will not happen. In the first place, with the rarest exceptions, it is no longer possible for the managers to realize such an aim, even if they have it. The chance to build up vast aggregates of wealth of the kind held by the big bourgeois families no longer exists under the conditions of contemporary capitalism. Lundberg shows that since the end of the first world war there has been only a single change in the listing of the first Sixty Families in this country; only a single newcomer has penetrated that stratum (and this closing of the doors to the top rank occurred much later in the United States than in the other great capitalist nations). The inability of a ruling class to assimilate fresh and vigorous new blood into its ranks is correctly recognized by many sociologists as an important symptom of the decadence of that class and its approaching downfall.

In addition, however, because of the structural changes within society, the future road toward social domination and control no longer lies in the massing of personally held capitalist property rights. Not merely is getting these rights on a big scale nearly impossible for newcomers, but also, if the aim is greater social domination and privilege, there are now and for the future more effective means for achieving the aim. With capitalism extending and ascendant, individual capitalists, together making up the ruling class, are, when they disappear, replaced by other individual capitalists. With capitalism collapsing and on its way out, the ruling capitalist class as a whole is being replaced by a new ruling class.

This need not mean (though it may) that those same individuals who are at present managers under capitalism will constitute that new ruling managerial class of the future. Very few of the leading capitalist families of the sixteenth century survived to become part of the ruling capitalist class of later generations. If the present managers do not themselves constitute the new ruling class, then other individuals will. But the other individuals will do so by themselves becoming managers, not capitalists, because the new ruling class will be the managerial class.

So far we have been considering the weakening of control by the big *bourgeoisie* and the increase of control by others, in particular the managers, within the field of what is usually called "private enterprise," the field of capitalist economy proper. The process is strictly analogous to what happened in the transition from feudalism to capitalism: in a constantly growing section of the total economy, control by the previously established ruling class diminishes, and control by another class is extended.

The somewhat blurred outlines of the picture so far drawn are at once sharpened when we extend our view from private to governmental (state) enterprise. The rapidity with which the economy is being removed from control by capitalists—that is, from organization in terms of capitalist economic relations—is unmistakable as soon as we pay attention to the role of government. Here, too, the example of the United States is all the more remarkable because in this country the development has gone much less far than anywhere else.

In capitalist society, the role of government in the economy is always secondary. The government acts in the economy chiefly to preserve the integrity of the market and of capitalist property relations, and to give aid and comfort, as in wars or international competition or internal disturbances, where these are needed. This we have noted in describing the general features of capitalist society. This restriction in the government's sphere of activity—whatever the form of the government, dictatorial or democratic, in the political sphere—is not a coincidence, but, it must be stressed again, an integral part of the whole social structure of capitalism. Capitalist economy is a system of *private* ownership, of ownership of a certain type vested in private individuals, of private enterprise. The capitalist state is therefore, and necessarily, a *limited* state.

The traditional and necessary capitalist role of government is, as everyone knows, now being quickly abandoned in all nations, has been altogether abandoned in at least one (Russia), and close to abandoned in several others. Government is moving always more widely into the economy. No matter who runs the government or for what, every new incursion of government into the economy means that one more section of the economy is wholly or partially removed from the reign of capitalist economic relations.

That this is the meaning of the governmental extensions into the economy can be seen from one very simple and obvious fact alone: All capitalist enterprises are run for profit; if, over a period, they do not make a profit, they have to stop running. But governments not only do not have to make a profit but on the contrary normally and properly run in the contemporary world at what is from the capitalist point of view a loss. When governments confined themselves to the narrower political sphere —army, police, courts, diplomacy—this might not have seemed so out of line (though in those days governments ran continuously at a loss only at the cost of going bankrupt, like any other capitalist institution): it could be thought that the government was a special expense chargeable to business like the private police force of a steel mill or the public-relations department of a utilities firm. But when we remember that government is now the biggest business of all, in the strictly economic as well as in other spheres, the demonstrated ability of government to keep running at a loss is intolerable from the standpoint of capitalism, and shows that the government functioning in the economy is implicitly a noncapitalist institution.

The government extension into the economy is of two kinds: First, government takes over fully, with all attributes of ownership, section after section of the economy both by acquiring already established sections and by opening up other sections not previously existing. There is little need to give examples: postal service, transportation, water supply, utilities, bridges, ship-building, sanitation, communications, housing, become fields of government enterprise. Among new fields that are opened up by government are such vast potential areas as what this country calls "conservation work" in order to hide the fact that it is a necessary part of contemporary economy.

What must be stressed is how much greater the area of government enterprise already is, even in the United States, than we commonly wish to recognize. It doesn't make any difference if we call WPA and CCC "relief," or biological and agricultural and meteorological surveys "research," or food stamp plans "distribution of surplus," or ash and garbage removal "municipal services"; they are all, in the contemporary world, part of the total economic process. For that matter, education may also be treated as an economic institution, and is, except for a negligible fraction, a governmental enterprise; and government, either directly or through subsidy, provides about half of the medical care in the United States. The immediate bureaucracy of the federal government includes over a million persons, double the number of a decade ago; but if we include the employees of state, county, and municipal governments, the army, navy, courts, prisons, the recipients of all types of relief, we find that already in the United States half or more of the entire population is dependent wholly, or in determining part, upon government for the means of living.

An equally striking symptom of the altered weight of government in the economy as a whole is provided by the figures for new capital investment. The ability of capitalism to handle the problems of the economic process was shown perhaps most accurately by the always-accumulating amounts of new capital investment, which indicated extensions of the capitalist economic area. During the past seven or eight years, however, new capital investment in private enterprise has been almost eliminated, the annual amounts totaling only a few hundreds of million dollars, while vast idle funds have piled up in the banks. This does not mean that new investment has not taken place. It has done so through government, and in state enterprise, where it is in effect measured by the increase in the national debt. Federal government investment during these years has totaled more than five times private investment, a plain enough signal where the economic future lies.

Outright acquisition by government of rapidly increasing areas of the economy is, however, only one phase of the process. Still more striking, and far more extensive in range, is the widening control by government of more and more parts and features of the economy. Everyone is familiar with this control, administered by the long list of commissions and bureaus and alphabetical agencies. There is control, to one or another extent, of agriculture and security issues, advertising and marketing practices, labor relations and utility rates, exports and imports, wages and banking rules.... In this matter of control without full ownership, also, the United States is far behind every other great nation; but even in the United States it has gone a long distance, and there is every reason to expect a vast speedup during the next immediate period. Nearly every one of these governmental controls imposes restrictions upon capitalist property rights, removes the objects and functions controlled to a greater or less degree from the unmixed reign of the market and capitalist property relations.

The actual, day-by-day direction of the processes owned and operated by the government or controlled, without full ownership, by the government is in the hands of individuals strictly comparable to those whom we have called "managers" in the case of private industry: the men of the innumerable bureaus and commissions and agencies, not often the publicly known figures, who may be decorative politicians, but the ones who actually do the directing work. In government enterprise, we have, in fact, the development outlined in the preceding chapter. Groups 3 and 4 (the finance-capitalists and the stockholders) disappear; and Group 2, with the executive functions stripped of profit-making, merges into the managerial Group 1. Direction is *not* in the hands of capitalists, nor does a directing position depend upon the possession of capitalist property rights in the instruments of production involved. Under present conditions in the United States it is true that the governmental managers do not have altogether free rein; but the process of the extension of governmental ownership and control nevertheless means a continuous increase of managerial dominance in the economy as a whole.

A clear witness to the truth of this last observation is provided by the growth in the number of "bright young men," of trained and educated and ambitious youth, who set out for careers in the government, not as politicians in the old sense, but as managers in the various agencies and bureaus in all the myriad fields where they now operate. A generation ago these young men would almost all have been headed for private enterprise, with the goal of making a name for themselves in business, industry, or finance, and perhaps of finding a place in the charmed ranks of the upper *bourgeoisie*. More and more of them understand now that security, power, or simply the chance to exercise their talents are not to be found in the old ways but must be sought elsewhere. The young men thinking and acting in this way include, significantly enough, many of the children of the capitalists themselves, who perhaps sense that the dominion exercised by their parents as capitalists can be continued by the children only through giving up capitalism.

*   *
*

I have been presenting so far only one side of this process: the process whereby, within the still-existing structure of capitalist society, ever greater percentages of the economy are getting wholly or partly out of control by the capitalists and subjection to capitalist relations, and coming under the control of new groups and new relations—in particular of the managers and relations suitable to the social dominion of the managers. Capitalists and capitalist relations do not, however, simply evaporate in the face of this process. They resist it, and, when resistance at any point gives way, try to turn what has happened to their own advantage. In the next chapter, we shall consider, among other things, why in the long run this resistance and the capitalist attempt to make use of the process will break down.

Here it remains to sum up once more the general meaning of the process. Marx once wrote that the basis of bourgeois domination was first built up "within the womb of the old (feudal) society." Thus, when the great political tests of war and revolution came, the battle was really decided in advance; the capitalists and capitalist relations had won out in the preparatory period. We have seen that the inability of the proletariat and the propertyless masses generally to build up in an analogous manner social dominion "within the womb" of capitalist society is one of the crucial reasons why socialism will not succeed capitalism.

However, disintegration of the social domination (that is, control over the instruments of production) of the capitalists is nevertheless going on within the very womb of capitalism, and domination by new groups, above all by the managers, is growing. On the world arena, which is the arena of modern society, the percentage of the economy controlled, as well as the completeness of the control, by the capitalists and capitalist social relations are alike diminishing at a rate which has rapidly increased since the first world war. It is the managers, with their allied or to-be-allied political associates, who are taking up the control as it slips from the capitalist grasp. This is not a shift scheduled for tomorrow. It began yesterday, continues today; and the only element of prediction lies in expecting it to be completed tomorrow.

The social revolution of today is not the revolution of the end of the Middle Ages, of the transition from feudalism to capitalism. There is no identity between what happens now and what happened then. But the decisive analogies between the two transition processes are just. The past in this case is able to teach us, if we wish to learn, what is happening and what is going to happen.

IX

THE ECONOMY
OF MANAGERIAL SOCIETY

IN THE LAST chapter I held that the extension of governmental (state) ownership and control (an extension no one could possibly deny, nor, especially if we are considering world economy, expect to be anything but speeded in the future) was, in its historical meaning, a decrease in capitalist ownership and control. This development is, in turn, part of the general process of social transition which is taking place, a process analogous to what happened in the transition from feudal to capitalist society. Through this process, the rate of which is markedly accelerated by war and revolution, I maintain that the position of the capitalists as the ruling class in society is being undermined and, before long, will collapse.

There are many who will agree with this interpretation of the growth of governmental ownership and control. Marxists, however, particularly Marxists of the Leninist wing (now represented by Stalinists and Trotskyists), will deny it; as will also, for very different reasons, many of the New Dealer type in this and other countries, who claim, when their own advocacy of the extension of government ownership and control is challenged, that, far from destroying capitalism, it helps preserve it. I wish to analyze here the argument of the Leninists.

The contemporary state, say the Leninists, is "the executive committee of the *bourgeoisie,*" the political agency for enforcing the capitalist rule of society. Therefore, when this state takes over some branch of the economy, or establishes economic controls, capitalist rule is in no way weakened—it is the capitalists' own state which does the taking over. On the contrary, capitalist rule is usually strengthened thereby.

Nothing could be simpler than this supposed demonstration. However, the whole show is given away when we compare the argument with a basic policy that is always also held by Leninists, as by all Marxists: the policy, namely, of advocating at all times that the government shall take over any and all parts of the economy.

Leninists, it is true, likewise say that what they want is a *new* government—a new state—which will be not the present "capitalist state" but a "workers' state"; and that government ownership will not "really" be in the interests of the masses and of socialism until such a new state is set up. It would seem, then, that they ought to wait for the arrival of such a workers' government before advocating government ownership and control. But this is not the case. They advocate that the *present* government, the executive committee of the capitalists, take over ownership and control. That is, they advocate what is, according to their ostensible theory, a measure which in no way weakens but on the contrary usually strengthens the social rule and domination of the capitalists and of capitalist social relations.

In this case as in so many others, practical politics are a better touchstone than theory. The truth is that the practical step of extending government ownership and control acts, in its longer-term effects, to weaken and finally do away with capitalism and capitalist rule. Leninists are against capitalism, and they *act* consistently, even if they do not *think* consistently, by advocating on all occasions this practical step. It would be forbidden by a strict interpretation of their theory. But the theory is part of an ideology; ideologies are not subject to the canons of science and logic; and with the help of "dialectics"—which are from one point of view simply a device for reconciling theoretical contradictions with the dictates of practice—the theory is adapted to the practical need.

In this respect the Leninists are the exact converse of the capitalists; and the attitude of the capitalists is no less revealing. Ninety-nine times out of a hundred, the overwhelming majority of capitalists are, at the outset, against any and every extension of governmental ownership and control of the economy. They speak, write, and act against it, and get others (teachers, editors, ministers) to speak, write, and act against it. When it comes anyway, they adapt themselves, or try to adapt themselves, to it; but they oppose its coming. Capitalists are *for* capitalism; and their practical policy, whatever theories accompany it, follows from their position and interests. They are against the extension of governmental ownership and control because, like the Leninists, they rightly sense that, in the long run if not at once, it is anticapitalist in its historical effects.

The historically anticapitalist nature of the extension of governmental ownership and control is the only basis from which we can plausibly explain the attitude of the capitalists themselves. Leninists are forced to the most complex and devious psychological fairy tales to get around the difficulties. When the capitalists, almost *en masse,* object, say, to some New Deal extension of the government into the economy, the Leninists are compelled to say that the capitalists, with their complaints, are only trying to "deceive" the people or are deceiving themselves about "their own best interests." Such explanations are logically possible but most unlikely, especially when there is a simpler one that fits the facts directly: the capitalists object because the measures *are* against their interests. Let us examine more carefully what happens:

We have already discussed the sense in which the Leninist theory of the state is correct, the sense in which it is permissible to speak, with proper caution, of the state in modern capitalist society as a *capitalist* state, as the state *of* the capitalists. Fundamentally this need mean only (though it may mean more than this) that, on the whole, most of the time and on the most decisive occasions, the state acts (through laws, courts, police, and so on) to uphold the general framework of capitalist social and economic relations: this is all that is necessary for the preservation of capitalism, since, given those relations, capitalism continues and the capitalists continue as the ruling class. When the state acts to enforce contracts or debt payments or to stop sitdown strikes (which negate the capitalist control of access to the instruments of production), the state may be described, somewhat metaphorically, as the "executive committee" of the capitalists. There is little doubt that the government (state) of the United States has been and may still be correctly described as a "capitalist state."

But we have also seen that, when the government takes over, either in full ownership or in some degree of control, some section of the economy, by that very fact that section of the economy is removed, entirely or partly, from the reign of capitalist economic relations. That section of the economy is no longer in the full capitalist sense a "profit-making institution," with the profits going in one way or another to individuals who have one or another form of "property right" in the given institution. The products (goods or services) of the state institution are not subject to the "laws of the market." They are not even, or do not need to be, "commodities" in the capitalist sense. Nor is the distribution of these products determined by capitalist property relations.

This is why most capitalists invariably oppose such acquisitions by the government. The situation here is entirely different from what it is when the government acts in the limited political sphere which is proper to a well-behaved capitalist government. When the government exercises police power, raises or lowers tariffs, goes to war or stays at peace, convicts or acquits a capitalist for some private economic offense, some (perhaps most) capitalists will object, others will approve; but none will raise a question "of principle," and there will seldom be a unified capitalist opinion on the matter. The measures may hurt some given group of capitalists and benefit others, may even hurt all capitalists; but they do not abridge the basic rights of property —control of access to the instruments of production and preferential treatment in the distribution of the products of those instruments—and they are consequently incidental to the main question of social structure and rule. The direct economic incursions of the government do, precisely, abridge or even eliminate those rights with reference to the section of the economy in question; they are therefore intolerable, so far as they go, incompatible with capitalism.

The capitalists oppose the economic incursions at the outset. When, nevertheless, for whatever reason, the incursions take place, the matter is not then ended. The capitalists, though they have lost ground, try to turn the loss to their advantage; and they are aided in the attempt because the government remains, on the whole, capitalist. For example: The government, through PWA or WPA or some similar agency, begins to build schools and apartments and roads and bridges. To the extent that this is fully a governmental enterprise it is out of the capitalist economy, and running it is not yielding capitalist profits to individual capitalists. But the capitalists can still turn it to capitalist advantage by supplying the materials that are used for the building (the materials still being turned out by capitalist enterprises), by selling the "relief workers" food and clothes paid for by the government wages, or by making profits from subcontracting where the government does not directly operate the work. The TVA can make electricity as a state enterprise; but, once made, a private capitalist concern can distribute the current, or a private capitalist factory can be built in the district to use its cheap rates. Again, it often happens that the section of the economy which the government takes over is one that private capitalists can no longer run except at a loss: the governmental incursion in such a case gets rid of the loss suffered by the individual capitalists—

which is possible, if for no other reason, because the government does not have to run at a profit.

Considerations such as these would seem to justify the Leninists (their theory, not their practice). Governmental incursions into the economy seem, in their light, not to weaken but usually to improve the position of the capitalists and of capitalism. This impression, however, disappears as soon as we turn from the frequent immediate effects to the full historical implications of the process.

The capitalists, for a long time, are able to make up for each separate loss, even often to seem to gain after it; but they do so only by exhausting their own resources. They operate further and further from shore, but meanwhile their own base is progressively narrowed. It is like a poker player, with a great pile of chips, covering and raising each bet of his opponent; the opponent meanwhile is getting *his* chips by sneaking them from the bottom of our player's pile. When the pile is big, the game can go on for a long time, but in the end there is no doubt about the victor.

Put it this way: The capitalists, as a class, base their power and privilege, their social dominion, on their control (ownership) of "private enterprise," which alone is capitalist enterprise proper, since in it alone do we find the characteristic capitalist social and economic relations. So long as government enters, either not at all or comparatively little, into the economy, and at the same time is either tolerant toward or the active defender of capitalist relations, the social rule of the capitalists and the continuance of capitalist society is assured and often immensely aided by government. Even when government takes over substantial but still minor percentages of the economy (either through outright ownership or growing but not complete control), the social rule of the capitalists can be continued, and government can still act primarily to their benefit. The capitalists will not benefit *directly* from governmental enterprise. But, having private enterprise as a base for leverage, governmental enterprise can be *indirectly* manipulated to benefit private enterprise and thus the capitalists.

This is simple enough when the relative percentage of governmental enterprise is low and that of private enterprise correspondingly high: private enterprise then easily outweighs governmental. But, especially since the first world war, the universal tendency, in the world economy as a whole and in that of each separate nation, is toward the relative extension of governmental enterprise at the expense, necessarily, of private. (Once again I must stress that such an extension is marked as much or even more by an increase in governmental *control* as by formal government "ownership": since control is the decisive factor in ownership.) This extension takes place continuously and progressively, just as the relative extension of bourgeois as against feudal control at the transition between the Middle Ages and modern times. The rate of the process is enormously speeded at certain points as in Russia in 1918, in Germany from 1933 on, and everywhere by the effects of the second world war. The base of capitalist leverage is undermined; the relative weights of governmental and private enterprise alter.

When, finally, the major part of the instruments of production come under governmental ownership and control, the transition is, in its fundamentals, completed. The "limited state" of capitalism is replaced by the "unlimited" managerial state. Capitalist society exists no longer or lingers only as a temporary remnant. *Managerial society* has taken its place.

The basis of the economic structure of managerial society is governmental (state) ownership and control of the major instruments of production. On a world scale, the transition to this economic structure is well advanced. All the evidence at our disposal indicates that the development will continue, will, in fact, proceed at a rate much speedier in the future than that of the past; and that the transition will be completed. We may not like this prospect; we may most bitterly resent it. But to think that it is not the most probable outcome is to judge history in terms of our desires and not of the evidence amply before us.

* *
*

What kind of economy will this be? What will be the specific economic relations within it? What group, if any, within it will hold most power and privilege, will be the ruling class?

It would be foolish to pretend that these questions can be answered in minute detail—the science of history does not, or should not, lay claim to the precision of physics. Nevertheless, sufficiently meaningful and accurate broad answers can be given. These answers need not be imaginative speculation. We have evidence, considerable evidence, upon which to base them: the experiences, namely, of what has already happened in the transition period. The past, after all, is the only source of knowledge about the future.

In contemplating an economic organization of society through state ownership of the major instruments of production, other writers have sometimes referred to it as "state capitalism" or "state socialism." I certainly wish at all costs to avoid disputes over words. Though I call it the "managerial economy" of "managerial society" I am perfectly willing to substitute any terms whatever, so long as there can be a common understanding of what is being talked about. However, as I wish now to show, the terms "state capitalism" and "state socialism" (it is ironic that both are used) are misleading in the extreme.

If by "capitalist economy" we mean (as we do mean) the economic structure which has prevailed from the end of feudal economy until recent years, there is no sufficient resemblance in any important aspect that would justify calling an economy of state ownership "capitalist." With this point, without further argument, I am sure that at least all capitalists would agree.

Apart from the absence of all those other features of capitalist economy discussed in Chapter II, you cannot call an economy of state ownership capitalist, because in it there are no capitalists A capitalist is one who, as an individual, has ownership interest in the instruments of production; who, as an individual, employs workers, pays them wages, and is entitled to the products of their labor. Where would, where could, such individuals be found in a state economy? Ownership would be vested in the state as an institution, not in individuals; men would "work for" the state as an institution, not for individuals; the state would control the products of their labor, not individuals. No individual with money would be able to use that money for capital to start a business and make a profit out of that business. What sense could there be in calling such a condition of affairs "capitalist"?

The term "state capitalism" seems to be due to a misunderstanding which we have already analyzed. When the state owns only a part, and a minor part, of the economy, with the rest of the economy remaining capitalist private enterprise, we might correctly speak of "state capitalism" in connection with that minor state-owned part: since, as we have seen, the economy remains in its balance capitalist and even the state-owned part may be directed primarily to the benefit of the capitalist part. But the "capitalism" in "state capitalism" is derived not from the state-controlled part of the economy but from the capitalist-controlled part. When the latter disappears, or becomes negligible, then the capitalism has disappeared. There is no paradox in saying that 10 times 10% state capitalism, far from equaling 100% capitalism, equals 0% capitalism. The multiplication is of *state,* not of *capitalism.* Though the mathematics would be much more complex, it would be nearer an analogy to say that, just as 10% *state* capitalist economy equals only 90% *capitalist* economy, so 100% (or even 80% or 70%) *state* economy would have eliminated capitalism altogether.

But it is equally deceptive to speak of "state socialism." According to traditional and historical usage, "socialism" *means,* so far as economic structure goes, an economically *classless* society. An economically classless society, as we have discussed, is a society in which no group of men, by virtue of special social or economic relations, has any special rights of ownership in the instruments of production—that is, any special degree of control over those instruments or any special preference in the distribution of their products. A state-owned economy *might* be economically classless. There is no *logical* impossibility in its being so. But there is not the slightest reason for believing that the particular form of state-owned economy now in the process of development *will* be economically classless.

For a state-owned economy to be economically classless, a situation along the following lines would have to exist: Ownership of the instruments of production would be vested in the state. But control over the state (and thus, indirectly, over what the state controlled) would have to be vested in everyone alike. No group or class in society would have any special advantage as against other groups or classes in controlling the state. This situation, it must be noted, would have to hold on a world scale; the natives of China, India, Africa, and central Brazil would have to have, with respect to control of state institutions, a position just as favorable as that of the inhabitants of the industrialized metropolitan centers. Any important deviation from this world group equality would constitute the more favored group or groups a privileged or ruling class.

It is not my intention to discuss the reasons why such a situation has no likelihood of coming about within the discernible future. At the very least, it would presuppose the presence of a superabundance of material and cultural goods for everyone in the world such as no one could sensibly expect for an indefinitely long time to come (especially when we remember that, as more goods become available, population increases, and more needs and wants arise: needs and wants are infinitely expansible), a general moral attitude of co-operation and self-abnegation such as no social groups have ever in history been observed to display, and a degree of intelligence, scientific knowledge, and education for everyone that can seem realistic to expect only in a daydream.

But it is not necessary to agree on the reasons. We have experiences of state ownership, in varying scales, to go by as well as the conclusions from the general economic trends which we have surveyed. They show us what we may justifiably expect. They prove that, though a state-owned economy might be classless, the form of state-owned economy which is now developing is, in fact, not classless and not going to be classless. There will not be a capitalist ruling class—there could not be—but there will be a ruling class. The privileged will not be bourgeois, but there will be those with privilege and those without.

Nevertheless, it may still turn out that the new form of economy will be *called* "socialist." In those nations—Russia and Germany—which have advanced furthest toward the new economy, "socialism" or "national socialism" is the term ordinarily used. The motivation for this terminology is not, naturally, the wish for scientific clarity but just the opposite. The word "socialism" is used for ideological purposes in order to manipulate the favorable mass emotions attached to the historic socialist ideal of a free, classless, and international society and to hide the fact that the managerial economy is in actuality the basis for a new kind of exploiting, class society. If the new rulers continue their present verbal usage, a book like this one is not going to change the linguistic outcome. For scientific purposes, however, the necessity remains to distinguish clearly the new economy (whatever it may be called) from the projected economy which was part of the traditional socialist ideal.

There is not a trace of a magic in the structure of state ownership which could in some mysterious and necessary way eliminate class rule and domination. On the contrary (and this is not a question of speculation but already shown by historical experience), an economy of state ownership can (though it need not) provide the basis for domination and exploitation by a ruling class of an extremity and absoluteness never before known. Those who control the state, those whose interests are primarily served by the state, are the ruling class under the structure of state-owned economy. Through the state, they will control access to the instruments of production. Through the state, they will control the distribution of the products of those instruments so that they themselves receive the privileged share. This ruling class, as what has happened in the past few decades already makes clear, will be, or at any rate its decisive section will be, those whom I have called the managers.

The managerial economy will be, thus, an *exploiting* economy. Here we must stop for a moment on the word "exploit." This word is often used in a moral or psychological rather than a mere neutral historical and economic sense. For example, a "bad" employer who pays his workers sweatshop wages is said to "exploit" his workers, whereas a "good" employer who pays union wages does not. As the word is used in this book, there is no moral or psychological reference of any kind. By an "exploiting" economy is meant simply an economy wherein one group receives a relatively larger share of the products of the economy than another. By "exploitation" is meant the processes, whatever they may be, whereby such an unequal distribution comes about, independently of any moral judgment or of the psychological motives of the individuals concerned. According to this definition, all class economies are exploiting; feudal and capitalist economies are exploiting; and the managerial economy will be exploiting.

The specific processes whereby exploitation takes place will not, of course, be the same as in capitalist (or feudal) society. No individual will be able to make money (profits) by using money as private capital in economic enterprise. "Capital," so far as it would be proper to use the term, will be supplied entirely, or almost entirely, through the state. Control over the instruments of production will be exercised by the managers through their *de facto* control of the state institutions—through the managers themselves occupying the key directing positions in the "unlimited" state which, in managerial society, will be a fused political-economic apparatus. Their preferential treatment in distribution will be allotted to them in terms of status in the political-economic structure, not in terms of the capitalist type of property rights (any more than of the feudal type). The experiences of Russia and Germany already show that this preferential treatment in distribution need not take an exclusively monetary form: the nominal monetary income of managers may be low, with privilege in the form of cars, houses, food and clothing, luxuries, and so on, being granted direct for "services to the state." It is the *fact* of preferential distribution that counts, not the form it takes or the means by which it is carried out.

In capitalist economy, preferential income distribution to the capitalists takes place through the fact that the owners of the instruments of production retain the ownership rights in the products of those instruments. Since these products can be sold on the market at a price higher than the cost of the labor that goes into making them, there is a surplus, and a large surplus, for distribution on the basis of claims other than those for wage-payments. According to capitalist practice, charges against this surplus are made in a great variety of forms, which obscure what is actually happening. Among these, however, such charges as interest, rent, dividends, bonuses, and high executive salaries assure the diversion to the capitalists of their preferential share in the national income.

Under a completely state-owned economy, preferential distribution could not take place in the same manner as under capitalism. But there would be no difficulty in working out new methods of exploitation. Freda Utley, in her remarkable book on Russia, *The Dream We Lost,* has shown some of the devices which are at present used in that nation. One is, in effect, a gigantic food tax. The state buys from the peasants, at fixed prices, the food which is to be processed and sold to the rest of the population (in some cases, in processed form back to the peasants themselves). The state then, as the sole important distributor, sells the food to consumers, also at fixed prices. The spread between the prices can be as large as the traffic will bear.

The second major device is made possible by the state's monopoly position in the production of nonagricultural goods and services. These also can be sold at fixed prices almost any percentage higher than the costs of production.

Through the price spread in both instances, the state is left with enormous funds at its disposal. Some of these must be devoted to such always-necessary social charges as depreciation, plant expansion, accepted social services, and so on. But the remainder can be so adjusted as to increase, relatively, the income of those who are actually controlling the state, the new ruling class. This is just what is done in Russia, and these two devices of exploitation are so simple and so easy, comparatively speaking, to control and manipulate that we may expect them to be very generally utilized in managerial economy. However, other equally effective devices can certainly be worked out. In fact, as the example of Germany (and of the New Deal, for that matter) is proving, more orthodox taxation methods are capable of very flexible use in redirecting income toward new channels, in violation of capitalist "laws" of profits and wages, even while capitalist relations remain nominally intact.

The system of managerial economy might be called a type of "corporate exploitation" as opposed to the "private exploitation" of capitalism. It is by virtue of its functional status that the managing group exploits the rest of society. There are, as I have mentioned, partial analogies in other cultures, for example certain cultures where a priest-group has been the ruling class. In some of these cultures, it was the corporate body of priests, acting as a group, which held social dominion; rights of rule were not recognized as attaching to the individual as such. (To a certain extent, the analogy would even hold for the medieval Church.) Qualifications for membership in the ruling priest-group were of diverse kinds: sometimes blood relationship, but often abilities of various sorts such as supposed supernatural abilities as marked by visions, trances, or other abnormalities. Naturally, the existing priest-group was able to control to a considerable extent the personnel of its recruited membership since the priest-group had the reins of wealth, power, and education in its hands.

There is a more limited analogy to be found in the Catholic Church's College of Cardinals, even today. The cardinals, by virtue of their status in the Church hierarchy, have, as a corporate group, the right to elect a new pope, in whose office is vested sovereignty over the Church as a whole. They do not possess this right, however, as individuals nor when acting as individuals; the right appertains to the corporate body, not to the separate individuals who make up this body. Within limits, the cardinals, with the help of their right and the powers which, as consequences, flow from it, can control the personnel of new members of the corporate body which they make up; and thus there can be, and is, a considerable human continuity in the make-up of the college.

Similarly, the managers will exploit the rest of society as a corporate body, their rights belonging to them not as individuals but through the position of actual directing responsibility which they occupy. They, too, through the possession of privilege, power, and command of educational facilities, will be able to control, within limits, the personnel of the managerial recruits; and the ruling class of managers will thus achieve a certain continuity from generation to generation.

An economic structure based upon state ownership of the major instruments of production provides the framework for the social domination of the managers. It must also be noticed that this apparently is the *only* economic structure through which the social domination of the managers can be consolidated. Within capitalist society the power of the managers is, as we have seen, extended, both in private enterprise and through the growth of governmental enterprise. But this power is interfered with, limited by the capitalists and by capitalist economic relations.

The manager is never secure. He can always be fired by someone or some group of persons possessing capitalist ownership rights. His plans for production must bow to the needs of a capitalist-profit-dominated market; he is prevented from organizing the technical co-ordination of different branches of industry in an efficient way. Moreover, he finds the chief rewards going, not to himself and his fellow managers, but to the owners. We have seen that the managers cannot solve their problems by becoming themselves capitalists. Nor does any other type of private property right seem to offer solution. Certainly the resumption of feudal forms, which could be adjusted only to a predominantly agricultural economy, is impossible for modern economy; and chattel slavery would be no less impossible. Fusion of the economy with the state, expansion of the state functions to comprise also control of the economy, offers, whether or not the managers individually recognize it, the only available means, on the one hand for making the economic structure workable again after its capitalist breakdown, on the other for putting the managers in the position of ruling class.

There are many millions of persons and many groups in the world today who consciously advocate state ownership of the instruments of production. They do so out of a variety of motives: some because they think it will bring a classless society and freedom, others because they think it will make possible universal material well-being, others from even more abstractly moral reasons. The attitude and actions of these persons and groups are one of the important social forces tending to bring about state ownership. Nevertheless, the *result* of state ownership does not depend upon the motives from which these persons advocate it. Under the given historical circumstances, the result will be not classlessness and freedom, not even universal material well-being, but a new form of exploiting, class society—managerial society.

On the other hand, many, perhaps most, of the present managers do not consciously want or favor state ownership. Nevertheless, the managers—if not the individuals who are today managers, then those who will be tomorrow—will primarily benefit from it. We have here an irony that is often repeated in history.

In the sixteenth century, many persons consciously wanted to get rid of the feudal lords and feudal exactions, to build strong national states, and so on. They wanted these things from diverse motives: a love of freedom, a wish for more material comforts, often from religious motives—a hatred and rejection of the Catholic Church. On the other hand, many of the capitalists of the time did not want these things. Their highest ambition was often to become feudal lords. They often were afraid that strong national states would interfere too much with the independent cities where their economic base had previously been. The majority of the great sixteenth-century financiers and merchants of south Germany were good Catholics, and supported the Catholic emperor and thus, indirectly, Rome in the religious wars. Nevertheless, the results, when won, in spite of motives, benefited primarily the capitalists—if not the individual capitalists who had taken part in the struggles, then other *capitalists.* Just so do the results of doing away with the capitalists, of establishing state ownership of the instruments of production, from whatever motives the aims are pursued, act to the primary benefit of the managers and toward the consolidation of a social structure in which the managers will be the ruling class.

Many persons want state ownership and control, but the tendency toward state ownership and control is not by any means dependent exclusively on the fact that many people want it and deliberately work toward it. There are persons who want to revive feudalism, who would like socialism, no doubt even those who wish for chattel slavery; but actual conditions prevent their wants from having any chance of being realized. The circumstances, problems, and difficulties of the present, however, all combine to furnish soil on which state ownership and control grow rapidly. Private enterprise proves unable to keep the productive process going; the state therefore steps in. Modern total war demands the co-ordination of the economy; this can be done only through state control. Private investment dries up; state investment takes its place. Private enterprise fails to take care of the unemployed; the state gives them jobs. Foreign trade cannot be conducted successfully and profitably on a capitalist basis; the state establishes export and import controls and monopolies. Private enterprise can no longer handle the great projects (roads, dams, steamship lines, electrical plants, shipbuilding...) required to keep contemporary society going; the state intervenes. There is nothing arbitrary about the extension of the state into the economy. It is not the result of a plot or a conspiracy. It seems to offer the only way of meeting the problems which actually arise; and consequently, however many may reject and oppose it, there are always some, and enough, ready to put it into practice.

Though a detailed sketch of the managerial economy is impossible to give in advance, some of its features and some of its possibilities are already clear. We have seen that its structure is based upon the state ownership and control of the major instruments of production, with the state in turn controlled by, and acting in the primary interests of, the managers. This in turn means the disappearance of capitalist private property rights vested in individuals.

From this structure it follows that it is no longer necessary for each branch of industry, or for industry as a whole, to operate at a profit in the capitalist sense. This will no doubt seem surprising or "contradictory" to those whose thinking on economic questions is determined exclusively by capitalist ideas. However, it is obvious enough when we reflect a little or consider the recent history of Russia and Germany. There is nothing in the nature of factories, mines, railroads, airplanes, radio transmitters that compels their operation to be dependent upon monetary profit. This dependence results merely from the specific economic relations of private enterprise, of capitalism. When these relations are gone, the need for profit is gone also. With the help of centralized state direction, managed currency, state foreign-trade monopoly, compulsory labor, and prices and wages controlled independently of any free market competition, branches of the economy or the whole economy can be directed toward aims other than profit. The managerial economy is no longer "the profit system."

In managerial economy, the role of money will be considerably restricted as compared with its all-pervasive influence in capitalist economy. In the first place, money will no longer function as individual capital, which is its distinctive and decisive use in capitalist economy. But even in exchange transactions the use of money, as we have known it, will be limited. How far these limitations will go in the future we cannot say in advance; but we already are acquainted with some of them.

Russia and Germany have shown how successfully foreign trade can be handled by a new type of "barter" method. It is argued by many economists that this barter method is clumsier and less efficient than the traditional capitalist methods which are dominated by the monetary aspect of the exchange, relatively free trading in currencies, and the help of gold to settle balances. This argument, however, holds only from a capitalist point of view: the barter method is "clumsier," less workable, only if we are thinking in terms of capitalist economic relations. Actually, these same economists refute themselves, for they go on to show, correctly, that the controlled barter method can be competed with only by adopting the same method. If it were in reality an inferior method, it would not raise the slightest competitive problem. The United States, for example, would be only too delighted that other nations made use of it, because its inferiority would guarantee that the United States, sticking to the old ways, would without trouble win out internationally. As everyone knows, just the opposite is the case.

Even in interior exchange transactions, the importance of money will decline. Where goods and services are supplied by the state without the consumer's paying directly in money for each unit of them, money is necessarily functioning more modestly than where it appears directly in each transaction. Many of such goods and services have been present for some while: roads, bridges, public sanitation services, parks, scientific aids, water, and others. Russia and Germany show (what could be predicted in any case) that the field of these public services is to be vastly enlarged under managerial economy. An increasing number of consumer goods and of services will be supplied without the direct intervention of money payment; that is, an increasing percentage of real income will not take monetary form. Theoretically, there would seem to be no limit in this replacement of money. In practice, however, the convenience of money, and especially its convenience in maintaining *differentials* in income, seem to guarantee its survival. However (as, again, experience already shows), money will become increasingly and perhaps altogether divorced from any metallic base. The Fort Knox gold pile may well be turned into a monument for posterity, like the Egyptian pyramids.

These developments in connection with money mean, from another point of view, that in managerial economy goods and services do not to such an extent or as fully as in the capitalist market function as *commodities*. Barter exchange, the allotment of goods and services without monetary intervention, both mean that the objects concerned are not treated simply as commodities —that is, as abstracted embodiments of so many units of exchange value—but as specific, qualitative entities fitted to serve certain needs and not others, independent, or partly independent, of exchange value.

Just as the *bourgeoisie* (capitalists) will be eliminated in the managerial economy, so will the position of "free workers" (proletarians), as known under capitalism, be greatly altered. The "freedom" of proletarians under capitalism is, of course, a curious kind of freedom. It means, in the first place, freedom from ownership rights in the instruments of production. There will be no change in this freedom: effective control of the instruments of production will be held not by workers but by the managers through their state. But proletarian freedom under capitalism also means, to a limited extent, freedom for the workers to sell their labor or not to sell it (though the alternative of not selling it, being starvation, is not too realistic), to sell it to one competing employer as against others, and to bargain over its price. These latter possibilities will not exist in anything like the same form under managerial economy. There being only one major employer (the state), there will be no bargaining among competing employers; and the assignment and transfer of jobs, as well as the fixing of rates of pay, will not be left to the accidents of market bargaining.

There seems no reason to believe that managerial economy will be subject to the capitalist type of economic crisis, since the factors involved in this type of crisis, which are all related to the profit requirement of capitalist economy, will be done away with. However, it is most probable that managerial economy will have its own form of crisis. Managerial crises will, it would seem, be technical and political in character: they will result from breakdowns in bureaucratized administration when faced with, say, the complicated problems of sudden shifts to war or peace or abrupt technological changes; or from mass movements of dissatisfaction and revolt which, with the state and economy fused, would be automatically at once political and economic in character and effect.

In managerial economy, the regulation of production will not be left to the "automatic" functioning of the market but will be carried out deliberately and consciously by groups of men, by the appropriate institutions of the unlimited managerial state. As we saw, the necessarily decentralized economy of private enterprise makes impossible such deliberate regulation of production as a whole. Under the centralized economic structure of managerial society, regulation (planning) is a matter of course.

If we compare these features of managerial economy with our

review, in Chapter II, of the chief features of capitalist economy, we see at once that all of the leading characteristics of capitalist economy are either not present at all or present only in a drastically modified form in managerial economy. This fact reinforces the rejection of the term "state capitalism."

Managerial economy would not be going to replace capitalist economy unless it could solve, at least in some measure, those key difficulties (which we noticed in Chapter III) that are faced by capitalism and make impossible the continuance of capitalism. We know, without waiting for the future, that managerial economy can do away with mass unemployment or reduce it to a negligible minimum. This was done, by managerial methods, in Russia and Germany at the same time that England, France, and the United States proved incapable of doing it by capitalist methods. The question here is not whether we "approve" of the way in which mass unemployment was or will be got rid of. We may think that unemployment is preferable to, for example, conscript labor battalions. Nevertheless, mass unemployment is the most intolerable of all the difficulties that any economy can face, sufficient, by itself, to guarantee the collapse of an economic system; and we are concerned with the fact, already sufficiently proved, that managerial methods and managerial economic relations can get rid of unemployment, whereas capitalist methods no longer can do so. The truth is that Russia, Germany, and Italy are not alone in having used the noncapitalist, managerial methods in handling unemployment. The CCC in this country is cut from the same pattern. Relief work in general is a half-hearted variant. If the United States had not resorted to such means, mass unemployment in this country would have been immeasurably worse and would already have sent the economic structure toppling.

Under managerial economy, the long-term production curve can again resume its advance after the decline under dying capitalism. Indeed, during the past decade, if we except small nations subject to special influences and without world economic significance, the degree to which nations have been able to build up a general production advance is closely correlated with the degree to which they have been transformed along managerial lines: Russia and Germany head the list of the great nations; the United States and France end it. Here, again, we are not concerned with *what* goods are produced, but with the volume of production relative to population and potential capacity. We may think that some of the goods produced (bombers and tanks, for instance) are not worth producing, are positively evil; we may think it is not "progress" to be able to produce more of them; but, nonetheless, the ability of one system of economy to produce relatively more goods than another system is a decisive indication of their relative survival value. Nor should we be so naïve as to imagine that the structural and institutional relations which permit the production of a greater volume of armaments do not also permit the production of a greater volume of other types of goods. If it were really true, as so many say, that the Nazi economy were solely an "armament economy," no one in the United States would be so worried, as all serious economists are worried, about Nazi *economic* competition *after* the war.

Similarly, managerial economy is in a better position than capitalist economy to make use of new inventions and technological devices. It is not restricted by the same profit requirements that often mean a disruption of the capitalist market through a too-sudden introduction of new inventions. This was not the least of the reasons why Nazi Germany was able to overcome, in part through the help of newly invented *ersatz* products, its seemingly hopeless inferiority in resources to France and England and why Germany developed more and better fighting machines.

Capitalist economy, we saw, is no longer able to use, for productive purposes in private enterprise, its own available capital funds. These idle funds will be no problem for managerial economy. The managerial state will either confiscate them, at once or gradually, or it will, for an interim period, compel their use on its own terms and for its own purposes.

Managerial economy will be able to exploit and develop backward peoples and areas in a way that, as we found, is no longer possible for capitalist economy. Capitalism, though it needs to exploit these peoples for its own preservation, is at the same time no longer able to do so profitably. Managerial methods, both economic and political, free from capitalist profit requirements, reopen Asia and Africa and Latin America to a new exploiting era.

Finally, as I have already mentioned, managerial economy, by virtue of centralized control of the economy as a whole, is able to *plan* for and with the economy as a whole in a way that is not possible for capitalist economy, with its system of divisive and unco-ordinated control. There comes into being a "five year" or "two year" or "four year" or "ten year" planning commission for the economy as a whole. Just as the very concept of such planning commissions is diametrically opposed to the individualistic ideologies of capitalism, so is the fact of their existence impossible for capitalism in any but a purely nominal sense.

These last pages might seem to suggest that the managerial economy is about to usher in an age of plenty, sweetness, and light such that no man in his senses could do anything but welcome with rapture the prospect of the future. With "all problems solved," milk and honey are apparently just around the corner. It is necessary to paint into this picture—which is, besides, only an economic picture so far—a few of the shadows.

I am not dealing in this book, let me repeat, with questions of "good" or "bad," of what "ought to be" or what we "ought to do." I am trying to present a theory, a hypothesis, which seems to me more probable than any other on the evidence available, about what is going on in society and where it is leading. I have no intention whatever of judging, in this book, whether what is indicated by this theory is "good" or "bad"; whether the transition from capitalism to managerial society constitutes "progress" or not, whatever "progress" may mean.

Moreover, even the apparently more modest question of whether managerial society will be "more beneficial to men" than capitalist society is in reality incapable of being answered. More beneficial in terms of what, to what men? When capitalism is finished, each man and each group of men necessarily loses both the distinctive goods and the distinctive evils that capitalism brought. A different organization of society will bring its own distinctive goods and its evils; it is not easy to know what evaluations men will make of what they have gained and lost.

It does seem possible to make two points: Managerial society will bring no benefits to the capitalists as a class, unless extinction is a blessing, since there will be no capitalist class in managerial society. And, second, there is good reason to believe that under managerial economy there will be a greater total output of material goods in relation to the total population than under capitalism, including such goods as supply the needs of warmth, food, shelter, and so on. This would seem to indicate that the masses on the average (not necessarily any particular section of the masses, and the result is not guaranteed) would have a somewhat higher material standard of living. Whether this would be considered compensation for other facets of managerial society is, of course, a quite different question.

That managerial society will, as I have stated, be able to solve certain of the major difficulties now faced by capitalism and incapable of solution under capitalism, seems to me highly probable. This does not, however, mean that managerial society will not have its own difficulties, including economic difficulties, and perhaps they will be judged more poignant than those of capitalism.

I have already suggested that, though managerial economy

will not be subject to the capitalist form of periodic crisis, it will have its own kind of crises. These may well be very devastating in their total social effects.

Another group of the problems of the future emerges from the following consideration: Under managerial economy it will be possible to *plan,* to a considerable extent, the general process of production. This will be possible because control of the economic process will be centralized: there will be the institutional mechanisms for translating deliberate planning into action. Neither the centralization nor the mechanisms exist under capitalism, and deliberate planning is therefore not possible, or possible only to a minor and partial degree.

But, contrary to a rather widespread popular misconception, there is no necessary social virtue in "planning." Before the meaning of a "plan" is understood, we must know what the plan is for, what ends it is to serve; there is no such thing as a "plan" in and by itself. Just as many new inventions can be used equally well to kill men or to grow better food, so may there be plans for freeing humanity or for enslaving it further.

A plan does not, of course, have to have one single and narrow aim. It may be directed simultaneously toward several aims, though it is quite possible that in such cases the different aims may interfere with each other. Unfortunately, we already know what two of the aims of managerial planning are: the more effective prosecution of war, and the support of the power and privilege of a new ruling class. There is no doubt that the ability to plan, which follows from the managerial structure, makes it easier to realize these aims, as well as other aims that may also be present. Theoretically, it is true, these aims might include greater happiness, security, and culture for mankind at large.

Even within the managerial planning, there will be plenty of confusion. The rulers of managerial society do not really proceed scientifically any more than has any other ruling group. Their social aspirations are hidden by ideologies, not clarified by a genuine social science. The ideologies mask what is happening, not only from men generally, but from the rulers themselves. When a process is not subjected to scientific control, there is no systematic means for the elimination of errors, no rational device for the resolution of conflicts: errors may accumulate into disasters; conflicts tend toward catastrophe.

No matter how scientific the administration of managerial society were made, difficulties would still remain. Managerial society is a class society, a society in which there are the powerful and the weak, the privileged and the oppressed, the rulers and the ruled. If we base ourselves upon what we know from the past and not on dreams of other worlds, there is no reason to think that the law which decrees that all social groups of any size try to increase their relative power and privilege will be suspended in managerial society. Even if the attempt is in fact hopeless, it will still be made, directly or indirectly, openly or covertly. Put in the crudest way, there will continue to be, as there has always been in human history, fighting over the spoils. The fight may translate, and thereby partly hide, itself into political and juridical, as well as physical, forms that we do not as yet suspect, but it will go on. And this is sufficient reason, if there were no others, why we should have as little faith in the promises of the ideologies of the managers—fascist or Leninist or Stalinist or New Dealer or technocratic—as we ought to have learned to have in those of the capitalists, when they tell us that following their pipe will guarantee a world of plenty and peace and freedom. The world of tomorrow will be very different from yesterday's; but if we choose to accept it—and most will accept it, whether or not they choose—there will be some satisfaction in doing so in terms of realities, not illusions.

X

THE MANAGERS SHIFT
THE LOCUS OF SOVEREIGNTY

ANY ORGANIZED society patterns its life according to certain rules—customs, laws, decrees. These rules may not be written down, may not be explicitly formulated even in verbal terms, but they must exist or there would be no sense in calling the society organized. The origin of many of the rules, at any given moment, is lost in a remote past; but there must be within the society some mechanism for enforcing those taken over from the past, and, since the rules are always changing and being added to or dropped, for stating and enforcing new or changed rules. A social group which makes and enforces its own rules for itself, and does not recognize rules made for it by an agency outside the group, is called "autonomous" or "sovereign"—such as the capitalist nations all claimed to be and the chief of them in fact were.

The "sovereignty" of the group, by virtue of which rules are made, cannot, however, simply float in the group air. It must be *localized,* concretized, in some human institution which is accepted as the institution from which rules (in complex society called "laws") come. In practice, this institution never includes all the members of the group: it might, for example, in a comparatively small and simple society, include all persons above a certain age meeting in "council," but it would exclude at least infants. In complex and large societies, the institution is always relatively small, sometimes a single person—a king, for instance, who publishes laws as personal royal decrees.

In large societies the situation is more complicated than might be suggested by the preceding paragraph. The particular institution (king or parliament or council of elders) where sovereignty is localized does not, in a broader sense, "possess" full sovereignty. Basic social power and privilege are possessed by the ruling class; the small institution is able to act as sovereign—to promulgate laws and have them enforced—not by virtue of the individual strength of its individual members (or member) but because, on the whole, it represents the interests of the ruling class and is, besides, able to gain acceptance or, at least, sufferance from a sufficient percentage of the population outside of the ruling class. Nevertheless, the question of the localization of sovereignty is by no means trivial in the history of societies. Some institution must be the public maker of the rules, the laws. Histories can be, and have been, written which center their attention on just this problem of where sovereignty is to be localized, and the many struggles which have as their political form the disputed claims to sovereignty of different institutions.

History shows that there are many kinds of institution which can serve the social purpose of the localization of sovereignty. However, within any given type of society there are fairly strict limitations to the possible varieties. One of the most obvious and important of these limitations is *technical:* the sovereign body must be able to handle its work, at least not too badly. It is a technical limitation which excludes infants—infants do not know enough to be lawmakers, even poor lawmakers—or which necessitates abandoning assemblies of all adults after a society gets beyond a certain size: there would be no place where they all could assemble, much less transact business if assembled. Moreover, a tribe that does nothing much else but hunt or fish has got to have a sovereign body that can handle at least those political problems that come up in connection with hunting or fishing.

But there are different sorts of limitation as well. For instance, the sovereign body must have a certain appropriateness of form in terms of the patterns of social thought, the ideologies. If it does not, it will be hard for it to get publicly accepted as sovereign. Furthermore, a new type of society will almost certainly have a different type of sovereign institution from that in which sovereignty was localized in the preceding society. This follows because the old institution becomes, over a long period, hardened in the ways of the old society, not sufficiently flexible to readapt itself to the new; and because mass hatred is directed against the old institution as representative of the old order. Though this is the case, the institution where sovereignty is shifted will usually have existed in the old society, though not as the sovereign institution. What will be new will be its possession of sovereignty, not its existence. This tends to be the case because social institutions in actuality change slowly, cannot be built up artificially overnight; and because the institution to which sovereignty shifts really represents in the old society those forces tending toward the new.

In an earlier chapter I have referred to the shift in the localization of sovereignty that occurred in connection with the transition from feudal to capitalist society. The result of this shift was to localize sovereignty more and more fully in "parliaments" (by whatever name they were, in different nations, called). History is not as tidy as a geometrical theorem; there is not a perfect equation between the development of capitalist society as a whole and the development of the sovereignty of parliament; but that there is a general correspondence, that in capitalist society sovereignty is *typically* localized in parliament,[1] could hardly be denied.

[1] In the United States, under the interpretation of the Constitution which became accepted during the early years of the nineteenth century, sovereignty has been, by and large, shared by Congress and the Supreme Court. Some historians would, indeed, hold that the Supreme Court alone has been the sovereign

There is, certainly, a historical and structural propriety in this fact. Parliaments (the "commons" or "third estate" only is in question here) existed in the late Middle Ages. They were simply the representative assemblies of the burgesses (the early capitalists) of the towns. They were called together, as infrequently as possible, by prince or king or great feudal lord, primarily when the prince wanted to get money from the burgesses, in return for which the burgesses would demand certain rights. Through this bargaining, the social power of the burgesses, and thus, on the political side, the sovereignty of their representative institutions, the parliaments, were built up. Historically there is no doubt about the status of parliaments as the typical political institution of the capitalists. In spite of changes and of the extension of the vote to sections of the population other than the capitalists, parliaments have retained the social marks of their origin. Constitutions, written and unwritten, and above all the control of basic power and privilege by the capitalists, have kept parliaments securely within the framework of capitalist society.

But in make-up and structure also, parliament has been a most appropriate institution for the localization of sovereignty under capitalism. Consider who are the members of parliaments. From the beginning probably a majority of them have been lawyers— that is, persons trained in the economic and juridical relations of capitalist society. They have been the kind of person you meet in businessmen's clubs—not clubs of the first rank, perhaps, but whose members are all the sounder and surer capitalist loyalists for the very reason of their second-rateness. In addition, there has been, especially in earlier days, a minority of powerful and brilliant political figures who identified the advance of their own political careers with the fate of capitalist society.

---

institution. This United States deviation from "pure" parliamentary sovereignty does not, however, affect the main course of my analysis, particularly since the aim of this analysis is to clarify the present shift of sovereignty *away from* those institutions where it has been typically localized in capitalist society to a type of institution which was, on any account, not sovereign within capitalism.

These persons, the members of parliaments, met, discussed, and concluded in circumstances very similar to those of many gatherings of capitalists in the economic field. When we read descriptions of the sixteenth-century meetings of parliaments, we cannot help being struck with the resemblance between them and the meetings of the bourses (exchanges) which were then starting in Antwerp and Lyons. The resemblance has continued. A law comes out of a parliament in a way not at all unlike that in which a price comes out of the bargaining on an exchange or other market.

Moreover, these men who were the members of parliaments, and the parliamentary methods of conduct, were fitted, well enough, for doing the law- and policy-making business of the "limited" capitalist state. This business, though often of the highest importance, did not as a rule need advanced technical, engineering or scientific training. Nor, except on rare occasions, was there much loss from the fact that the procedure was slow and cumbersome. In what the parliaments had to do, time out for party disputes, faction wrangling, speeches from dozens of persons, compromises and attempts at compromise, could usually be afforded. The economic process went on, in any case, at its own pace and under its own direction, largely outside the parliamentary province. States moved ponderously in their own element.

It is no news to anyone to point out that during the generation since the first world war, sovereignty has been slipping away from parliaments. No development of this period is more obvious and indisputable; yet, for some reason, it has received far less attention than its unquestionably major importance deserves. It is a remarkable comment on men's unwillingness to face the facts of their own time that, though in recent decades hundreds of books and articles have been written on the history of how parliaments won sovereignty, there is scarcely a handful of serious studies of how, today, parliaments are losing it or of the implications of this loss.

In four of the major nations of the modern world (Germany, Russia, Italy, France) sovereignty has already altogether departed from parliament; in two (Japan and England) parliament retains a small shred; and even in the last refuge, the United States, parliamentary (Congressional plus Supreme Court) sovereignty is more than half way into its grave.

In Germany, Russia, Italy, and France, it is true that a parliament, in form, is retained as part of the state apparatus. These parliaments occasionally meet and even pass a few motions—unanimously, of course. But, even juridically, not to speak of *de facto,* these parliaments are no longer regarded as possessing the attribute of sovereignty. The rules (laws) for the societies do not issue from them. Their meetings are simply propaganda devices, like a parade or a radio and press campaign. Often the parliaments meet only to hear a speech or two: they provide a sounding board, in a ritualistic way symbolizing the nation. Sometimes they take a vote "approving" or "accepting" the speech. But they never initiate any measure; their acceptance is always of something already done by another agency. However, even this nominal, *ex post facto* acceptance is rare. The parliaments take no part of any kind in almost all the actions of the regimes.

The example of Russia is particularly instructive, because revolutionary Russia made an attempt to continue parliamentary sovereignty: not a sovereignty localized in the Duma, the parliament of the old regime, but in the Congress of Soviets, which was thought to be the fitting representative of the new order. The Congress of Soviets, in 1917, was made up of representatives of local soviets which, in turn, were elected primarily by workers and peasants in the various local districts. In the Congress of Soviets which met at the beginning of November, 1917, the Bolshevik party had a majority. This Congress then declared itself to be "the government": that is to say, it claimed *sovereignty* and declared that sovereignty was no longer possessed by the Kerensky government which was based upon the remnants of the old Duma. The Soviet Congress then proceeded to enact the chief initial measures of the new regime and to elect an executive —the Council of Commissars.

It would seem, then, that sovereignty was still localized in a parliament; and, for a short time, this was more or less the case. But this state of affairs did not last. Parliamentary sovereignty proved inappropriate for a nation that rapidly developed in the direction of *managerial society*. Within a few years, well before the death of Lenin and the subsequent exile of Trotsky, the Soviet Congress had lost, one by one, all the attributes of sovereignty. Its nominal rehabilitation in the "Stalinist" Constitution of 1937 changed nothing and left the Soviet Congress the mere minor propaganda instrument which it continues to be.

The development was indicated at least as early as the so-called "Kronstadt revolt," which took place in 1921. The opposition platform of the sailors and populace of the Kronstadt area had as its key plank, "new elections to the soviets." This demand was in reality an effort to return sovereignty to the soviets and the Soviet Congress and an implicit recognition that these institutions no longer possessed sovereignty. The demand was rejected by the true sovereign institutions of the soviet state, and the dissidents answered by armed suppression. I am not here raising any question about who was "justified" in this famous dispute—a problem which has been so hotly and so often debated. I mention the incident to bring out only the point that it revealed the loss of sovereignty by the Soviet Congress, that is, the parliament.

In this shift of sovereignty away from parliament in Russia, which seems to have taken place without any very clear intentions on anyone's part, several important factors were involved. Experience shows that localization of sovereignty in parliament presupposes the existence of more than one legal political grouping (political party or some organized group comparable to a party). When there is more than one party, even if one of the parties is an overwhelming majority, parliament has always at least a minimum real function, since it provides a forum where the majority defends its policy against minority criticism. But where there is only one party, there is really nothing much left for parliament to do, and its political significance cannot be more than propagandistic. The politically significant body will be the controlling institution of the one political party, whatever that institution may be. The decisions of the party institution, when the one party monopolizes political life, complete the political job. The parliament can only reflect these decisions to whatever extent is thought propagandistically expedient. Even in this minor work, the parliament's sphere will dry up, since there is no use in merely having parliament duplicate tasks that are actually done elsewhere. From one point of view, and for certain types of activity, sovereignty shifts into the hands of the key party institutions.

But this is not the whole story. We are not asking here who or what in some ultimate sense "runs things" in a society (as a matter of fact, as we have seen, in the more general sense things are run by and for the ruling class). Often in a society where sovereignty is localized in a parliament, the decisions later adopted by parliament are actually made by some institution of a firm majority party. Nevertheless, the phenomenon which I have called the "localization of sovereignty" is understood within a society, even if not by that name. Whoever may run things ultimately, some given institution or group of institutions is commonly recognized and accepted as the public lawmaker, the proclaimer of the rules for society. A political party or parties must work *through* this institution or group of institutions, at the least. In capitalist society the typical institution of this sort is the parliament. We are asking what institution or group of institutions replaces parliament in this matter of the localization of sovereignty. We are not concerned here with where "real" power may be. History has shown the enormous *symptomatic* importance of shifts in the localization of sovereignty, and that is all that is necessary for our present purposes.

In the case of Russia, as of Germany and Italy, the rules, regulations, laws, decrees, have more and more issued from an interconnected group of administrative boards, commissions, bureaus —or whatever other name may be used for comparable agencies. Sovereignty becomes, *de facto* and then *de jure* also, localized in these boards and bureaus. They become the publicly recognized and accepted lawmaking bodies of the new society. When you want to know what the law is, you look up the records not of parliament but of a Four Year Plan Commission or Commissariat of Heavy Industry or Bureau for the Colonies.... Similarly, the place of "committees of parliament" is filled by subcommissariats and subsidiary bureaus. Sovereignty has shifted from parliament to the administrative bureaus.

There are many who think that this development is the special result of the activities of communist and fascist politicians who by means of "subversive" activities have overthrown the old parliamentary order. As soon as we turn our eyes back to the United States we should begin to realize the incompleteness of such a view. Exactly the same process has been going on in the United States as everywhere else, though it is today at a different stage from that reached in Russia or Germany. This fact is enough to show that the process has deeper historical roots than the deliberate schemes of revolutionaries.

In the United States, sovereignty may still be chiefly located in Congress (together with the Supreme Court), it may still be the principal "lawmaking" body; but no one with eyes open during the past generation and especially the past decade will believe that its claims are today undisputed. "Laws" today in the United States, in fact most laws, are not being made any longer by Congress, but by the NLRB, SEC, ICC, AAA, TVA, FTC, FCC, the Office of Production Management (what a revealing title!), and the other leading "executive agencies." How well lawyers know this to be the case! To keep up with contemporary law, it is the rulings and records of these agencies that they have chiefly to study. How plainly it is reflected in the enormous growth of the "executive branch" of the government—which is no longer simply executive but legislative and judicial as well—in comparison with that of the other two branches. Indeed, most of the important laws passed by Congress in recent years have been laws to give up some more of its sovereign powers to one or another agency largely outside of its control.

The process is, naturally, not yet completed in the United States. Congress is not yet the same as Hitler's Reichstag or Stalin's Soviet Congress. But it has gone much further than Congress itself would be willing to realize. Congress still occasionally "revolts," still now and then "disciplines" an administrative agency or even abolishes it; but these acts are like the petty tyrannies of an already close-to-powerless old man. Very little control over the state is actually, today, possessed by Congress. The last year has shown that even the question of making war, most crucial of all the attributes of sovereignty, is, in spite of the Constitution, in reality beyond the power of Congress. Wars, also, are no longer conducted according to the parliamentary code.

In the new form of society, sovereignty is localized in administrative bureaus. They proclaim the rules, make the laws, issue the decrees. The shift from parliament to the bureaus occurs on a world scale. Viewed on a world scale, the battle is already over. The localization of sovereignty in parliament is ended save for a lingering remnant in England (where it may not last the next few months), in the United States, and certain of the lesser nations.

There is no mystery in this shift. It can be correlated easily enough with the change in the character of the state's activities. Parliament was the sovereign body of the limited state of capitalism. The bureaus are the sovereign bodies of the unlimited state of managerial society. A state which is building roads and steel mills and houses and electric plants and shipyards, which is the biggest of all bankers and farmers and movie producers, which in the end is the corporate manager of all the major instruments of economic production, can hardly be run like the state which collected a few taxes, handled a leisurely diplomacy, and prosecuted offenders against the law. Nor can the same kind of men run it. The new agencies and new kinds of agency are formed to handle the new activities and extensions of activity. As these activities overbalance the old, sovereignty swings, also, over to the new agencies. If a state is running steel plants, this is a more influential activity than punishing murderers; and the institution directing the steel plants has more social weight than that which makes laws about murderers.

In theory, even under these circumstances, the locus of sovereignty might remain in parliament. Parliament might continue to exercise representative sovereignty rights with respect to the great issues of general policy, providing a basic guide for all the agencies and bureaus. But this, which might well prove awkward in any case, is ruled out in practice for other reasons.

The shift in the locus of sovereignty is only a symbol of the shift in basic social relations, the shift from the rule of the capitalists to the rule of the managers. As has happened in the other comparable historical transitions, managerial society does away with the representative political institution of the old society, not merely because a new type of institution is technically better for the new society, but precisely because the old institution represents the old society; it becomes despised and hated, and the resentment of the masses is turned against it (look at France in the early summer of 1940); psychologically, ideologically, it is not suited for the new rule.

Equally important, the administrative bureaus have the same kind of general appropriateness for localizing *managerial* rule as the parliaments had for localizing capitalist rule. For that is the real significance of the shift in sovereignty toward the bureaus: it is simply one of the phases, in the field of political structure, of the transition from capitalist to managerial society.

The old-line parliamentarians do not do well in the bureaus.

One or two of them may be present, as figureheads, for decorative purposes. But the actual directing and administrative work of the bureaus is carried on by new men, a new type of men. It is, specifically, the *managerial* type, the type we noticed also when considering the structural developments in "private enterprise." The active heads of the bureaus are the managers-in-government, the same, or nearly the same, in training, functions, skills, habits of thought as the managers-in-industry. Indeed, there is less and less distinction between the two: in Russia, managers-in-industry and managers-in-government are one and the same, since there is no (important) industry apart from government. In all countries, as government expands, it incorporates the tasks and fields which were before left to private industry.

Moreover, even before the state has swallowed all of the economy, the way in which the new administrative agencies conduct their affairs is, by the nature of the case, close to the way in which the managers act elsewhere—certainly far closer than a parliament's way, which is at an opposite extreme from the managers' habits. In structure, mode of functioning and personnel, the administrative agency, board, or commission appears as the typical institution for the localization of sovereignty in managerial society, as parliament did in capitalist society.

It is clearly to the advantage of the managers that the localization of sovereignty should be shifted to the administrative bureaus. These institutions are of a sort with which the managers can most easily collaborate; in fact, these bureaus have, in their leading staffs, got to be peopled primarily by managers—it is a managerial function that the bureaus are performing. Thus the social rule of the managers as a class can be best assured when sovereignty is recognized as pertaining, *de facto* and to a considerable extent *de jure* as well, to the bureaus. The social position of the managers is buttressed in the bureaus both against the claims of the capitalists and also against the pressure of the masses, neither of which groups can function effectively through the bureaus.

Here, as before in the case of government ownership, the practical attitude of the capitalists is most revealing. Just as, in their overwhelming majority, the capitalists oppose every extension of government ownership, so do they oppose the setting up of new bureaus, boards, and commissions or the extension of the powers of those already set up. They inspire a constant stream of propaganda against them, including a continual effort to belittle their accomplishments and to picture them as ridden with graft, red tape, and inefficiency compared with "private business"—which, when it is true (as it usually is not), is most often so because the bureau work has been interfered with by private capitalists. Following the customary pattern, when the agencies are nonetheless set up and functioning, the private capitalists then try to keep control of their activities in order to benefit primarily themselves. So long as the transition is in its early stages, so long as the dominant sectors of the economy still are those of private enterprise, this can be done. But when the balance swings, when the greater amount of economic life is subject to the bureaus' control, the base of leverage is lost, the capitalists' vantage point is undermined, and the managers through the bureaus swing into dominance. For just as the capitalists cannot continue as the ruling class, cannot continue even to exist, under a system of state ownership and control of the economy, so they cannot rule through a structure where sovereignty is localized primarily in the bureaus.

It would, I think, be difficult to exaggerate the significance of this shift in the localization of sovereignty. It is, perhaps, a secondary phenomenon in the entire social revolution through which we are going. But it is a secondary phenomenon of a symptomatic character. Just as, in the case of the outward and evident symptoms of so many diseases, the nature of the disease is most plainly grasped by observing the symptom, minor in itself, so does this historical symptom reveal plainly to us the nature of the social revolution we are studying.

XI

TOTALITARIANISM
AND MANAGERIAL SOCIETY

THOSE NATIONS—Russia, Germany, and Italy—which have advanced furthest toward the managerial social structure are all of them, at present, *totalitarian* dictatorships. Though there have been many dictatorships in the past, none of them, in a complex culture at any rate, has been so extreme in form as totalitarianism. Others have been as severe within the limited realms of social life to which the dictatorship extended. But what distinguishes totalitarian dictatorship is the number of facets of life subject to the impact of the dictatorial rule. It is not merely political actions, in the narrower sense, that are involved; nearly every side of life, business and art and science and education and religion and recreation and morality are not merely influenced by but directly subjected to the totalitarian regime.

It should be noted that a totalitarian type of dictatorship would not have been possible in any age previous to our own. Totalitarianism presupposes the development of modern technology, especially of rapid communication and transportation. Without these latter, no government, no matter what its intentions, would have had at its disposal the physical means for co-ordinating so intimately so many of the aspects of life. Without rapid transportation and communication it was comparatively easy for men to keep many of their activities, or even their entire lives, out of reach of the government. This is no longer possible, or possible only to a much smaller degree, when governments today make deliberate use of the possibilities of modern technology.

Totalitarianism is so striking a feature of the present social transition that it seems, to many persons, to define the character of the transition. They tell us that the "issue" is "totalitarianism vs. democracy"; and, if a revolution is taking place, they call it the "totalitarian revolution." This is a very superficial point of view. No matter how important totalitarianism may be, it is still necessary to separate from the problem of totalitarianism the question of *what kind of society* is being totalitarianized: for whose benefit and against whom, with what economic and political institutions, with what ideologies and beliefs? When we hear, merely, that Russia or Germany is "totalitarian," there is not much that we have learned about them.

It is particularly difficult, in a discussion of totalitarianism, to exclude all moral and emotional considerations, as throughout the present book I am rigorously excluding them. Everyone has such powerful feelings, such acute moral opinions, for or against totalitarianism that scientific understanding is gravely hindered. It is legitimate to believe that there is often an element of hypocrisy or illusion in these feelings. Frequently, in the United States, it is not totalitarianism but Russian or German, in general "foreign," totalitarianism that is being objected to; a 100% American totalitarianism would not be objectionable. And it is not at all clear, from historical experience, how much the masses are devoted to democracy when compared with other values such as jobs or food or reasonable security. In the terrible and bloody history of mankind, modern totalitarianism is not so startling an innovation as many spokesmen of the moment try to make it appear. Lies, cruelty, terrorism, brutality are, after all, normal, not exceptional, ingredients of human history. For the purposes of our analysis, for the clarification of our central problem, we must treat the question of totalitarianism as we treat all the other questions. Our business is not to judge it good or bad, not to express likes or dislikes, but to analyze it in its relation to the problem of what is happening to society.

For us, there are two chief questions in connection with totalitarianism which must be raised and answered. First, we must ask whether the development of totalitarianism is not in conflict with one of the principal contentions of the theory of the managerial revolution. According to this theory, the ruling class of the new society now being born is the *managers*. But under totalitarianism does it not seem that not the managers but political bureaucrats— Stalins and Hitlers and Goerings and Goebbels and Mussolinis —are the rulers? Is it not a "bureaucratic" society rather than a "managerial" society that is coming into being?

Second, we must ask whether totalitarianism is to be the permanent political frame of managerial society or whether we may expect that totalitarianism will disappear, and the political organization of managerial society be achieved along different lines. In the preceding chapter we have seen one decisive feature of the political organization of managerial society which there is good reason to regard as permanent: namely, the localization of sovereignty in administrative boards or bureaus. This, however, is not necessarily identical with totalitarianism, certainly not with an extreme type of totalitarianism. We must ask whether, on the basis of such a localization of sovereignty, totalitarianism will be eliminated or considerably modified.

We have defined "ruling class" as consisting of the group of persons which has (as a matter of *fact,* not necessarily of law or words or theory), as against the rest of the population, a special degree of control over access to the instruments of production and preferential treatment in the distribution of the products of those instruments. In many societies, the members of the ruling class in question have also, in their own persons, administered the state: that is, have been the governing officials in the state apparatus. In feudal society, for example, this was usually the case. But it has not always been the case. In some societies, the state has been administered, its chief offices have been occupied, by persons who were not themselves members of the ruling class, or rather who were distinctly subordinate members of the ruling class. This has been the situation most of the time in capitalist society. As we have defined "ruling class," there is no doubt at all that usually the chief members of the ruling class were not to be found in high governmental office. The chief members were the great industrialists and financiers.

This peculiarity is puzzling to many people and causes much confusion in social thinking. The nominal rulers—presidents and kings and congressmen and deputies and generals and admirals —are not the actual rulers. This is often the fact. *Why* it should be so does not have to occupy us. Certainly it does seem odd that those officials who, apparently, are able to command the armed forces of the state—upon which, in the last analysis, the social structure rests—nevertheless are not themselves the chief rulers. That they are not presupposes a whole set of established social beliefs and attitudes which condition and limit their actions. But, however odd, there can be no doubt about the fact itself. In capitalist society, the big industrialists and financiers get the chief preferential treatment in distribution (get the largest proportionate share of the national income), not the politicians. It is the capitalists who, more than anyone else, control access to the instruments of production: if the owner of a factory wants persons kept out of his plant, he has the right to keep them out; and the armed forces of the state will back him in that right. It is in such ways that the capitalist state acts as a political agency of a ruling class which is not identical with the state.

How will it be in the new society? Will it be the managers or the political bureaucrats who are the ruling class?

In the first place, we may observe that it really doesn't make very much difference which of the two groups is correctly to be regarded as the new ruling class; whether, as we might put it, the bureaucrats are to be the servants of the managers or the managers of the bureaucrats. In either case, the general structural and institutional organization will be the same. The same type of economy, the same ideologies, the same political institutions, the same position for the masses would be found whether the state were "bureaucratic" or "managerial."; so that the difference may well be largely one of words. Moreover, modern politicians —that is, politicians of the types found in the present Russian and German regimes and their counterparts in other nations— are in reality not unlike modern managers. They direct masses of people in ways analogous to those used by managers in directing production; they have similar habits of thought, similar methods, similar manipulation of the possibilities of advanced technology. Stalin or Hitler prepares for a new political turn more or less as a production manager prepares for getting out a new model on his assembly line.

Indeed, the very raising of the question of who will rule, the bureaucrats or the managers, indicates the persistence of modes of thinking carried over from capitalist society and not strictly applicable to managerial society. The fact that in capitalist society the ruling class was a different group from the governing political administrators is largely the reflection of more basic structural features of capitalist society to which I have several times referred. Capitalist economy proper was the arena of private enterprise, and the capitalist state, we saw, was a *limited* state. The rulers of capitalist society, as in every society, were those who ruled the economy; and these were not the persons who held the offices of political administration. By the nature of the case, the latter, no matter how supreme they were in their own limited realm, were, in the entire social process, subordinate to the former.

In managerial society, however, politics and economics are directly interfused; the state does not recognize its capitalist limits; the economic arena is also the arena of the state. Consequently, there is no sharp separation between political officials and "captains of industry." The captain of industry is, by virtue of his function, at the same time a state official. The "supreme planning commission" is indistinguishably a political and an economic institution. In capitalist society, the capitalist controlled the state indirectly, in the sense that the state backed up, when necessary, the capitalist rule over the (private) economy and kept in force the capitalist economic, social, and legal relations. In managerial society, the managers become the state. To say that the ruling class is the managers is almost the same thing as to say that it is the state bureaucracy. The two have, by and large, coalesced.

This need not mean that the same *individuals,* in any given nation, who are today or yesterday managers under capitalism will be managers under managerial society. This will often be the case, but we are interested in the class, not the particular individuals who make up the class. The situation is no different from that in the formative period of capitalism. If the present managers do not, in the course of the social transformation, take up the controlling positions in the new society, other individuals will take their place—some capitalists, no doubt (as some feudal lords became capitalists), some newcomers, some who will be rewarded for services in the managerial political movements. But, and this is the important point, the managers who are dislodged from ruling positions will be replaced by other *managers;* just as, formerly, the individual capitalist who lost his place in the ruling class was replaced by another *capitalist.*

In spite of the fusion between the state and the economy, there will remain a certain differentiation between the "politicians" and the "managers." At the very least, there will be a certain differentiation in function: some persons will be primarily concerned with such activities as war, propaganda, diplomacy, policing, and so on; whereas others will be directing primarily the immediate instruments of economic production such as railroads and factories and farms and the rest. This differentiation can easily be exaggerated. It is partly based upon moral prejudices against regarding war and propaganda and diplomacy and policing as "economically productive" processes; though, in a complex society, above all in a society so integrated as that under a managerial structure, no clear line can be drawn between them and the remainder of the economy. Armies and police forces and courts and fireside chats and prisons can be looked on as among the means whereby society produces goods, when we are observing how goods are actually produced and not how we might like them to be produced. But let us still grant a difference, though minimizing it.

Insofar, then, as there is a differentiation between the political bureaucrats and the managers in the new society, we must conclude that it is the managers, not the bureaucrats, who are the leading section of the new ruling class.

Political bureaucrats (in the narrower sense of those who concern themselves primarily with such functions as war, propaganda, diplomacy, and policing) cannot exist in isolation. They must, on the one side, secure some measure of acceptance from a considerable portion of the masses (a task which is peculiarly their own to fulfill); but, in addition, they must collaborate with other groups which occupy a privileged and important place in the society. Otherwise the bureaucrats would have nothing to operate with and would be left stranded. During the Renaissance, the state power became increasingly dependent upon, finally subordinate to, the capitalists, in part for very simple reasons. For example, the princes and kings of the time had to have money to pay the mercenary armies with which they fought their wars or to equip voyages of exploration. They could get sufficient money only from the capitalists. The bureaucrats of today and tomorrow may think, in their own minds, that they pursue an independent course; but their projects, their wars and displays and manipulation of mass sentiment, all require enormous resources. In practice these can be assured only through their collaborating with, and in the end subordinating themselves to, those who are actually directing the processes of production, to the managers. The sources of wealth and power are the basic instruments of production; these are to be directed by the managers; and the managers are, then, to be the ruling class.

We shall return to this question in other connections, but we may note here that Russia, Italy, and Germany already provide evidence for this view, though an element of speculation undoubtedly remains. So far as "preferential treatment in distribution" (one of the two decisive tests of rule) goes, there is no question that in Russia, the nation most advanced toward managerial structure, it is the managers—the directors of factories and state trusts and big collective farms—who as a group are getting the largest proportionate share of the national income. In Italy and Germany, there are still capitalists getting a considerable share, but the tendency is steadily toward a diminution of their numbers and importance, while the share of the managers is big and increasing. As a *group,* the managers probably already receive much more than the remaining capitalists, and of course much more relative to their numbers than any other section of the population including the political bureaucrats.

Even in the matter of control of access to the instruments of production, the relations are similar in spite of appearances. In both Germany and Russia, the managers decide in practice who shall be denied access to a factory or a mine or a large farm. Arms are in the hands of soldiers and police, but the soldiers and police in practice ordinarily back up the decisions of the managers, just as they back up decisions of the capitalists in a capitalist nation. (Once again, we are not concerned with *why* those with arms in their hands do not take all privileges for themselves; the fact is that they do not.) It might be properly pointed out that at any time the GPU or the Gestapo may oust a manager from his position and send him to execution or a concentration camp. But, relatively speaking, such cases, though conspicuous, do not happen so very frequently. And, even more important, though the individual manager may be removed, it is not a soldier or a policeman but *another manager* who takes his place and who, *as a manager,* takes on power, responsibility, and privilege.

The last reference suggests that there are conflicts between the interests of the political bureaucracy, in the narrow sense, and those of the managers. These conflicts are not unlike those which existed during the earlier periods of capitalism (when a king might decide to behead or imprison a capitalist) and, in fact, to some extent all through capitalism. There will be other sources of conflict as well in managerial society. From the point of view of the managers, for example, the political bureaucracy will often seem (already seems) too irresponsible, too much addicted to graft and waste, too unstable. Such conflicts presage changes within the structure of managerial society. But in such changes there seems to be every reason to believe that it will be the managers, whose position is upon a firm technical and functional foundation in modern society, who will display the greater degree of stability and who will more and more gather unambiguously into their hands the realities of social rule. Stalin, Hitler, Mussolini, and the Stalins and Hitlers of tomorrow, will go, some of them with violent political convulsions. The class of managers will remain. From the vantage point which their functional role in modern economy gives them, the managers will strengthen and consolidate their social position, and will establish society on a strong basis that will guarantee their rule, whoever may be the figures who stand in the political limelight.

These last considerations are by no means unrelated to the second question: Is totalitarian dictatorship to be a permanent characteristic of managerial society, or is it likely to be replaced by some other political form, specifically, by some form of democracy? Before trying to answer this question, it will be useful to make sure that we know what we mean by "democracy."

"Democracy" is sometimes thought to be the equivalent of

such vague abstractions as "freedom" or "liberty." These latter words, however, do not contribute to clarification. "Freedom" is by itself an incomplete term; there is no such thing as freedom pure and simple; it must always be freedom *from* something and *for* something. Freedom along certain lines always implies restrictions along other lines. If I want to be free from hangovers, I must restrict my freedom to drink large amounts of alcohol. If a worker wants to free himself from a job he doesn't like, he will usually have to restrict his intake of food, since he will have nothing to get food with. A capitalist in capitalist society is free from feudal levies but subject to capitalist taxation. When the slaves of the South were freed from chattel servitude, the planters were no longer free to own slaves. It is physically and logically impossible for any person or group to be free from *everything;* to be so would mean not to exist. In all societies, different groups of men are free to do certain specific things and not free to do other specific things. The specific freedoms present change from society to society and are different for various groups within any given society. It is really hard to see what it could mean to say— as so many people get emotional satisfaction from saying—that one kind of society is, without qualification, more "free" than another. In actuality, all we can properly say is that one society is more free in certain ways—and less free in other ways—than another. In any case, the notion of "freedom" does not help us understand what "democracy" is.

Sometimes, also, we speak of "social democracy" and "economic democracy." But here, too, we are seldom clear to ourselves or others. Historically, "democracy" has stood for a certain type of *political* institution or structure in society. I shall accordingly restrict the term to its political sense.

There are many who would take it for granted that political democracy means "majority rule." If, however, we examine those political systems to which we actually apply the term "democracy," it is certain that majority rule is not, by itself, an adequate definition. There is no possible way of proving that many political systems which we all agree in calling dictatorial, including several of the dictatorships of the present day, are not accepted by majorities, often, perhaps, by larger majorities than accept the prevailing political order in democracies. One may doubt this in particular cases, but no one can deny it for all instances.

The key characteristic of "democracy" as we use the word (whatever it may have meant to the Greeks who invented it) is the granting of the right of political expression to *minorities*. More fully: democracy is a political system where policy is decided, directly or indirectly, by a majority, *and* where minorities, differing in their opinion from the majority, have the right of political expression and the opportunity, thereby, of becoming a majority. It is necessary to add—because this is not obvious—that, under democracy, majorities and minorities are determined by simple arithmetic summation, by an adding up of individual opinions where each individual counts as one (as by a show of hands or a marking of ballots).

It can be seen at once that there has never been—and in practice will never be—a 100% democracy. Democracy is a matter of degree, of more or less; and it varies in several dimensions. It can differ, for example, in the percentage of the total population out of which the majority is determined; in the number of minorities to which the rights of political expression are extended; in how fully these rights are extended and how many different kinds of question they apply to; and in the degree to which minorities are given facilities of public expression equal to those of the majority.

No society has included the entire population in determining majorities and minorities for political purposes. Children are almost always excluded up to a certain arbitrarily decided age. There are usually, in fact if not in law, additional restrictions as well: sex and property and class and birth qualifications. In the much-talked-about Athenian democracy, suffrage was the prerogative of the members of the original tribes of Attica. The slaves, who made up half of the population, were excluded, as well as the numerous "foreigners," many of whose families had been residents for generations. In the Florentine democracy of the late Middle Ages, during certain periods only the members of the great guilds voted; for a while, oddly enough, even the nobles were excluded by law and in fact. Those regarded as insane and certain classes of criminals are almost always excluded.

No democracy has extended the right of public political expression to any and all minorities. A minority must, as a rule, be of a certain sufficient size: a minority of one is usually put in an asylum, not accorded political rights. Moreover, there is a variation in the extent of the public-expression rights given to minorities. In the theory of a "perfect" democracy, a minority should no doubt receive just the same public-expression rights as the (temporary) majority—otherwise the population as a whole does not have a fully adequate basis for deciding between majority and minority. In practice it does not happen this way, and probably could not: in the modern world this would mean that the minority would have the same opportunities (and be provided with the material means for these opportunities) in the press, radio, schools, churches, movies, and all the other mediums utilized by the majority. Furthermore, there are always, in fact, restrictions about the limits of democratically acceptable opposition. When the minority goes beyond these limits it is not given rights to propagate its views but suppressed as "subversive" or "criminal" or "vicious."

It is necessary to review these features of democracy in order to stress the point that there have been many kinds and degrees of democracy. Democracy such as England and France and the United States have recently known is only one kind among many others. Democracy as a political system, moreover, is in no way incompatible with class rule in society. On the contrary, all the democratic systems of history have operated in conjunction with one or another type of class rule. And, naturally, the general social character of the democracy differs in accordance with the different structure of the society in which it is found. The democracy of Athenian slave society is not the same in general social character as the democracy of capitalist England. Modern totalitarianism, since it denies any rights of public political expression to all minorities, is certainly not, by our definition, a democracy. But when we ask whether, in the future development of managerial society, totalitarianism will give way to democracy, we are not asking whether a democratic system exactly like what we have had in the United States will be revived. If managerial society becomes democratic, it will have its own kind of democracy, not a kind that accompanied a previous social structure.

There have been many democracies, differing in kind and degree, in history; and there have been many dictatorships. (It is not, of course, our task to inquire into the moral problem of which is the "better" form of political rule.) Dictatorships have occurred under many historical circumstances. But there seems to be one type of situation out of which dictatorships very readily develop: namely, a period of social crisis and major transition. This seems rather natural, when we come to think about it. When established institutions and ideas are falling to pieces, are being sharply challenged by opposing institutions and ideas, society loses cohesiveness. Strong and ruthless hands reach in to pull it together again. The present is such a period of social crisis and major transition.

The analogies between the dictatorial politics of the present and the politics of the period of transition from feudalism to early capitalism are striking. Then, too (in the sixteenth and early seventeenth centuries, for example), there was a succession of conspicuous dictators whose ruthlessness and brutality have been obscured only because of the glamorous way in which romantic historians have written about them. Their dictatorships were not totalitarian, it is true, because they did not have at their disposal the technological means for totalitarian politics, but they were extreme enough in their own terms. Francis I, Charles V, Henry VIII, the kings of Spain and Portugal...a dozen could be named without difficulty. Their actions parallel surprisingly, in terms of their own age, the actions of contemporary dictators. They expropriated the property of institutions they opposed (Henry VIII and the Church property), converted the Inquisition into a political instrument (Spain, Italy), lied and broke faith and treaties, held public trials of dissenters (Thomas More, Bruno, Campanella), demanded "loyalty oaths" from everyone, harried and pillaged and put to death tens upon tens of thousands of opponents (peasant wars, wars of religion, persecutions of heretics)....

The parallel is even more remarkable in that we find it extends also to the *ideological* realm. Today we are told about the "leader principle," which is used to ideologize the political position of the dictator. In the sixteenth century, men were told about the doctrine of "the divine right of kings," which was used to ideologize the political position of the dictators of that time. (Even Shakespeare, in his plays, reinforced the "divine right" ideology.) The doctrine of the divine right of kings was, from one most important point of view, simply a sixteenth-century version of today's theory of "leadership."

The social problem which the managers and the coming managerial society face is, in general, analogous to that faced in the sixteenth century by the early capitalists and the rising capitalist society—though the capitalists did not and the managers do not, needless to say, face their problem explicitly and scientifically. The capitalists of the sixteenth century were, we might say, carrying on a triple battle: against the feudal lords, whose interests were bound up with the decaying social order; against the masses, who, though obscurely, were a social force working against oppression and class rule of any kind; and against each other for first prizes in the new world. The battle was carried on with the help of dictatorial political methods. The feudal lords were reduced to social impotence. The struggle with the masses continued always in one way or another, but, after armed and bloody suppressions and, above all, after the new capitalist institutions and new ideologies contributing to the defense of these institutions became consolidated, was less acute. The third aspect of the triple battle went on; though, after the reduction to a subordinate place of Italy, Spain, Portugal, and Germany, and as long as many new sections of the world remained open for adventure, it, too, was less sharp and dangerous. With the firm consolidation of the new society, the dictatorial political systems began to give way—sometimes gradually, sometimes to the accompaniment of civil wars—to democratic systems.

Today the managers are carrying on a similar triple battle (let us recall here, as always when we use the language of the class struggle, the partly metaphorical character of that language): against the capitalists, whose interests are bound up with the decaying social order; against the masses, who, obscurely, are a social force tending against oppression and class rule of any kind; and against each other for first prizes in the new world. The hold of the capitalists on the instruments of production must be smashed. The masses must be curbed, and as many as possible of them diverted so that their weight is thrown into the scale on the side of the managers and of the new social structure. The various sections of the managers contend with each other, on a world scale, for mastery. This is a complex process with its elements so intertwined that it is often hard to see through to the major forces. But comparable processes in history indicate that it is worked out by wars and revolutions and persecutions and terror, and by the clash also of rival propaganda and ideologies, all under a bewildering variety of slogans and ostensible motivations.

In such a period political rule tends to concentrate under the form of dictatorship. We already know, without speculating about the future, that this is what is happening today. But when the transition is accomplished, the situation changes. The capitalists will be eliminated or rendered impotent and negligible. The new institutions and ideologies will be consolidated on an at least semistable basis. The masses will be curbed, partly by armed suppression, partly through the consolidation of the managerial institutions and ideologies, which will have, as one effect, the shifting of the struggle of the masses from the revolutionary aim of the transition period—when the old society is going to pieces—to reformist aims within the now-established structure of a new society that has a historic period still before it. The contests among different sections of managerial society will still continue; but the elimination of the first of the elements of the triple battle and the lessening of the second will make the third less devastating in its over-all effects on social structure.

Historical analogy, then, suggests that with the consolidation of the structure of managerial society, its dictatorial phase (totalitarianism) will change into a democratic phase.

This conclusion is reinforced by two additional considerations. In the first place, it would seem that the managers, the ruling class of the new society, will for their own purposes require at least a limited democracy. The managerial economy cannot operate without a considerable degree of centralized planning. But in planning and co-ordinating the economic process, one of the factors that must be taken into account is the state of mind of the people, including something of their wants and of their reactions to the work they are doing. Unless these are known, at least roughly, even reasonable efficiency in production is difficult. But totalitarian dictatorship makes it very hard—as Russia especially already proves—to get any information on the actual state of mind of the people: no one is free to give unbiased information, and the ruling group becomes more and more liable to miscalculate, with the risk of having the social machine break down. A certain measure of democracy makes it easier for the ruling class to get more, and more accurate, information.

Secondly, experience shows that a certain measure of democracy is an excellent way to enable opponents and the masses to let off steam without endangering the foundations of the social fabric. Discontent and opposition, under an absolute dictatorship, having no mechanism for orderly expression, tend to take terroristic and, in times of crisis, revolutionary forms. The example of capitalist parliaments shows how well democratic possibilities are able to make discontent and opposition harmless by providing them with an outlet. Faced with the threat of trouble from the submerged and underprivileged groups, and with the need for mediating conflicts within its own ranks, the new ruling class will doubtless prefer a controlled democracy rather than the risk of social downfall.

Important internal requirements of managerial society thus unite with historical analogy to indicate that totalitarianism is temporary and will be succeeded by some type of democratic political system. There are, however, certain special factors that seem to weigh against this prediction.

Democracy, within a class society, must be so limited as not to interfere with the basic social relations whereby the ruling class maintains its position of power and privilege. In some democracies, this is accomplished by the easy device of restricting political rights altogether or for the most part to members of the ruling class itself (to, for example, slaveholders in a slave society or landholders in an agricultural society). When the vote has been extended to wide sections of the population, including a majority that is not members of the ruling class, the problem is more difficult. In spite of the wider democracy, however, control by the ruling class can be assured (as under capitalism) when major social institutions upholding the position of the ruling class are firmly consolidated, when ideologies contributing to the maintenance of these institutions are generally accepted, when the instruments of education and propaganda are primarily available to the ruling class, and so on. In such cases the governmental changes brought about through democratic processes may be real enough, but they do not threaten the fundamental structure of society: they all revolve within the given framework of basic institutions and ideas.

The capitalists kept in control of society, including, on the whole, the various governments, through their *de facto* control, in their own names, of the major instruments of production, a control which was recognized and accepted by society through the recognition and acceptance of the chief institutions and ideas of capitalism. But the managers, in managerial society, are in an entirely different relationship. Ownership of the instruments of production is formally vested in the state. The managers can maintain their ruling position only, then, through assuring for themselves control of the state, and thus, indirectly, of the instruments of production. But to guarantee this control of the state without dictatorship, with democracy—that is, freedom for public minority political expression—is not so simple. So far, the development toward managerial society has been everywhere accompanied by the tendency toward a one-party monopoly in the political arena, a tendency which has reached completion in most countries. A one-party monopoly would seem to be incompatible with democracy, since public political expression for minorities means the existence of opposition parties whether or not they are called parties. It is not yet clear whether the social relations of the new society could be guaranteed in any other way than through a one-party monopoly.

Moreover, the economic structure of managerial society seems to raise obstacles to democracy. There is no democracy without opposition groups. Opposition groups cannot, however, depend for their existence merely on the good will of those who are in power. They must have some sort of independent institutional base in society so that they can put up meaningful resistance and not be wiped out at an official's casual nod. In decentralized economies, oppositions are able to base themselves on some section of the economy, since no one and no group controls the economy as a whole. Oppositions can be based on one large branch of the economy as against others, on agriculture as against industry, on heavy industry as against light industry, on labor as against capital. But the centralization of the economy under the managerial structure would seem to remove these possibilities. All major parts of the economy will be planned and controlled by the single integrated set of institutions which will be the managerial state. There would seem, then, to be no independent economic foundation for genuine opposition political groups. Democracy will, perhaps, have to seek a different kind of institutional base from that which has traditionally supported it.

The problem is added to when we keep in mind the political institutions of the new society, which we have already discussed. Sovereignty, we have seen, is localized in boards or bureaus, and there seems every reason to think that this will continue to be the case. How, then, in terms of political institutions, would democracy be able to function? It would have to be a nonparliamentary democracy. The 1937 Soviet Constitution nominally revived parliament, but kept the one-party monopoly and the localization of sovereignty in the bureaus. The result was a foregone conclusion, whatever were the intentions of the drafters of the Constitution: the parliament (the two-house Soviet Congress) is a mere sounding board and propaganda agency, and not a fraction of a step was made toward democracy.

It may be that democracy could be introduced through the localization of political opposition in such institutions as syndicates, co-operatives, technical associations, or others of the same order perhaps not yet known. These institutions would then become, in reality, opposition political parties, though the fiction of a one-party monopoly could be kept up. The governmental bureaus would feel the impact of their influences, and mechanisms could easily arise for mediating conflicts. This is not at all an empty speculation. Something of this kind already takes place in the totalitarian nations. In spite of the surface rigidity, it represents a democratic intrusion, capable of indefinite development, in the totalitarian political systems. Democracy grown along these lines would be able to function, up to a point, without being a dangerous threat to the social rule, the power and privileges, of the managers or to the foundations of the new society.

On the whole, it seems to me that a later democratic development in managerial society is likely. It would, however, be an error for those who like democracy to be over-optimistic about it. It is not certain on the evidence so far. And it does not seem indicated for the next day or year or decade. This much is clear: The democracy of capitalist society is on the way out, is, in fact, just about gone, and will not come back. The democracy of managerial society will be some while being born; and its birth pangs will include drastic convulsions.

XII

THE WORLD POLICY OF
THE MANAGERS

UNDER THE political system of capitalism, we have seen, there
existed a comparatively large number of comparatively large
nations. Each of these nations claimed sovereignty for itself. On
a world scale, a considerable part of the world's territories and
peoples was controlled, in a subject status, by the few most
powerful of the advanced nations.

It does not take a prophet to know that under managerial
society this political system is to be radically altered. A prophet
is not needed because the radical change is already taking place,
at mounting speed since the beginning of the second world war.
One after another of the sovereign capitalist nations are being
either wiped out altogether or stripped of the attributes of sovereignty. What is to be the outcome of this process in terms of
world political structure? This is the question which I propose
to examine, and answer, in the present chapter.

Sovereignty for a nation implies that the nation makes laws
for itself and recognizes no superior lawmaker. It means that the
nation sets up tariffs and other import and export controls, regulates its own foreign policies and its own currency, and maintains
civil, diplomatic, and military establishments. The simultaneous
existence of many sovereign nations in the modern world necessarily means an anarchic situation in world politics. This must

be because, since each sovereign nation recognizes no lawmaker superior to itself, there is in the end no way except by force to mediate the deep conflicts that are bound to arise among the various nations.

Experience has shown that the existence of a large number of sovereign nations, especially in Europe (and with somewhat less acuteness in Latin America), is incompatible with contemporary economic and social needs. The system simply does not work. In spite of the fact that the post-Versailles European arrangements were set up and guaranteed by the most powerful coalition in history, which had achieved victory in the greatest war of history, they could not last. The complex division of labor, the flow of trade and raw materials made possible and demanded by modern technology, were strangled in the network of diverse tariffs, laws, currencies, passports, boundary restrictions, bureaucracies, and independent armies. It has been clear for some while that these were going to be smashed; the only problem was who was going to do it and how and when. Now it is being done under the prime initial impulse of Germany.

Anyone who believes that there is the slightest chance for the restoration of the pre-1939 system in Europe is living in a world of fantastic dreams, not on the earth. The United States can keep declaring from now forever that it will never recognize alterations of boundaries brought about by force (the only way in which important alterations have ever been brought about in history, including those alterations accomplished by the United States), and London and Washington can continue "accepting" the dozen refugee governments that run from one capital to another and will doubtless end up at the North Pole; but these highly moral fictions are not going to pump back one drop of blood into the veins of a political system which is already dead.

* *
*

If political problems were settled by scientific reasoning, we should, most probably, expect that the political system of managerial society would take the form of a single world-state. In this way the anarchy necessarily following from conflicting sovereignties would be wholly eliminated. World production could be organized on the most efficient plan with the maximum utilization of world resources and the most effective division of labor. Unnecessary duplications could be avoided, and land, climate, peoples, and resources could be exploited in the most fruitful way. Such a world-society is a goal which Marxists, pacifists, and many others before them have had. If we stick to formal and moral arguments, a powerful case can be made out for it.

Even when we come down to cruder realms, it is not improbable that some of the managers and their political colleagues are also looking toward a world-state, if not as a triumph of justice and logic, then as an aim of power. In particular, it may well be that Hitler and some of his associates have something of the sort in mind; and some at least among the bolder spirits in the United States. Moreover, it is likely that wars will be fought which will have a monopoly of world power as the aim of the participants.

Nevertheless, it is extremely doubtful that the world political system of managerial society will be organized, within the discernible future, as a single world-state. If we leave words and get closer to practical details, the organization of the entire world under a single sovereign-state power seems to present difficulties that are close to insuperable. These difficulties are of many kinds.

First, there are technical and administrative difficulties. The centralized direction of the whole world and all its peoples would be a task beyond the technical ability of any human group so far as we can judge from the behavior of human groups in the past. The job is just too vast. Second, there is the military and police problem: There seems no reason to believe that any state can organize a military group sufficiently large and sufficiently cohesive to be able to patrol the whole world. Even if, by a lucky chance, some one power might win what would look like a world victory, it could prove only temporary. The disintegrative forces would be sufficient to pull it rapidly to pieces. Third, the ethnic, cultural, social, and climatic diversities of the world are so considerable as to preclude its reduction to a political unity; and these diversities, even if they are not permanent, will continue for as long as we can sensibly pretend to predict about. A world state would presuppose a large measure of general social unity among men: in interests, in culture, in education, in material standards of life. No such unity exists, nor, under the class structure of managerial society, can be expected to develop.

At the same time the capitalist system of a comparatively large number of sovereign states cannot continue, and is, in fact, collapsing right now. What is going to take its place?

The answer, in general terms, is not obscure; and, as with so many other questions, does not have to be given by idle speculation about the dim future. The working out of the answer started some time ago and is now going on quickly before our eyes. The comparatively large number of sovereign nations under capitalism is being replaced by a comparatively small number of great nations, or "super-states," which will divide the world among them. Some of the many nations which are eliminated in *fact* may be preserved in *form;* they may be kept as administrative subdivisions, but they will be stripped of sovereignty. Sovereignty will be restricted to the few super-states.

It might seem rash to try to predict just how many of these super-states there will be. Certainly we cannot be sure just how long it will take to consolidate the world political system of managerial society or just what stages will be gone through. Nevertheless, the main outlines and the sketch of the final result are already clear.

If we look at an economic map showing the occupations of mankind, a decisive fact is at once apparent. Advanced industry is concentrated in three, and only three, comparatively small areas: the United States, especially its northeastern and north-central regions; Europe, especially north-central Europe (Germany, the Netherlands, Belgium, northern France, England);

and the Japanese islands together with parts of eastern China. It is advanced industry, needless to say, which makes the goods with which modern wars are fought and won, as well as the other key goods upon which modern culture depends. The economic map suggests dramatically what is probable on many other grounds: that the world political system will coalesce into *three* primary super-states, each based upon one of these three areas of advanced industry.

This does not necessarily mean that these three super-states will be the United States, Germany, and Japan as we know them today. This may well be the case, but it need not be so. In these nations there may be internal convulsions which, together with foreign military struggles, will seem to break their continuity with the past. New names may be used. This would, however, be of secondary importance in the long run.

It should go without saying that the mechanism whereby this new political system will be built is and will be war. War is the only mechanism that has ever been employed for similar purposes in the past, and there is not the slightest indication—certainly not at the opening of 1941!—that any other is going to replace it.

*   *
*

We are now in a position to understand the central historical meaning of the first two world wars of the twentieth century. We might put it, over-simplifying but not distorting, in this way: The war of 1914 was the last great war of capitalist society; the war of 1939 is the first great war of managerial society. Thus both wars are transitional in character, are wars of the transition period between capitalist and managerial society. In both wars we find both capitalist and managerial elements, with the former predominant in the war of 1914, the latter immensely increased in the war of 1939.

This political characterization of the two wars correlates with and reinforces the conclusions we have reached in our economic analysis, and again motivates our selection of the year, 1914, as the beginning of the social transition to managerial society. We found that from the late Middle Ages until the first world war, the percentage of world economy under the control of capitalists and capitalist economic relations had continuously increased; but from that time on has, also continuously and at a growing speed, declined. Looked at politically, we may say that from the midst of the first world war came the first great abrupt jump toward managerial society—the Russian Revolution. That war and its aftermath (the "Versailles system") gave the final proof that capitalist world politics could no longer work and were about to end.

From the war of 1939 are coming at least two more of the major political leaps toward managerial society: first, the political consolidation of the European Continent, which involves also the smashing of England's hold on the Continent; and, second, the breakup of the British Empire, chief political representative of capitalist world society. Though it is not yet understood in this country, both of these steps were assured when France surrendered in June, 1940. The dominant position of capitalist England has always depended upon its acting as middleman between the European Continent and the rest of the world, including most prominently its own great Empire. From this dependence followed the "balance of power" policy which England has been compelled to uphold during the entire capitalist era. This policy demands that no single nation shall dominate the European Continent; or, rather, that England shall dominate the Continent through balancing Continental nations against each other. England's domination can be achieved in no other way, since its comparatively meager national resources and its small population make impossible direct domination through its own force. But the balance of power on the Continent is possible only when the Continent is divided up into a number of genuinely sovereign and powerful states. Such a division ended, for all time, when France surrendered. Consequently, whatever happens during the remainder of the present war, whether or not Hitler's regime is overthrown, whether or not new revolts take place, the old system is finished, and England can never again be dominant in Europe or the controlling political center of a vast world empire.

But the war of 1939 is only the first, not the last, war of managerial society. There will be much still to be decided after the present struggle is over—though, since war and peace are no longer declared, it may be hard to know when this struggle is over and the next one begins. The immediate war will not even complete the consolidation of the managerial structure of society; and after it is completed there will still be wars, for there will remain plenty to fight about.

I have predicted the division of the new world among three super-states. The nuclei of these three super-states are, whatever may be their future names, the previously existing nations, Japan, Germany, and the United States. It is of great significance to note that all three of these nations began some while ago their preparations for the new world order. The preliminary period is one of the consolidation of strategic bases—which means, above all, the three areas of advanced industry, together with the positions necessary for the protection of these areas. Since entering Manchuria, Japan has got hold of almost all of her area and is branching out from it. Germany widened her base at first without open war (the Saar, Austria, Czechoslovakia...) and now is completing its consolidation through the war. The United States began on the ideological front, with the Pan-American conferences and the propaganda of the "hemisphere policy," and is recently beginning to make up for lost time by taking more practical steps, such as the defense agreement with Canada (in reality the reduction of Canada to a satellite), the acquisition of the Atlantic bases (through the formula of a lease), and the concrete implementation of the hemisphere policy.

However, the "consolidation of the strategic bases" is only the first phase. The fundamental theme of the wars of the future—

into one of which the second world war was already evolving by the latter part of 1940—will be the clash among the three areas which constitute the three main strategic bases. Ostensibly these wars will be directed from each base for conquest of the other bases. But it does not seem possible for any one of these to conquer the others; and even two of them in coalition could not win a decisive and lasting victory over the third.

What will be actually accomplished by these wars will not be a decision as to who is to rule the bases—for Americans are going to rule here, Europeans in Europe, and Asiatics in Japan and East China—but decisions as to what parts and how much of the *rest* of the world are going to be ruled by each of the three strategic centers. It might be thought that a "rational" solution could be worked out along "natural" geographic lines, dividing the world into three parts, as the pope in the sixteenth century tried to divide the non-European world between Spain and Portugal. But men do not solve their problems in such a way in the twentieth any more than in the sixteenth century. Geography gives certain advantages to each of the contestants in certain areas: to the United States in the northern two-thirds of the two Americas; to the European center in Europe, the northern half of Africa and western Asia; to the Asiatic center in most of the rest of Asia and the islands near by. But there is much left over, and, besides, the rivals will not be willing to admit any "natural" geographic right. As in the sixteenth century, the wars that are coming, not a pope, will draw the maps.

This struggle among the three strategic centers for world control will be the fundamental theme of the coming wars of managerial society. Naturally, the fundamental theme will be obscured and complicated, and will be played with variations. The theme only begins to emerge during the present war—though it is daily clearer. Capitalism is not yet dead, and the wars of the present are not "pure" managerial wars. They are also completing the destruction of capitalism, not merely by the effects of military defeat, but also by the internal consequences of war regimes under modern conditions. And the consolidation of the three super-states, even within their immediate strategic areas, is not by any means finished. In Europe, for example, even if Germany is fully victorious in the present war, there still remain Russia and Italy; and Russia is also in Asia along with Japan.

Everyone knows, however, that Italy is a subordinate, incapable of a really independent sovereign policy. There is every reason to believe (as we shall discuss in Chapter XIV) that Russia will split apart, with the western half gravitating toward the European base and the eastern toward the Asiatic. But even if a coalition of the future, combined with internal disturbances, should overthrow the Germany of the present, this would be secondary to the main scheme. The result of such a development would not alter the political system toward which managerial society tends. It would merely change the name and some of the leading personnel of one of the super-states.

The coming years will also include wars of another type—indeed, these began several years ago: wars of the metropolitan centers against backward areas and peoples. The backward areas, which include a majority of the territory and people of the world, are not going to line up automatically behind one or another of the three centers or merely stand aside while the three fight over them. In the dissolution of the capitalist world political structure and during the internecine conflicts of the great managerial states, the backward peoples will attempt to break free altogether from domination and to take their destiny into their own hands. Often such uprisings will occur in connection with wars among the chief managerial powers. However, it is doubtful that any of the backward peoples will be able to win independence (except, perhaps, in form and title). They do not have the technological resources to conduct modern war successfully or to compete more or less evenly from an economic point of view—which is also necessary for independence today. They will have to gravitate toward one or another of the great camps, even if they have some temporary success in a struggle for independence.

This is already seen during the course of the second world war. There is no doubt that the Indian masses want independence from Great Britain and sovereignty for themselves. Under the given circumstances, however, they are held back from a struggle for independence, not merely by the cowardice of many of their leaders, but because many of the leaders correctly understand that Indian independence could not be firmly established. Revolt against Britain would link them and finally subordinate them to Germany or Russia. A similar dilemma confronts the Arabs of the Near East. In Latin America the situation is analogous: the nations, unable to stand on their own feet in the coming world, shilly-shally back and forth. With Britain, formerly the most influential nation in Latin America, dissolving, the only realistic alternative they face is subordination to the United States or to the new European center. Their own choice as to this alternative does not make much difference, since the issue will be decided by the relative strength of the United States and the European center.

These remarks would seem to apply to the whole world. Everywhere, men will have to line up with one or the other of the super-states of tomorrow. There will not be room for smaller sovereign nations; nor will the less advanced peoples be able to stand up against the might of the metropolitan areas. Of course, polite fictions of independence may be preserved for propaganda purposes; but it is the reality and not the name of sovereignty about which we are talking.

The managers under the structure of the new economy will be able to solve one of the difficulties which we saw has been confronting capitalism and which is an important element in the downfall of capitalism: namely, capitalism's inability any longer to exploit and develop the backward areas successfully. Capitalism cannot do it today (as, for example, the United States in Latin America) because it is no longer profitable from a capitalist standpoint. There is no longer the profit incentive sufficient to draw idle private funds from their present unfruitful storehouses. Even now, when the war has left the Latin American door wide open, business men and bankers in the United States do very little. They cannot be persuaded to pump in large investments or to undertake important enterprises. And they are right, for they know from hard experience of late years that this would be unprofitable. The government, through such devices as the Export-Import Bank, and other grander devices to come, has to take over. The managerial state does not have to make a capitalist profit; and as the capitalist relations are liquidated the managerial state will move ahead to a new stage in world colonial and semicolonial development.

Germany, in its economic relations with lesser and subordinate nations, has already shown some of the ways in which it can be done. For years all of the orthodox economists have been proving that German trade dealings with the Balkans, South America, Russia, and so on "hurt" German economy rather than helped it—because, of course, these dealings are "uneconomic," that is, unprofitable in a capitalist sense. This conclusion follows only when the reasoning is carried out in terms of capitalist economic relations. The fact is that the dealings keep people employed in both Germany and the subordinate nations, and bring about exchanges of goods and services held to be of value by both sides, especially by Germany. To prove that such trade cannot be carried on profitably is not to prove that it won't be carried on but only that it will not be under capitalism.

Such political predictions as I have herein outlined are very much resented in the United States. Our official doctrine still continues in the Wilson tradition: international law and morality; rights of small nations; nonrecognition of territories acquired by force. Washington continues to be crowded with diplomatic representatives of nations which no longer exist. I have no wish to quarrel with the way people like to talk and think and feel, or how they like to use words; my purpose is to discover what is probable on the evidence. In spite of what our spokesmen in the United States say, I do not really think that there are many serious persons here or anywhere else who do not judge the probabilities pretty much as I do.

Does any serious person seriously think that the European Continent is again going to be divided up into a score of sovereign nations, each with its independent border guards, tariffs, export restrictions, currencies, forts, armies, bureaucracies... ? I doubt that anyone really thinks so. If it didn't work after Versailles, when conditions were a hundred times more favorable, when mounting mass unemployment and permanent economic depression were not yet inescapable features of capitalism, it is certainly not going to work today or tomorrow. It is not a question of what we would like, but of what is going to happen. Even the British propagandists have been compelled to speak in terms of a "United States of Europe"—that is, a European consolidation under the dominance of England in which the participating states would necesssarily give up the rights of sovereignty. The only thing wrong in this conception is the notion that this consolidation could be achieved under a capitalist social structure with the British Empire remaining capitalist and undisturbed. And what are all these schemes of "Union Now" but polite phrases for a possible way of consolidating one of the superstates of the future under United States control?

It is still more important, and ironic, to observe that for all the talk by the official spokesmen, the United States *acts* today in accordance with the predictions of this chapter. The United States is consolidating its strategic base in the northern two-thirds of this hemisphere and preparing to do battle against either or both of the two great rivals—the European center and the Asiatic center—for its share in the new world. That its actions are more hesitant than those of its rivals, especially the European rival, is due simply to the fact that the United States today still retains more of capitalism and that capitalists and capitalist ideologies still are more powerful in the United States than managers and managerial ideologies. But in spite of this, the realistic calculations of the leaders, and particularly the future leaders, of the United States are based upon predictions the same in content as these I have stated. It could hardly be otherwise, since these are plainly written by the facts of yesterday and today. In politics, acts and the consequences of acts are far more revealing than words.

XIII

THE MANAGERIAL IDEOLOGIES

ALL ORGANIZED societies are cemented together, not merely by force and the threat of force, and by established patterns of institutional behavior, but also by accepted ways of feeling and thinking and talking and looking at the world, by ideologies. No one today will deny the crucial social function of ideologies, though we are always more critical about others' ideologies than about our own. Indeed, many of us like to feel ourselves free from the influence of any ideology, though we are seldom prepared to grant such enlightenment to anyone else. A society cannot hold together unless there is a fairly general acceptance on the part of most of its members, not necessarily of the same ideology, but, at any rate, of ideologies which develop out of similar root concepts as starting points.

Scientific theories are always controlled by the facts: they must be able to explain the relevant evidence already at hand, and on their basis it must be possible to make verifiable predictions about the future. Ideologies are not controlled by facts, even though they may incorporate some scientific elements and are ordinarily considered scientific by those who believe in them. The primary function of ideologies—whether moral or religious or metaphysical or social—is to express human interests, needs, desires, hopes, fears, not to cover the facts. A dispute about scientific theories can always be settled, sooner or later, by experiment and observation. A dispute between rival ideologies can never be thus settled. Arguments about ideologies can, and do, continue as long as the interests embodied by them are felt to be of any significance.

After that, they become curiosities to be studied by philosophers or anthropologists. There can never be, as there are in the case of scientific theories, satisfactory tests for the "truth" of ideologies, since in reality the notions of truth and falsity are irrelevant to ideologies. The problem with an ideology is not, when properly understood, whether it is true, but: what interests does it express, and how adequately and persuasively does it express them?

However, though ideologies are not controlled by facts, they are nevertheless subject to controls. In particular, the major ideologies of a class society must be able to perform two tasks: (1) They must actually express, at least roughly, the social interests of the ruling class in question, and must aid in creating a pattern of thought and feeling favorable to the maintenance of the key institutions and relations of the given social structure. (2) They must at the same time be so expressed as to be capable of appealing to the sentiments of the masses. An ideology embodying the interests of a given ruling class would not be of the slightest use as social cement if it openly expressed its function of keeping the ruling class in power over the rest of society. The ideology must ostensibly speak in the name of "humanity," "the people," "the race," "the future," "God," "destiny," and so on. Furthermore, in spite of the opinion of many present-day cynics, not just any ideology is capable of appealing to the sentiments of the masses. It is more than a problem of skillful propaganda technique. A successful ideology has got to seem to the masses, in however confused a way, actually to express some of their own interests.

In a period of social transition, the ideologies of the old society are under attack by the rising ideologies of the society-to-be, just as the institutions of the old society and the economic and political power of the old ruling class are under attack. The rising ideologies naturally devote much of their attention to the negative task of undermining mass acceptance of the old ideologies.

The major ideologies of capitalist society, as we noted briefly in an earlier chapter, were variants on the themes of: *individualism;* opportunity; "natural rights," especially the rights of property; freedom, especially "freedom of contract"; private enterprise; private initiative; and so on. These ideologies conformed well to the two requirements stated above. Under the interpretations given them, they expressed and served the interests of the capitalists. They justified profit and interest. They showed why the owner of the instruments of production was entitled to the full product of those instruments and why the worker had no claim on the owner except for the contracted wages. They preserved the supremacy of the field of private enterprise. They kept the state to its limited role. They protected the employers' rights of hiring and firing. They explained why an owner could work his factory full time or shut it down at his own discretion. They assured the right of owners to set up factories or to buy and sell wherever they might choose, to keep money in a bank or in cash or in bonds or in active capital as seemed most expedient. So long as ideologies developed from such conceptions as these were not seriously and widely questioned, the structure of capitalist society was reasonably secure.

At the same time, these ideologies were able to gain the acceptance and often the enthusiasm of the masses. Men who were not capitalists were willing to swear and die by slogans issuing out of these ideologies. And, as a matter of fact, the way of life embodied in these ideologies was for some while beneficial to large sections of the masses, though never to the extent advertised or in any way comparable to what it was for the capitalists.

The capitalist ideologies are today in a very different position from that which they held even a generation ago. The differences are plainly written on the surface of events.

Once these ideologies provided the slogans for what nearly

everyone would call the most "progressive" groups in society—among them the English and French and American revolutionists —and in later times for groups which in any case were not the most conservative. Today the same slogans, proceeding from the same ideological bases, are found most often and most naturally among the words of what everyone recognizes to be the most conservative, or even reactionary, groups in society—those whom the New Dealers call the "Tories," without much regard for historical propriety.

In the United States, it is the Hoovers, the Lippmanns, the Girdlers and Weirs and Willkies, the New York *Herald Tribune* and the Chicago *Tribune,* the leaders of the Chamber of Commerce and the National Association of Manufacturers, who speak most readily in these terms. The "Liberty League" was their organization. There are many who are outraged by this phenomenon. They think that this sort of talk from these sources is shocking hypocrisy and a fake. But this is a naïve analysis, made by those who do not know how to relate words to social realities. There was nothing fake about the Liberty League. The claim of the Tories to these slogans and these ideologies is one hundred per cent legitimate. These are the slogans and ideologies of capitalism, and the Tories are the bona fide representatives of capitalism. The slogans mean for them what they have always meant in practice for capitalism; it is the world, not they and their ideas, that has changed. If these slogans are now associated, and correctly associated, with the most conservative (that is, backward-looking) sections of society, that is because the old structure of society, once healthy, is now breaking up and a new structure is being built; an old class is on its way out and a new class marching in.

But, second and even more revealing, the capitalist ideologies and slogans have largely lost their power to appeal to the masses. This is not in the least a subjective and personal opinion; it may be perfectly well established by impersonal observation.

Perhaps the most striking proof of the falling off in mass

appeal is provided by the complete failure of voluntary military recruiting in England (as well as the entire British Empire) and in the United States. This failure would in itself be remarkable enough. When we remember that voluntary recruiting was tried in England and in the United States at a time when millions were unemployed, and with the help of all the instruments of modern propaganda technique, the significance of the failure is immense. The recruiting was conducted under slogans drawn from the capitalist ideologies. The youth, though it had no jobs and no prospects, simply did not respond. The armies must be gathered by compulsion. No one can challenge the fact; and no one who is honest about it can doubt the significance of the fact.

A second equally demonstrative proof is provided by the advance of Hitler prior to the war and without war. In 1933, in Germany itself, no group among the masses was willing to risk life to stop the Nazi assumption of power; Hitler took power without a civil war. The capitalist ideologies did not provide a sufficient incentive for heroism. In the Saar and in the Sudetenland, the masses had had their experience of capitalism and capitalist democracy. They chose Hitler and Nazism. There is not the slightest doubt that overwhelming majorities in both were in favor of becoming part of Hitler's Germany. It may be granted that terrorism and skilled propaganda methods played some part in influencing opinion. But to imagine that these were the full explanation would be shallow and absurd. Terrorism and skilled technique cannot by themselves put across an ideology that has no roots in mass appeal. The fact is that Nazism was preferred by the masses to the capitalist ideologies.

A third set of proofs is provided by the war itself, above all by France. The masses in France could not be stirred to enthusiasm for a war for "democracy" (that is, capitalism). They rejoiced at Munich. They were passive when the war started, and all through the war. They did not have the will to fight. The Nazi military machine might well have defeated France whatever the state of mind of the French people. But the French army was not armed with bows and arrows. It is incredible that the defeat should have been so swift unless we admit, what is undeniably true, that the masses in France did not want to fight the war. They did not want to because the capitalist slogans no longer could move them.

The United States is finding a similar difficulty. Several years of intensive and able war propaganda fail to meet with really enthusiastic mass response. Heads of colleges and preachers and statesmen and librarians of Congress rebuke the American youth for being cynics, for its unwillingness to sacrifice, for its indifference. But no one can scold the masses into enthusiasm. The youth will not fight willingly because it does not believe in what it is being asked to fight for, that is, in the slogans of the capitalist ideologies. The point is not whether the youth is "justified" or not in its feelings. These *are* the feelings; that is what is decisive.

When old ideologies wear out, new ones come in to take their place. The capitalist ideologies are now wearing out, along with the capitalist society of which they are the ideologies; and many new ideologies are contending for the jobs left vacant. Most of the new ideologies don't get very far, because they do not fulfill the requirements for great social ideologies. The new "agrarianism," medievalism, regionalism, religious primitivism pick up a few recruits and may have a few months of notoriety, but they remain the preoccupation of small sects. At the present time, the ideologies that can have a powerful impact, that can make real headway, are, naturally, the *managerial* ideologies, since it is these that alone correspond with the actual direction of events.

The general basis of the managerial ideologies is clear enough from an understanding of the general character of managerial society. In place of capitalist concepts, there are concepts suited to the structure of managerial society and the rule of the managers. In place of the "individual," the stress turns to the "state," the people, the folk, the race. In place of gold, labor and work. In place of private enterprise, "socialism" or "collectivism." In place of "freedom" and "free initiative," planning. Less talk about "rights" and "natural rights"; more about "duties" and "order" and "discipline." Less about "opportunity" and more about "jobs." In addition, in these early decades of managerial society, more of the positive elements that were once part of capitalist ideology in its rising youth, but have left it in old age: destiny, the future, sacrifice, power.... Of course, some of the words of the capitalist ideologies are taken over: such words as "freedom" are found in many ideologies since they are popular and, as we have seen, can be interpreted in any manner whatever.

These concepts, and others like them, help break down what remains of capitalism and clear the road for the managers and managerial society. They prepare the psychic atmosphere for the demolition of capitalist property rights, the acceptance of state economy and the rule of a new kind of state, the rejection of the "natural rights" of capitalism (that is, the rights of the capitalists in the private market place), and the approval of managerial war. When enough people begin thinking through these instead of the capitalist categories, the consolidation of the managerial structure of society is assured.

Starting from such concepts as these, many dialectical and "philosophical" variations are possible, just as there were many variant developments of the capitalist concepts. There will be no *the* managerial ideology any more than there was a *the* capitalist ideology. The several managerial ideologies will, however, revolve around a common axis, as the capitalist ideologies revolved around a common and different axis. Cultural background, local history, religion, the path taken by the revolution, the ingenuity of individual propagandists will permit a considerable diversity in the new ideologies, just as they have in those of past societies.

We already have examples. Fascism-Nazism and Leninism-

Stalinism (communism or Bolshevism) are types of early managerial ideologies which have been given organized expression and have already had great success. In this country, Technocracy and the much more important New Dealism are embryonic and less-developed types of primitive, native-American managerial ideologies. All of these are well known—or, at any rate, are easily available if anyone wishes to know about them instead of believing the parodies of them published in the daily press—so that I do not intend to waste time with a lengthy discussion of their contents. They are all managerial ideologies in one or another stage of development, and all, with greater or less clarity, make use of the elements which I have listed above.

Let us consider the position in which the managers, and those who from ability and ambition and actual or potential training would like to be managers, find themselves during the last decade in capitalist nations; and let us consider also how they themselves see their own position in the world. (We can easily verify our results by talking to a few managers.) From their point of view, they are the ones who are actually running modern society, making it work, providing its brains, keeping it going. Nevertheless, they do not get rewards, in terms either of unchallenged power or of percentage of the national income, commensurate with what they feel to be their functional role. In particular, the capitalists, even though they may never come near a factory or a mine, get far more.

The institutional setup of capitalism—whether or not the managers realize this explicitly—deprives the managers of rewards in keeping with what they take to be their merits, and at the same time prevents the managers from running things as they would like to. They are often interfered with, by those whose only relation to production is one of capitalist ownership, for the sake of aims that have nothing to do with the managers' conception of how to run the economy. The managers' training as administrators of modern production naturally tends to make them think in terms of co-ordination, integration, efficiency, planning; and to extend such terms from the area of production under their immediate direction to the economic process as a whole. When the managers think about it, the old-line capitalists, sunning themselves in Miami and Hawaii or dabbling in finance, appear to them as parasites, having no justifiable function in society and at the same time preventing the managers from introducing the methods and efficiency which they would like.

The masses, also, are, through the trade-union and other devices introduced under capitalism, interfering with the managers' control and plans. Besides, the masses seem to the managers stupid, incapable of running things, of real leadership. The managers know that with the technological means at their disposal it would be perfectly easy for them to put everyone to work; but the existing setup prevents them from acting. They naturally tend to identify the welfare of mankind as a whole with their own interests and the salvation of mankind with their assuming control of society. Society can be run, they think, in more or less the same way that they know they, when they are allowed, can run, efficiently and productively, a mass-production factory.

It is out of such a vision of life, which is that undoubtedly held by very many managers and would-be managers—above all, managers functioning in the governmental apparatus—that the managerial concepts and managerial ideologies arise. It is not the managers themselves who make the ideologies explicit, draw out their implications, systematize them. That is the task of intellectuals. So long as capitalism is providing the managers with large incomes, so long as the social structure doesn't seem to be cracking to pieces, the managers may accompany these feelings I have sketched with much of the traditional ideology of capitalism. But capitalist ideology is hollow in their living experience. They readily adapt themselves to the new ideologies because the new ideologies correspond much better to their experience, to their way of looking at the world and themselves. Indeed, the intellectuals, without usually being aware of it, elaborate the new ideologies from the point of view of the position of the managers.

That an ideology should be a *managerial* ideology, it is not necessary that managers should be its inventors or the first to adopt it. Capitalists did not invent capitalist ideologies; and intellectuals were elaborating them when the ambition of nearly every capitalist was still to be a feudal lord. It is the social effects that count. The effects of managerial ideologies, such as the three types I have named, are to aid in the establishment of that structure of society which I have called managerial, where the managers are on top. Certainly there can be no doubt that under Nazism, Stalinism, and New Dealism, the group in society which has done better (however well or badly) than any other group is the managers; above all, the managers who have had sense enough to become integrated in the state.

Before going further, I must pause briefly on an issue over which there has been much controversy. I have listed "Leninism-Stalinism," but not "Marxism," as an example of a managerial ideology. This raises the question of the relation of Marxism to Leninism and of Leninism to Stalinism. Historically, the social movement, which both in organization and ideas traced its source to the activities and writing of Marx, separated, through a division which started during the last years of the nineteenth century and culminated in 1914, into two main streams: a reformist, "social-democratic" wing; and a revolutionary wing in which for the first decade after 1914 Lenin was the most conspicuous figure. I do not any longer consider it fruitful to dispute over which of these is "genuine" Marxism. Historically, they both spring from Marx.

What happened seems to be the following: The views of Marx, in their implications and consequences, were historically ambiguous. In addition, he proposed a social goal—a free, classless international society—which cannot be reached in the present period of history. Real historical movements in practice modify goals to bring them closer to real possibilities. The Marxist movement separated along the lines of the great division of our time, capitalist society and managerial society. Both wings of Marxism retained, as often happens, the language of Marx, though more and more modifying it under new pressures. In practice, the reformist wing lined up with the capitalists and capitalist society, and demonstrated this in all social crises. The Leninist wing became one of the organized movements toward, and expressed one of the ideologies of, managerial society. The reformist wing is a somewhat inconsistent defender of capitalism, it is true, because by its retention of much of the ambiguous language of Marx it also contributes to popularizing managerial concepts. But this is the main line of the division.

Lenin died, and Stalin headed the managerial wing. The ideology and practices were further modified. There has been much dispute over whether Stalin is the legitimate heir of Lenin; and I, for some years active in the Trotskyist political organization, long took part in that dispute. I have come to the conclusion, however, that the dispute has been conducted on a pointless basis. The historical problem is not whether Stalin or Trotsky (or someone else, for there are many other claimants) comes closer to the verbally explicit principles enunciated by Lenin. A dispute on such a level has never been and will never be settled, since Lenin said many things and did many things. It is like arguing over the legitimate interpretation of the Bible or the Koran. So far as historical development goes, there really cannot be much question; Stalinism is what Leninism developed into—and, moreover, without any sharp break in the process of development. Stalinism is different from Leninism, and so is a youth from a child; the difference is to be accounted for by the change in the background against which development took place. Nazism is much more different from Italian fascism than Stalinism is from Leninism, as might be expected from the differences in origin and conditions of development. But it is clear enough that Nazism and fascism are closely related as general social movements and as social ideologies.

The most conservative capitalist spokesmen have for years identified "communism" (that is, Stalinism), "Nazism," and "New Dealism." This identification has been the cause of bitter resentment among liberals. It is certainly true that the grounds presented by capitalists in justification of the identification are often superficial. It is also true that what is usually at issue in arguments of this kind are not ideologies in general but some specific proposal (more relief, the Wagner Act, government ownership of utilities...) about which there is a specific difference of opinion. The broader ideological concepts are brought in by the two sides primarily for their emotional effect for or against the specific proposal.

Nevertheless, so far as the general ideological question is involved, there is no doubt that the capitalists—as is ordinarily the case—are correct in their attitude no matter how absurd they may be in the explicit reasons they give for the attitude. What the capitalists sense, and are in the best position to sense, is that the final implications in all these ideologies are anticapitalist, destructive of the ideologies which are the psychological cement of capitalist society. There is, in truth, not a formal identity, but a historical bond uniting Stalinism (communism), Nazism (fascism), and New Dealism. Against differing developmental backgrounds and at different stages of growth, they are all *managerial* ideologies. They all have the same historical direction: away from capitalist society and toward managerial society. Of the three, New Dealism is the most primitive and least organized;

it retains most from the capitalist ideologies. But the direction is what is all-important; and New Dealism points in the same direction as the others.

Once we get even a short way beneath the surface, it is easy to recognize in both Stalinism and fascism the same set of assumptions and key concepts—the concepts out of which we have noticed that managerial ideologies develop. The critiques of capitalist society made by communist and fascist theoreticians are, for practical purposes, identical. There are certain verbal and metaphysical differences, but these are of no serious importance. The anticapitalist pages of fascist and communist analyses could usually be interchanged without anyone's being able to tell which came from which. This holds for the critiques of capitalist economy, politics, and ideologies. The two ideologies are the same also—and this is most influential in developing patterns of attitude—in their scorn and contempt for "capitalist morality," in their scathing dismissal of "natural rights" as capitalism understands these rights.

They unite to attack "individualism," root and branch. In both ideologies, the "state," the "collectivity," "planning," "co-ordination," "socialism," "discipline" replace the "individual," "free enterprise," "opportunity," as attitude-terms to hammer into the consciousness of the masses.

Fascist and communist ideologies denounce in the same words the "chaos" and "anarchy" of capitalism. They conceive of the organization of the state of the future, their state, exactly along the lines on which a manager, an engineer, organizes a factory; that is, their conception of the state is a social extension generalized from managerial experience. And they have identical conceptions of "the party"—their party, with a monopoly in the political field.

The idea of the party is of special importance, for the problem of the party is the center of the direct struggle for power. There is a most striking and thorough similarity in both the theory and practice of communists and fascists on the problem of the party. A communist could subscribe to nine-tenths at least of Hitler's careful discussion of the party in *Mein Kampf;* and the Nazis, on their side, took over many of their ideas on the party direct from the communists. The structure of the party, the techniques of its operation, the utilization of "sympathizers" and "peripheral" organizations, the building up of "cells," the penetration of mass organizations, the "fraction" method whereby a small tight party group can control a huge mass movement, the culminating "one-party dictatorship" within the state as a whole: all are the same. And, in passing, the capitalist methods of party organization do not stand a chance against them.

Both communism and fascism claim, as do all great social ideologies, to speak for "the people" as a whole, for the future of all mankind. However, it is interesting to notice that both provide, even in their public words, for the existence of an "élite" or "vanguard." The élite is, of course, the managers and their political associates, the rulers of the new society. Naturally the ideologies do not put it in this way. As they say it, the élite represents, stands for, the people as a whole and their interests. Fascism is more blunt about the need for the élite, for "leadership." Leninism worked out a more elaborate rationalization. The masses, according to Leninism, are unable to become sufficiently educated and trained under capitalism to carry in their own immediate persons the burdens of socialism. The masses are unable to understand in full what their own interests are. Consequently, the "transition to socialism" will have to be supervised by an enlightened "vanguard" which "understands the historic process as a whole" and can ably and correctly act for the interests of the masses as a whole: like, as Lenin puts it, the general staff of an army.

Through this notion of an élite or vanguard, these ideologies thus serve at once the twofold need of justifying the existence of a ruling class and at the same time providing the masses with an attitude making easy the acceptance of its rule. This device is similar to that used by the capitalist ideologies when they argued that capitalists were necessary in order to carry on business and that profits for the capitalists were identical with prosperity for the people as a whole. So long as the masses believed this, they were ardent defenders, not only of capitalism in general, but even of bigger and better times (power and privilege) for the capitalist ruling class. The communist and fascist doctrine is a device, and an effective one, for enlisting the support of the masses for the interests of the new élite through an apparent identification of those interests with the interests of the masses themselves.

The historical bond between communism and fascism is much clearer today than it was fifteen years ago. The difference in origin obscured the similarity of direction. But the events of these fifteen years, as they took place under the pressures of our time, clarified the direction until the second world war offered definitive proof. Fascism and communism slough off differences one by one, approach a common norm, and show their full historical significance. Leninism, for example, at first denied, in words at least, the doctrine of a one-party political monopoly. Following the development of a one-party regime in practice in Russia (well before the death of Lenin), Leninist theory was altered to explain why a one-party monopoly was "necessary": because, the argument runs, all parties but the Bolshevik party turn out to be counter-revolutionary. Stalinism now incorporates the doctrine in the Soviet Constitution. Leninism formally attacked the "leader-principle"; but in practice—not only within the Soviet Union, but also in communist movements, Stalinist or non-Stalinist, outside Russia—a leader invariably appears. Leninism called for free and autonomous trade-unions; but in practice the unions became incorporated in the soviet state just as in the fascist states; and, in other nations, the unions become party adjuncts, before state power is won, wherever fascist or communist parties make headway in them (as must, indeed, follow from the technique of party operation).

Impressive evidence of the historical bond between communism and fascism is also to be found in the similar conclusions that are drawn from them on specific practical issues, often at the very same time that they are most fervently denouncing each other in words. I wish to cite two from the dozens of major examples:

Prior to Hitler's assumption of power in January, 1933, on several occasions the Communist party of Germany and the Nazi party jointly opposed the Social-Democratic (reformist-Marxist) candidates in the Prussian elections, and thereby brought about the defeat of the Social-Democrats. The reformist party was, as we noted, a capitalist party (in spite of its verbal Marxist ideology). On the verge of a social overturn the communists, in practice, found themselves drawn to the Nazi side against the reformist: that is, the managerial representatives held together against the capitalist.

The most important of all examples, and a crucial one, is however the Stalin-Hitler pact of August, 1939, which precipitated the second world war. How are we to interpret this pact? The truth is that, in spite of a few predictions that Hitler and Stalin were going to get together, nearly everyone in the capitalist world thought, and had thought for years, that the main contestants in the approaching war were going to be Germany and Russia. All serious calculations were made with that expectation. So powerful was this opinion that during the first six months of the war it continued unshaken: nearly everyone considered the war between England and Germany a "fake" war, and waited for Russia to "change sides." So far as the past propaganda of Nazis and Stalinists went, the view was certainly justified. These were the ultimate enemies. In fact, liberal journalists have since the pact spent a great deal of time rebuking Stalin and Hitler for "inconsistency," for "betraying their own principles" —a rather odd charge from the liberals.

If we try to understand ideologies by merely taking their words at face value, as if they were scientific statements of fact, we can never comprehend history and politics. Nor can we do any better by explaining great events as "inconsistencies" and hypocrisies. Faced with an ultimate challenge, with the first great opening war of managerial society, Hitler and Stalin acted altogether correctly, from their point of view. Hitler's first job is to drive death wounds into capitalism—into the "plutocratic democracies"—and to consolidate his strategic base in the European area. The contest with Russia, which, whether carried on by instruments of war or peace, will be a managerial conflict in a much fuller sense than the present war, belongs to a later stage, even though that stage may be reached before the end of the present war. Before getting on with the new, there must be assurance of the disintegration of the old. Representatives of the managerial future come temporarily together to grapple with the capitalist past before getting at each other's throats.

There is no other sensible explanation of the pact.

It may be added that the conduct of the Stalinists and Nazis in all nations during the course of the war is in general a confirmation. They are not identical: the interests of Germany and Russia are by no means the same in every respect. But when it comes down to practical issues, they equally work to weaken the war efforts of the old-line capitalist countries and to strengthen those of the nations closest to managerial social organization.

New Dealism is not, let me repeat, a developed, systematized managerial ideology. The New Dealers, most of them, protest frequently their devotion to capitalism and "private enterprise." But just as the New Deal *actions* (to which we shall return in Chapter XVI) have been toward the managerial revolution, so is the managerial direction of the ideology of New Dealism clear as soon as we refer it back to root concepts. In its own more confused, less advanced way, New Dealism too has spread abroad the stress on the state as against the individual, planning as against private enterprise, jobs (even if relief jobs) against opportunities, security against initiative, "human rights" against "property rights." There can be no doubt that the psychological effect of New Dealism has been what the capitalists say it has been: to undermine public confidence in capitalist ideas and rights and institutions. Its most distinctive features help to prepare the minds of the masses for the acceptance of the managerial social structure.

Interestingly enough, as New Dealism develops it draws always closer to the other managerial ideologies. The notion that there is only one party—the New Deal party—that can represent the American people is no longer unfamiliar. The successful propaganda for a third term was simply a native expression of the doctrine of an indispensable leader. In each Roosevelt election the ideological line has been sharper. It was fascinating to observe that when Roosevelt appealed to "the people" in his brilliant 1940 election speeches, he called for the support of all classes, including "production men," "technicians in industry" and "managers," with one most notable exception: never, by any of the usual American terms of "businessmen" or "owners" or "bankers" or even "industry," did he address himself to the capitalists. It was Willkie's speeches that were defending "businessmen" and "private enterprise," and the words and phrases correctly expressed the social reality.

What is very revealing, moreover, is the fact that attempts of New Dealers to utilize the old capitalist slogans are never successful. These are the slogans of the Tories; the Tories have the historical right to them; and the public in its own way recognizes this right. The New Dealers never win any votes when they appeal to "free enterprise" and "opportunity" and the safeguarding of property. Every heart that can be stirred by such phrases was swept into Willkie's "Great Crusade" (no one seemed to remember that the original Crusades were also lost). The New Deal mass support depends upon, is aroused and held, through the New Dealers' use of the managerial ideas and slogans.

Technocracy is another example of an American variant of the managerial ideologies. Technocracy has not had a very wide direct public influence, but much has been taken over from it both by New Dealism and also by communism and fascism.

As a matter of fact, Technocracy's failure to gain a wide response can be attributed in part to the too-plain and open way in which it expresses the perspective of managerial society. In spite of its failure to distinguish between engineers and managers (not all engineers are managers—many are mere hired hands—and not all managers are engineers) yet the society about which the Technocrats write is quite obviously managerial society, and within it their "Technocrats" are quite obviously the managerial ruling class. The theory is not dressed up enough for major ideological purposes. It fails also in refusing to devote sufficient attention to the problem of power, which so prominently occupies communism and fascism. However, the developed native-American managerial ideologies of the future will doubtless incorporate Technocratic propaganda, for it seems on the whole well adapted to propaganda needs in this country.

But what about the bitter disputes among the various types of what I have stated are all managerial ideologies? How can these be explained if the ideologies are all "the same"? Are the disputes, thought so notorious, "unreal"? I wish to guard against possible misunderstanding. These disputes are not "unreal" and the ideologies are not "the same." Such a contention would be ridiculous and easily disproved. What I am maintaining is simply this: Communism (Leninism-Stalinism), fascism-Nazism, and to a more-partial and less-developed extent, New Dealism and Technocracy, are all *managerial ideologies*. That is, in short: as ideologies they contribute through their propagation to the development of attitudes and patterns of response which are adverse to the continuance of capitalism and favorable to the development of managerial society, which are adverse to the continued social acceptance of the rule of the capitalists, and favorable to the social acceptance of the rule of the managers. The fact is, moreover, that they and ideologies similar to them are securing wide public acceptance throughout the world while capitalist ideologies are losing support; and that this support is much more intense than that given to the capitalist ideologies, making believers willing to sacrifice and die for managerial slogans while fewer and fewer are willing to sacrifice and die for capitalist slogans. This shift in public attitude is itself a very important symptom of the general breakup of capitalist society and the advance of managerial society.

There are, however, great, and by no means illusory, differences among these managerial ideologies. A number of these differences will be discussed in the course of the next three chapters. The differences have various sources: the special local circumstances under which the managerial transition takes place (Russia is not Germany nor either the United States); the way in which the transition takes place (the stages in the Russian and German way have been not at all alike: there are several roads to the managerial goal); the oppositions, present and to come, among the various sections of the new ruling class; differing cultural traditions and psychological equipment which lead the formulators of the ideologies to express themselves differently.

If we were making a logical or etymological analysis, we might well stress the differences among the ideologies rather than the similarity. But there is nothing strange in the differences, or even in their causing disputants to kill each other over them. In the Middle Ages, there were immense differences between realists and nominalists, between Augustinians and Scholastics; the disputes were not by any means confined to words. It would be a crude error to discount these differences as "unreal," and for many purposes they are what is most important. Yet medieval realism and early nominalism, Augustinianism and Scholasticism, were from a sociological point of view all variant types of feudal ideologies; they all started from shared concepts; they all contributed to the formation of attitudes favorable to the maintenance of the feudal system and the rule of the feudal lords. The differences among Calvinism, Lutheranism, Presbyterianism, Anabaptism, Episcopalianism, Quakerism...were not trivial in the sixteenth and seventeenth centuries and on many occasions led from philosophical debate to bloodshed. But these were all, at least as against medieval Catholicism, capitalist religious ideologies, all contributing in variant ways to the development of attitudes favorable to capitalist society as against feudal society. How many bitter disputes over "natural rights" have occurred in the modern world, without nevertheless questioning a natural-rights foundation that assumed a capitalist social order! The analysis which I make here is what is appropriate to the central problem of this book; it would be irrelevant and distorting if transferred to the context of another kind of problem.

The development of managerial ideologies has not come to an end, needless to say with contemporary Stalinism and Nazism, any more than capitalist ideologies froze in the sixteenth century. As New Dealism is primitive alongside them, they will seem primitive to the ideologists of the future. There are indefinite possibilites for philosophical elaboration, and there will be plenty of intellectuals anxious for the task. Managerial ideologies will have their Cartesian and Rousseauistic and Kantian "revolutions." But the main direction can be known now, is to be seen now in what is already at hand.

XIV

THE RUSSIAN WAY

THERE HAS been an immense stack of books written about contemporary Russia and Germany, but few of these have served to clarify their subject matter. The reason is evident: people are not interested in understanding Russia and Germany but in expressing their feelings about them. Passionate loyalty or equally passionate hatred seem to be the only two feelings that men today can have toward these two nations. In fact, no other nations have been able to excite half so extreme a loyalty or so bitter a hatred as these two. This singularity ought itself to suggest that within these nations is to be discovered the historical key of these last years.

Passionate feeling, unfortunately, however appropriate it may be for some purposes—winning or losing a war, for instance—is a poor foundation for understanding. A scientist may hate the plague which he is studying; but he must not permit that hatred to juggle the results he gets in his laboratory. The subject of this book is knowledge, not passion. We are trying to find out what is happening, in Russia and Germany as elsewhere, not what to feel about it or what to do about it.

Once we look carefully and impersonally, it is not hard to find out. True enough, almost all the news that comes out of Russia and Germany is distorted in accordance with the propagandistic aims of the regimes. The statistics cannot be trusted,

and statistics in many fields are not given out at all. But a physi-
cian does not have to know the chemical condition of every cell
in his patient's body in order to diagnose smallpox. We can find
out *enough* about Russia and Germany for our purpose, and
that is all that can be required. If our purpose were different—
if we wanted to predict exact price movements over the next
six months in Germany and Russia or to estimate exactly how
much butter or petroleum were on hand—there is not enough
information available to fulfill such purposes. But we are interested in the problem of what is happening to society, in
discovering what social structure, in terms of major economic
and political institutions and major ideologies, is going to prevail
in the comparatively near future and for the next period of history. We have at our disposal, if we want to use it, enough
information about Russia and Germany to relate developments
in those nations to our problem.

The theory of the managerial revolution does not hold that in
the present historical period there will be no mass revolutions,
or no mass revolutions carried through under the slogans and
ideas of socialism. On the contrary. There have already been
several mass revolutions, some under socialist slogans, in the
period of rapid transition which began in 1914. Others are doubtless to be expected. A social revolution does not necessarily have
to be accompanied by overt mass revolutionary movements, but
it often, and perhaps usually, is. The primary question for us,
however, is not the mass revolutionary movements, and above
all not the slogans under which these develop, but rather the
consequences of these movements in terms of social structure.

The consequences of a mass revolution seldom coincide with
the slogans and ideas under which it takes place. Capitalism was
introduced or strengthened in many places in the world to the
accompaniment of mass revolutions. I have never read or heard

of such a revolution's proclaiming in its slogans that its object was to introduce capitalism. There was, it is true, a certain relation between the slogans and what happened; they were, as we saw in the last chapter, slogans which tended to develop attitudes favorable to capitalist institutions and capitalist rule; but the relation is indirect. Similarly, an ostensibly socialist mass revolution does not at all have to lead to socialism. These preliminary remarks are indispensible to clarity about what has happened in Russia.

We saw that the managers, and the future managerial society, are faced with a triple problem: (1) To reduce the capitalists (both at home and finally throughout the world) to impotence; (2) to curb the masses in such a way as to lead them to accept managerial rule and to eliminate any threat of a classless society; (3) to compete among themselves for first prizes in the world as a whole. To solve the first two parts of this problem (the third part is never wholly solved) means the destruction of the major institutions and ideologies of capitalist society and the substitution for them of the major institutions and ideologies of managerial society along the lines that we have already surveyed. To accomplish this solution, large sections of the masses must be enlisted, under suitable slogans, on the side of the managers and of the managerial future. Like the capitalists, the managers do not as individuals do the bulk of the fighting which is part of the process of social transition. This they leave to the masses. Even the fighting which, in addition to the change in ideology, is needed to curb the masses is done by one section of the masses in combat against other sections.

To the extent that the first two parts of the triple problem are solved, managerial society has replaced capitalist society. Their solution, by whatever means, *is* the managerial revolution. The structure of managerial society is not, however, firmly consolidated until it is dominant in the world as a whole: that is, in the three "central" areas of advanced industry which we noticed in Chapter XII.

These three parts into which I have analyzed the managerial problem do not coincide with any particular order in time. The solution can be achieved in differently arranged stages. All three parts are ordinarily mixed together, in varying degrees, at every stage. War, especially world war, throws them almost inextricably together and vastly speeds up the whole process.

One pattern of development is illustrated in surprisingly schematic fashion by the events in Russia since 1917. What has happened in Russia is the following: The first part of the triple problem was solved quickly and drastically. The capitalists were not merely reduced to impotence but, most of them, physically eliminated either by being killed or emigrating. They were not replaced by other capitalists—if we discount a socially unimportant continuation of small-scale capitalists, especially during the so-called NEP (New Economic Policy) period. The capitalists were got rid of not merely as individuals but as a class, which is the same thing as to say that the chief economic institutions of capitalism were done away with, that the economic structure of society was changed.

In another sense, it is true, this drastic solution of the first part of the problem was only partial. It was the home capitalists, not all capitalists, who were eliminated, whereas a full solution for the managers anywhere requires a reduction to impotence of capitalists and capitalist institutions everywhere—or at least in all major areas. This the Russians soon discovered (their leaders knew it in advance) when the great capitalist nations, including the United States, dispatched armies to Russia in order to try to overthrow the new regime. But the regime defended itself with considerable success and reached an uneasy truce with foreign capitalists which lasted until the second world war.

The second part of the managerial problem—the curbing of the masses—was left suspended until this solution, or partial solution, of the first part was achieved. Or, rather, the masses were used to accomplish the solution of the first part just as the capitalists in their early days used the masses to break the power of the feudal lords. In a new stage, the beginning of which merged with the first, the solution of the second part of the problem was carried through. The masses were curbed. Their obscurely felt aspirations toward equalitarianism and a classless society were diverted into the new structure of class rule, and organized in terms of the ideologies and the institutions of the new social order.

The third part of the managerial problem—the competition with other sections of the managers—still lies primarily in the future. The preparations for meeting it, always implicit in the activities of the sections of the Communist International (which are simply agencies of the Russian rulers) throughout the world, are being greatly speeded up during the course of the war. Russia, the first managerial state, prepares to defend its rights of seniority in the managerial wars of the future.

The Russian way, the Russian pattern, may thus be summed up as follows: (1) Speedy reduction of the capitalist class at home to impotence (and, after a sharp struggle, an armed temporary truce with capitalists elsewhere); (2) the curbing of the masses in a more gradual and piecemeal manner, over a considerable number of years; (3) direct competition, in the days still to come (though the preparations started some while ago), with the other sections of the rising managerial world society.

This pattern, and relative timing, is, it may be remarked, not necessarily confined to Russia. It may well be reproduced elsewhere, especially if conditions comparable to those of 1917 in Russia are repeated. Among the factors that prominently determined it in Russia may be mentioned: a relatively weak development of capitalism internally, with a correspondingly weak and small capitalist class; the association of the capitalist class with the discredited and also weak political regime of Czarism; and the devastating social, economic, and human crisis brought about in Russia by the first world war.

The rise of Stalin from his obscurity of the first years of the revolution corresponds roughly with the carrying out of the second part of the managerial problem: the curbing of the masses and the consolidation of the rule of the new group. As so often happens in history, the new stage in development was marked by the discarding of the leaders of the preceding stage and the assumption of key positions by formerly subordinate or even altogether unknown men. Those who had carried the burden of the first stage, the reduction of the capitalists, were first stripped of effective power in the faction struggles of 1923-29; and then, in the more recent trials and purges, for the most part killed. The great public trials gave, we might say, a formal flourish to the solution of the second part of the problem, which left the masses properly subordinated in the new social structure, and the power, privileges, and greatest share of the revenues in the hands of the new rulers—the managers and their associated bureaucrats. In a sense, the mass purges were largely symbolic and ideological in purpose. The purgees had already been broken, and were most of them personally prepared, through one or another rationalization, to go along with the new order.

We must not make the mistake of supposing that the Russian changes were dependent merely on the presence of one or another individual, on the personal wickedness or nobility (depending on our point of view) of, for example, Stalin. If Lenin himself had lived, there is no reason to think that the process would have differed greatly. After all, there is more than passing significance in the fact that, for many years, probably the most intimate colleague of Lenin's, the man with whom he exercised hidden control over the Bolshevik party underneath the party's formal apparatus, was the brilliant and successful engineer—the manager—Krassin. But the death of all the early leaders was an important ritual act in establishing the mass attitudes of managerial society and in strengthening the foundations of the managerial institutions.

The pattern of the Russian way to the managerial revolution is illuminated by the history of the revolutionary concept of "workers' control." "Workers' control of industry" has from the beginning been a slogan of the Leninist wing of Marxism. The reason why is easy to understand. According to the formal ideology of socialism, private ownership (control) in industry is to be eliminated—that is, as socialism understands it, control is to be vested in the masses as a whole. The crucial revolutionary act, therefore, would presumably be the actual taking over of control in industry by the workers themselves. Hence the slogan.

Now, in the course of the Russian revolution (as in the many other attempts at mass revolution which followed it during the past twenty-three years), the workers acted quite literally in accordance with the slogan of "workers' control." In the factories, shops, mines, and so on, the workers, through committees elected from their own ranks, simply did take over control. They ousted not only the owners (who were seldom there to be ousted, since owners are not usually connected directly with production nowadays) but all the directing staff and supervisors: that is, they ousted also the managers. The workers thought, in their own way, that the revolution was designed to rid them of all rulers and exploiters. They recognized that the managers as well as the owners were among the rulers and exploiters both of the past and, above all, of the future. The workers set about running the factories themselves.

This state of affairs did not, however, last long. Two issues were at stake. In the first place, the separate factories and other instruments of production were not run very well under workers' control exercised at the source; and there were even greater difficulties in the co-ordination of the efforts of various factories. It is needless to speculate on exactly why this was so. Elected committees of the workers themselves, the members of which are subject to momentary recall and who have, besides, no technical training for, or background in, the managerial tasks, do not seem to make a good job of running modern factories or mines or railroads. It is even harder for them to collaborate effectively in directing entire branches of industry or industry as a whole. Perhaps new democratic mechanisms and sufficient time to gain experience would overcome the troubles. As things actually work out, time is not granted, and the mechanisms are not available.

Second, the perspective of workers' control of production at the source, if it should be proved in the end successful, would mean the elimination of all privilege, all differentials of power in society, would mean, in short, a classless organization of society. Thus the drive for class power in society needs to get rid of workers' control, and finds rational motivation in the evidences of the inefficiency of workers' control—above all, because the movement toward workers' control occurs in periods of intense social crisis, or war and civil war, when efficient industrial organization seems an imperious need.

If the temporary workers' control is replaced by the old control of capitalist owners (as happened in the two revolutionary crises in Germany at the end of, and a few years after, the first world war), then society, after a crisis, has simply returned to its previous capitalist structure. If workers' control is replaced by the *de facto* control of the managers, backed by a new kind of state, then capitalism, after a transitional crisis, has changed into managerial society. The latter, through a series of intermediary steps, is what happened in Russia.

For a while after the revolution in Russia, in many factories and other enterprises—for a very short while—the factories were run by the workers through their elected committees, called "Factory Committees." Then the "technical" direction of operations was turned over to "specialists" (that is, managers), with the Factory Committees remaining in existence and still exercising substantial control through a veto power over the managers and jurisdiction over "labor conditions." Meanwhile, bureaus and commissions and individuals appointed from above by the new (soviet) government were beginning to take over the job of co-ordinating the efforts of various factories and branches of industry. Gradually the powers of the managers and managerial co-ordinators increased, necessarily at the expense of "workers' control" and the Factory Committees. The Factory Committees lost their veto powers. Their prerogative, "labor conditions," became more and more narrowly interpreted. The Committee composition was changed to include one state representative, one managerial representative, and one man nominally representing the workers—though this last was pretense. Finally, even these Committees lost all real power and remained as mere formalities, to be dropped altogether in 1938. Workers' control had been transformed into managerial control.

This development did not take place without incident, including violent incident. The workers, or some of them, sensed its meaning: that the freedom and end of privilege, which they had thought the revolution was to bring, were giving way to a new form of class rule. They tried to prevent power from getting out of the hands of their Committees. They refused to accept the managers, sometimes drove them out or even killed them. But at each decisive step, the state (the "workers' socialist state"), whether under Lenin or Stalin, backed not the workers but the managers. A wide campaign of "education" was undertaken to show the people why "workers' rule" meant, in practice, managers' rule. Where necessary, the education by the word was supplemented with education by firing squad or concentration camp or forced labor battalion.

Lenin and Trotsky, both, in the early years of the revolution, wrote pamphlets and speeches arguing the case of the specialists, the technicians, the managers. Lenin, in his forceful way, used to declare that the manager had to be a *dictator* in the factory. "Workers' democracy" in the state, Lenin said in effect, was to be founded upon a managerial dictatorship in the factory.

Perhaps Lenin did not realize the full irony of his position. He, as a Marxist, believed—correctly—that the roots of social power lie in the control over the instruments of production. And he, as the head of the new state, helped to smash workers', popular, control over those instruments and to substitute for it control by the managers. And, of course, the managers of individual plants became subordinate to the big managers, to the boards and bureaus directing entire sectors of industry and governing industry as a whole. Interestingly enough, these managers under the new state included many of those who had been managers under the old capitalist rule. Lenin and Trotsky poured scorn on "infantile leftists" who were against making use of the "services" of the "bourgeois specialists" (as they called them). The workers needed them—to run the plants. Lenin regretted that there were so few left and that in Russia there had never been an adequate staff of trained specialists. Most favorable terms were given to foreign "bourgeois specialists" who were willing to come to work under the new regime. The class of managers that steadily rose was not altogether a new creation; it was the development and extension of the class which, as we have seen, already exists, and is already extending its power and influence, under capitalism, especially during the latter days of capitalism.

We shall deservedly place the greatest stress upon what happened to "workers' control." Moreover, the Russian experience is plainly typical. There have not yet been any other revolutions just like Russia's; but there have been a dozen revolutionary situations of the same general nature. In them all, the same tendencies are displayed. In them all—Germany, the Balkans, China, Italy, Spain—the workers, in the crisis, start to take over control of the instruments of production, to take it over directly, into their own hands on the spot. Always a formula is found to explain to them why this cannot continue; and, if the formula is not enough, the guns come later.

The question for us is not whether it is a "good idea" for the workers to take control. We are concerned merely with noticing, first, that they try to take control; and, second, that they do not succeed in maintaining control. Their inability to maintain control is one more demonstration that socialism—a free, classless society—is not now scheduled. The control, and the social rule which goes with it, when it leaves the hands of the capitalists, goes not to the workers, the people, but to the managers, the new ruling class. A parallel of the Russian process can be observed with particular clarity in connection with the events in Loyalist territories during the recent Spanish Civil War, above all in Catalonia. There, just as in Russia, the workers and peasants began taking over direct control of the factories and railroads and farms. There too, not at once, but during the course of the first two years of the Civil War, the *de facto* power slipped from the workers' hands, sometimes voluntarily given up at the persuasion of a political party, sometimes smashed by arms and prison. It was not the troops of Franco who took control away from the people of Catalonia; they had lost control well before Franco's army conquered.

These experiences have, as a matter of fact, received recognition in Leninist doctrine (both the Stalinist and Trotskyist variants), not so much in public writings as in the theories elaborated primarily for party members. "Workers' control," the doctrine now reads, is a *"transition* slogan," but loses its relevance once the revolution is successful and the new state established. By calling it a "transition slogan" it is meant that the slogan, and the act, of establishing workers' control are useful in arousing mass sentiment against the existing capitalist regime and in bringing about the downfall of the capitalist order—both undoubtedly the case; but that, when the new regime is functioning, workers' control must step aside. Naturally!

The *ideological* explanation offered by Leninism for this turnabout is that, while workers must rightly defend themselves with the help of workers' control against the enemy capitalist state, they will have no need to defend themselves against the new regime which will be "their own" state, a workers' state busily constructing a true socialist society. This explanation is to be interpreted in the same manner we interpret all aspects of all ideologies. What is really involved is a very important consequence of the pattern of the Russian way to managerial society, which we are here studying. This pattern, we saw, calls for first reducing the capitalists to impotence and then curbing the masses.

The masses are of course used in accomplishing the first step; and "workers' control" is a major maneuver in breaking the power of the capitalists. But workers' control is not only intolerable for the capitalist state: it is, if long continued and established, intolerable for any state and any class rule in society. Consequently, the consolidation of managerial power in the new state requires the breaking down of workers' control, which was so important an influence in finishing up the old society. Leninist doctrine expresses in terms of a managerial ideology the lessons of the Russian and similar experiences from the point of view of the interests of the managers.

Russia has without doubt been the chief political enigma of the past generation; and on no other enigma have so many attempts at explanation been spent. Everyone has been wrong in predicting what was going to happen to Russia. What kind of society is it? What sort of revolution was the Russian Revolution? What is it leading toward? These questions have remained mysteries. That the revolution was made under the leadership of radical Marxists who professed as their aim the establishment of the free, classless, international society of socialism, everyone knows. And everyone knows also that there is not the trace of a free and classless society or of internationalism in Russia today.

Russia speaks in the name of freedom, and sets up the most extreme totalitarian dictatorship ever known in history. Russia calls for peace, and takes over nations and peoples by armed force. In the name of fighting fascism Russia makes an alliance with the world's leading fascist. Proclaiming a fight against power and privilege, Russia at home drives a great gulf between a stratum of the immensely powerful, the vastly privileged, and the great masses of the people. The only country "with no material foundation for imperialism," in theory, shows itself, in practice, brutally and—for a while at least—successfully imperialistic. The "fatherland of the world's oppressed" sends tens of thousands to death by the firing squad, puts millions, literally millions, into exile, the concentration camp, and the forced labor battalions, and closes its doors to the refugees from other lands The one country "genuinely against war" performs the act that starts the second world war. The nation "dedicated to the improvement of labor's conditions" invents, in Stakhanovism, the most intense form of speedup known. The government which denounced the League of Nations as a "den of brigands" enters the League and becomes its most ardent champion. The state which asked the peoples of the world to form a popular front of democracies to stop aggressors overnight walks from the camp of the democracies to that of their sworn and mortal enemies. And yet, in spite of the reiterated predictions, from friends and enemies, of its quick downfall, the regime has endured, without a break, for more than twenty-three years.

The mysteries and puzzles that are found in connection with Russia, the failure of predictions about her future course, can be accounted for in just the same way that similar mysteries and puzzles and failures are accounted for in other fields: by the fact that the phenomenon of Russia is treated from the point of view of false theories. The false conclusions drawn, the bewilderment, show us that the theories from which they proceed are wrong. Commentators, in desperation, fall back on the "morbid Russian soul" to excuse their inability to understand events. Disappointed friends of Russia keep complaining that the Russian government is "inconsistent with its principles," that it has "betrayed" socialism and Marxism—in short, that it has failed to do what these disappointed friends had hoped and expected it would do. How much simpler (and science always prefers the simpler answer if it is to be found), after all these years of *historically* continuous development, to substitute for these strained and paradoxical apologies a theory which shows that Russia, far from being inconsistent with its principles, acts uniformly in accordance with them, that Russia could never have betrayed socialism because its revolution never had anything to do with socialism!

Russia was and still remains a mystery because the theories that tried to understand it were false. These theories all revolved around one or the other of the two predictions which we discussed and rejected earlier in this book: the prediction that capitalism is going to continue; or the prediction that capitalist society is about to be replaced by socialist society. *Both* of these predictions share the assumption which I analyzed in Chapter IV: that "the only alternative" to capitalism is socialism—that capitalism and socialism are the only two possible forms of social organization in our time. On the basis of this assumption and either of these predictions, Russia had to be judged socialist if it were not to be regarded as capitalist. No matter what happened to Russia, it had to be thought still socialist unless one were willing to accept the view—as some have in recent years— that it had reverted to capitalism.

The Russian Revolution was regarded by almost everyone, when it happened, as a socialist revolution. Almost everyone, also, agreed at the beginning that it would thereafter have to develop either toward socialism (a free, classless, international society), or return to capitalism. On the basis of the common assumption, and of either of the two predictions, this expectation, shared alike by friends and enemies of the revolution, inside and outside Russia itself, was certainly justified. But *neither* development has in fact occurred. After twenty-three years it is time to recognize that this failure proves the common assumption, and both predictions, to be false. It is false that socialism is "the only alternative" to capitalism. It is false that capitalism will continue. It is false that socialism will replace it.

Russia has not reverted to a capitalist social structure. None of the major distinguishing features of capitalist society is to be found within Russia. The non-capitalist elements of Russian life have been enormously increased and strengthened, not weakened, with the years. Everyone said that the growth of privilege in the new Russia would "inevitably" bring about the reintroduction of capitalism. Privilege has grown, but capitalism has not come back. There are no capitalists of any importance in Russia. Not even imperialist expansion beyond the national borders brings any tendency to return to capitalism; just the contrary.

And at the same time there has been not the slightest tendency toward the free, classless society of socialism as socialism was defined in the prior expectations. There is no democracy in Russia. There is no control, social or economic or political, exercised by the masses. There is a stratification in power and privilege which exceeds in degree that to be found in many capitalist nations. There is in Russia, as we have seen, not merely graft and corruption but systematic class exploitation on the basis of the state-owned economy. Russia came by far its closest to socialism in the months immediately following the revolution. In every decisive respect, every year since then has found it further away, not nearer socialism as defined by the fathers.

It is the business of a correct theory to clear up mysteries. If once we get away from ungrounded assumptions, unjustified predictions, if we stop mistaking ideologies for scientific hypotheses and recognize them for the expressions of social interest that they are, then we can get rid of bewilderment over Russia. Russia is not a mystery from the point of view of the theory of the managerial revolution. The Russian development, in broad outline, is exactly what may be expected from that theory and is a powerful confirmation of the theory.

The Russian Revolution was not a socialist revolution—which, from all the evidence, cannot take place in our time—but a managerial revolution. It was not the only possible kind of managerial revolution, but it was one kind, the kind the pattern of which this chapter has explained. The sharp revolutionary crisis has been succeeded by the consolidation of the new class regime in a manner altogether analogous to a number of the capitalist revolutions. The outcome of the revolution is the development of a new structure of society—managerial society, a new order of power and privilege which is not capitalist and not socialist but that structure and order which this book has described. Leninism-Stalinism ("Bolshevism") is not a scientific hypothesis but a great social ideology rationalizing the social interests of the new rulers and making them acceptable to the minds of the masses. There is nothing inconsistent between this ideology on the one side and the purges, tyrannies, privileges, aggressions on the other: the task of the ideology is precisely to give fitting expression to the regime of those purges, tyrannies, privileges, and aggressions.

Today Russia is the nation which has, in structural aspects, advanced furthest along the managerial road. In its economic and political institutions, Russia comes closest to the institutional types of the future. It should not, however, be thought that Russia is now an example of a finished and fully consolidated managerial state. Managerial society is still hardly out of the womb. The present situation in Russia, moreover, is conditioned by the backward cultural and economic inheritance of the Russian Revolution and by the fact that its political regime is suited to a period of social transition and sharp recurrent crises. But, structurally at any rate, the institutions of present-day Russia, more fully than any others in the world, give the direction toward the future. It is along such lines that the institutions of established and consolidated managerial society will evolve.

Who are the rulers of Russia? They are, of course, the men who are running its factories and mines and railroads, the directing members of the commissariats and subcommissariats of heavy and light industry and transportation and communication, the heads of the large collective farms, the expert manipulators of the propaganda mediums, the chiefs of the dozens of "mass organizations," the managers in short: these and their bureaucratic and military and police associates. The power and privileges are under their control. For them the capitalists at home have been got rid of or reduced to impotence; and for them the capitalists abroad were fought off and forced to an uneasy truce. It is they who have curbed the masses and have instituted a social structure in which they are on top, not by virtue of private property rights in the instruments of production, but through their monopoly control of a state power which has fused with the economy. It is they who now await the contests of the future with the other sectors of the world managers.

It is these managers, with their political and military associates, who have been extending their regime beyond Soviet boundaries during the course of the second world war. The events in the little border nations have reproduced on a laboratory, and somewhat grotesque, scale the pattern of the Russian Revolution; and, also like a laboratory experiment, the events have done so under the firm guidance of the experimenter, not at their own sweet will. The local workers and peasants (in the Baltic nations, eastern Poland, Bessarabia), as the Red Army marches, begin to take control of the local industries and farms and to oust the capitalists who have not already fled. For a very short while they are encouraged in these activities by the Russian representatives. A semblance of "workers' control" appears. The first part of the triple managerial problem is solved—the capitalists are reduced to impotence—which is not so major a task in the tiny states concerned. Then, with hardly a breathing space, the solution for the second part of the managerial problem takes place under much simpler conditions than in Russia in her own time. The masses are curbed: today the army and the GPU that supervise the curbing are large and experienced in solving this part of the problem. The new rulers—not new capitalists, naturally, but Russian managers and their representatives—walk in to run their newly acquired factories and mines and banks. Workers' control is transformed into a name, and the soldiers and police back the dictates of the managers. The whole process, which took in Russia itself so many strenuous years, is completed in a couple of months.

What will happen to Russia in the days to come?

There is no doubt that the revolutionary Russian regime has shown astounding strength surpassing all estimates. Disaster has been a hundred times prophesied, but the regime still stands. It came into existence in the nation which had suffered most, and immeasurably, from the first world war. It fought off the armies of intervention sent by the greatest powers; and it held its own against their always-continuing intrigues and hostility. It won out in a civil war that lasted years, during which for a while its authority was reduced to a small province of the vast Russian territories. It did not fall in the midst of famines that wiped out millions of persons, and many and devastating plagues. It was able to exile, emprison, or shoot millions of its own citizens, including the majority of the officers of its armed forces, without being seriously challenged by internal revolt. There is in history scarcely a record of another regime that has been able to go through such events unscathed. That the Russian regime has done so can only be understood as a demonstration of the strength of the managerial organization of society—of its strength as against the capitalist organization, for the Russian regime has not been tested yet against other managerial states. Moreover, Russia has mighty potential resources in raw materials, land, and people.

The possible overthrow of the Russian regime has, in keeping with the assumption which we have examined, always been thought of as meaning the restoration of capitalism, either through conquest by foreign capitalist nations or by internal "counter-revolution." By now the evidence is fairly conclusive that there is not going to be a capitalist restoration in Russia. Internally the tendencies to capitalist restoration, so often expected, have failed to appear on a serious scale and have been weakened steadily with the years. There is no reason to look for them in the future, above all when we realize that capitalism on a world scale is just about finished. Externally, there were certainly threats in great number; and some of these might once have led to the conquest of Russia by capitalist powers. But when Britain and France failed to attack Russia during the Finnish war, this marked the close of the period during which foreign *capitalist* nations might have hoped to restore Russia to capitalism by armed might.

It does not follow, however, that the present Russian regime will long continue. In spite of the demonstrated sources of strength in Russia, there are even graver weaknesses. In the first place, the industrial and technological development of Russia was extremely primitive at the time of the revolution. The undoubted successes of the new regime in industrialization leave it still backward compared to the most advanced industrial regions. The backwardness of the industry is to be measured not merely in terms of the physical equipment, which is relatively none too good or extensive, but equally in terms of the relative scarcity of competent workers and technicians. The latter weakness is a phase of the more general cultural backwardness which would require not years but generations to overcome. Third, the Russian managers, the new ruling class, are qualitatively weak. This results in part from the fact that in pre-revolutionary Russia, because of the low industrial and cultural level, there were few competent managers; and of these, the revolution failed to absorb a large part. The managerial class had to be built up too rapidly, without an adequate leavening of trained men and without proper facilities for training and experience. All of these factors, finally, gave openings to an unusually low grade of careerist in the new state apparatus. Graft, corruption, terrorism, and downright stupidity, which always are found in every bureaucracy, are unusually widespread in Russia. Because of this, the bureaucrats make many mistakes and at the same time excite the resentment of the masses.

If the question of foreign intervention were ruled out, these weaknesses would be enough to suggest that internal convulsions would be probable. These would have as their object, not the restoration of capitalism, but the drastic reform of the new regime, a reform which the totalitarian character of the political institutions makes almost impossible by peaceful means. It should be noticed that such reforms would be to the interest both of the masses and also to the more competent of the managers, since some of the methods of the present political bureaucracy are annoying and cumbersome for the best managers as well as grievous for the masses.

However, the question of foreign intervention cannot be ruled out. The capitalist nations have shown by their actions that they have no confidence in their ability to carry through war against Russia. But world society is now in the process of being transformed along managerial lines. The advantages which the managerial structure gave Russia against capitalist nations disappear when Russia is confronted with other managerial or near-managerial states which are not burdened by Russia's weaknesses. There seems good reason to believe, as I stated in Chapter XII, that during the course of the next years Russia will split apart into an eastern and western section, each section gravitating toward one of the key areas which constitute the strategic bases of the super-states of the future.

Indeed, this process has already started. Siberia is so far away from Moscow and so badly connected with European Russia that it naturally swings toward the East as it has for some years been conspicuously doing. Its future brings it into always-closer integration with the East Asian central area of advanced industry. And similarly, at an increased rate since the Nazi-Soviet pact, European Russia swings toward the central European area. Feelers move out from both sides of the border. The Russian boundaries advance toward the west. At the same time, economic and social relations with Germany increase. German technicians, managers, move into the Russian industrial enterprises. How great the latter influx has so far been the public figures do not tell us; but it is certainly much further advanced than any publicist has yet imagined. This infiltration of German managers is a large step in the road toward fusion of European Russia with the European center. We may be sure that the completion of the fusion, under whatever nominal auspices it comes, will find Russia subordinated to the European center, not, as the spinners of Bolshevik nightmares tell us, the other way around. The development of the fusion begins in a dozen ways, beneath the surface. Its accomplishment will, presumably, include war, one or more of the managerial wars of tomorrow, the preparations for which are so plainly around us.

NOTE—In spite of the Russo-German war, it has seemed to me advisable to leave the text as it was written in 1940, and first published in the Spring of 1941. The intent of this book is not journalistic but scientific. From a scientific standpoint, the theory of the managerial revolution is much better tested by its ability to make events intelligible before they happen, rather than by the ease with which it can doctor up references to what has already occurred.

The outbreak of the Russo-German war, and its course, seem to me a confirmation of the fundamental analysis presented in this chapter, and in particular of the political analysis summarized in Chapter XII. This war, to use the language of the theory, is part of the means whereby the western half of Russia is being "integrated into the European superstate." However, the impression that the text gives is of a later beginning of war between Russia and Germany than actually turned out to be the case—and, so far as I can recall, this impression corresponds with the opinion I held in 1940. I believe that this error in "time schedule" resulted from a too schematic application of the sociological and economic analysis to the problem, with insufficient attention to strictly military considerations. That a large part of Russia should be drawn within the west-European orbit, and that war would be part of the process of fusion, followed from the whole course of contemporary history. Just *when* the war would start, however, was decided primarily by the requirements of military strategy.—J. B.

XV

THE GERMAN WAY

WHEN WE HAVE finished expressing our emotions about Germany by calling its society "nihilism" or "barbarism" or whatever similar epithet we prefer, we are still left with the scientific problem of describing just what kind of society it is and where it is going. It is obvious, when we think about it, that no organized society—and Nazi Germany is certainly a form of organized society—can actually be "nihilistic"; and "barbarian," by etymology and ordinary usage, means simply "foreign," different from ourselves.

The serious attempts to analyze contemporary German society reduce to two. The majority view has been that Nazism is a type of capitalism, usually considered decadent capitalism, the degenerate last stage of capitalist society. A small but recently growing number of critics holds that Nazism is an early stage in a new form of society. This latter group, however, has not been clear about what kind of society this new form may be. Does the spectacular energy of present-day Germany represent the hideous convulsions of a death agony, or the—also hideous, let us remember—pangs of birth? This is a question that we must answer if we are to understand what is happening in the world.

The dispute can easily become merely verbal. No one will deny that there are in German society elements which it shares with traditional capitalist society; and, equally, no one will deny that there are many other elements in German society not found in traditional capitalism. It might seem, therefore, that we could give either answer that we might choose. But for us the problem is not verbal. We have defined what we mean by capitalism, by socialism, and by managerial society. We are interested, here as elsewhere, not in the static condition of the moment, but in the trend of development, the direction of change. With this background, we are enquiring into facts, not words, when we ask whether Germany today is a type of capitalism or whether it is in the first developmental stages of a new order of society—specifically, managerial society.

A preliminary observation, to which I have already referred, must be repeated. By a "decadent" society, I shall mean no more than a type of society which is nearing its end in time and history. There are many who call Nazi Germany decadent because its rulers lie a great deal, are treacherous, break treaties, exile, imprison, torture, and murder worthy human beings. It is a fact that the Nazi rulers often carry out such actions—though such actions are more common among all rulers of all times than our moralists like us to believe. But it is not at all a fact that such actions are typical signs of decadence. It would be altogether impossible to establish any necessary link between lies, terror, tyranny on the one side and historical decadence on the other. Indeed, if historical experience establishes any correlation in this matter, it is probably a negative one: that is, the young, new, rising social order is, as against the old, more likely to resort on a large scale to lies, terror, persecution. Tragedy always seems more heroic than worldly success; ideal characters we usually are taught to find on the losing side. Hector was the noblest hero of the Trojan War; it was the Greeks who introduced the treacherous Trojan horse; but the Greeks won. The splendid personal traits of many of the late feudal lords did not prevent them and their system from going down in ruins. By the time of Cervantes those traits were the subject for nostalgic ridicule, not for imitation. There is no historical law that polite manners and "justice" shall conquer. In history there is always the question of *whose* manners and *whose* justice. A rising social class and a new order of society have got to break through the old moral codes just as they must break through the old economic and political institutions. Naturally, from the point of view of the old, they are monsters. If they win, they take care in due time of manners and morals.

All orthodox Marxists believe that Nazi Germany is a form of decadent capitalism. They put it in this way: fascism is the political organization of capitalism in decay; it is the extreme end point of "monopoly finance-capitalism." In reality, this opinion follows simply from the crucial assumption which we have so frequently met, the assumption that "socialism is the only alternative to capitalism." Nazism certainly is not the free, classless society of socialism. Consequently, by virtue of the assumption, it *must* be a type of capitalism. This deduction, granted the assumption, is perfectly sound, and saves all the bother of a careful examination of what is actually happening.

This belief is by no means confined to Marxists. It is held also by many capitalists. In particular it was held, prior to 1933, by a large section of the German capitalists who were, after all, the ones most intimately concerned. The opinion of this section was summed up by a remarkable article published in the late summer of 1932 in one of the journals of German heavy industry, and reproduced in *The Brown Book of the Hitler Terror*.[1] This article is well worth quoting at some length:

The problem of consolidating the capitalist regime in post-war Germany is governed by the fact that the leading section, that is,

[1] This book was published in 1933 by Alfred A. Knopf, Inc., with whose kind permission I am using the quotation.

the capitalists controlling industry, has become too small to maintain its rule alone. Unless recourse is to be had to the extremely dangerous weapon of purely military force, it is necessary for it to link itself with sections which do not belong to it from a social standpoint, but which can render it the essential service of anchoring its rule among the people, and thereby becoming its special or last defender. This last or 'outermost' defender of bourgeois rule, in the first period after the war, was Social Democracy.

National Socialism has to succeed Social Democracy in providing a mass support for capitalist rule in Germany.... Social Democracy had a special qualification for this task, which up to the present National Socialism lacks.... Thanks to its character as the original party of the workers, Social Democracy, in addition to its purely political force, also had the much more valuable and permanent advantage of control over organized labor, and by paralyzing its revolutionary energies chained it firmly to the capitalist State....

In the first period of re-consolidation of the capitalist regime after the war, the working class was divided by the wages victories and social-political measures through which the Social Democrats canalized the revolutionary movement.... The deflection of the revolution into social-political measures corresponded with the transference of the struggle from the factories and the streets into Parliament and Cabinets, that is, with the transformation of the struggle 'from below' into concessions 'from above.'

From then onwards, therefore, the Social Democratic and trade union bureaucracy, and with them also the section of the workers whom they led, were closely tied to the capitalist State and participation in its administration—at least so long as there was anything left of their post-war victories to defend by these means, and so long as the workers followed their leadership.

This analysis leads to four important conclusions:

1. The policy of 'the lesser evil' is not merely tactical, it is the political essence of Social Democracy.

2. The cords which bind the trade union bureaucracy to the State method 'from above' are more compelling than those which bind them to Marxism, and therefore to Social Democracy; and this holds in relation to the bourgeois State which wants to draw in this bureaucracy.

3. The links between the trade union bureaucracy and Social Democracy stand or fall, from a political standpoint, with parliamentarism.

4. The possibility of a Liberal social policy for monopoly capitalism is conditioned by the existence of an automatic mechanism for the creation of divisions in the working class. A capitalist regime which adopts a Liberal social policy must not only be entirely parliamentary, it must also be based on Social Democracy and must allow Social Democracy to have sufficient gains to record; a capitalist regime which puts an end to these gains must also sacrifice parliamentarism and Social Democracy, must create a *substitute* for Social Democracy and pass over to a social policy of constraint.

The process of this transition, in which we are at the moment, for the reason that the economic crisis has perforce blotted out the gains referred to, has to pass through the acutely dangerous stage, when, with the wiping out of these gains, the mechanism for the creation of divisions in the working class which depended on them also ceases to function, the working class moves in the direction of Communism, and the capitalist rule approaches the emergency stage of military dictatorship. . . . The only safeguard from this acute stage is if the division and holding back of the working class, which the former mechanism can no longer adequately maintain, is carried out by other and more direct methods. In this lie the positive opportunities and tasks of National Socialism. . . .

If National Socialism succeeds in bringing the trade unions into a social policy of constraint, as Social Democracy formerly succeeded in bringing them into a Liberal policy, then National Socialism would become the bearer of one of the functions essential to the future of capitalist rule, and must necessarily find its place in the State and social system. The danger of a State capitalist or even socialistic development, which is often urged against such an incorporation of the trade unions under National Socialist leadership, will in fact be avoided precisely by these means. . . . There is no third course between a re-consolidation of capitalist rule and the Communist revolution.

In connection with this brilliant analysis, let us note in passing its confirmation of the estimate we have previously made of the social role of Social Democracy (the reformist wing of Marxism) as a capitalist movement. But let us remark, second, that this analysis coincides exactly with the Leninist analysis. If its source were not given, there would be no way of telling whether it came from a capitalist or a Leninist pen.[2] (Naturally, neither reformism nor liberalism could produce such a critique.) Most important of all, along with Leninism it shares the basic assumption: socialism (communism) is the only alternative to capitalism. It is its reliance upon this assumption that finally brings the analysis, in spite of its brilliance, to grief. Even, however, apart from the assumption, the analysis was plausible in 1932, when it was made. It expressed, we might say, a chance, and the only chance, for capitalism to take. But 1941 is nine years later. We have the experience of nine more years to learn from. The lesson of this experience conclusively refutes the analysis of 1932.

The view that Nazism was a type of capitalism, a late, or the last, stage of capitalism, had a reasonable probability on the evidence a decade ago. It was a belief capable of verification. The verification would have been found in the tendency of Nazism to strengthen or at least maintain the typical institutions of capitalism and the power and privileges of the capitalists. The Italian experiences had not been conclusive. There was no way to decide the problem with confidence beforehand. By now it has been decided. The decision refutes the theory that Nazism is a form of capitalism.

The view that Nazified Germany is decadent capitalism, the political organization of capitalism in decay, is *prima facie* implausible in 1941, no matter how legitimate a guess it was in 1932. As compared with the undoubtedly capitalist nations of France (before her fall) and England (and the United States, too), and relying upon the analogies that may be drawn from comparable

---

[2] As a matter of fact, the analysis may be from a Leninist pen. I have been unable to verify the authenticity of the quotation. Since *The Brown Book* was a Comintern propaganda document, designed to justify the Stalinist policy in Germany, it is possible that the source of this quotation, as of so many others, is the fertile brain of the GPU. However, this would not alter the point I am making, inasmuch as many German capitalists undoubtedly, in 1932, *did* hold the views expressed in the quotation.

historical situations, Germany exhibits the signs not at all of decadence but of social revolution, of the transition to a new structure of society.

Before reviewing some of the more important of these signs, let us recall the extraordinary handicaps faced by Germany at the conclusion of the first world war. She had just been defeated in the greatest war fought up to that time and had been compelled to sign the harshest peace terms in modern European history. Important sections of her territory had been lopped off, and she had been surrounded by satellite states of her enemies. She had been stripped of her colonies, her merchant marine, and her navy; and her army was reduced to a minimum figure. Her people had been exhausted by the war and by the famine which occurred during its last year. She was saddled with reparations not merely in money—which she could and did pay largely through borrowings—but in kind, which latter meant the loss of material goods. Her opponents had carved up all the juiciest slices of the world in what they took to be their own interests. It is against this background that we must place contemporary Germany.

Nazi Germany eliminated unemployment within a couple of years from Hitler's ascension to power. The means whereby this was done are irrelevant to our inquiry; the fact that it was done is crucial. Mass unemployment is the primary indication of the collapse of a given form of society. The great capitalist powers have proved that they cannot get rid of mass unemployment under capitalist institutions. Even after a year and a half of war, after more than half a year of the "Battle of Britain," there were still, according to official figures—which probably understate the facts and besides do not include so-called "unemployables"— nearly a million unemployed in England. Nazi Germany's elimination of unemployment is, in and by itself, a sufficient proof that Germany has left the basis of capitalism and entered the road of a new form of society. Everyone knows and many have stated that it is not by virtue of the capitalist elements remaining in German culture that unemployment has been got rid of, but through the introduction of noncapitalist methods.

Similarly, Germany has broken through the restrictions of capitalist finance. According to all the "laws" of capitalism, Germany should have been bankrupt five years ago; its currency should have gone into a wild inflation; it should have been impossible for the state to finance its vast undertakings. But, under the state control of finance, none of the "laws" held. Again, through state control of imports and exports, Germany has been able to carry on foreign trade without the means, according to capitalist standards, of doing so. And huge outlets—primarily in state enterprises—have been found for the investment funds that sit idly in the banks of the great capitalist powers.

In territory, Germany has been expanding rapidly, first in peace and now in war. The expansion is not confined to lands brought formally within the boundaries of the Reich but includes also the nations drawn within the Reich's sphere of influence. Rapid territorial expansion has always been a sign not of decadence—societies break up in their decadent period—but of renewal.

Germany makes war better than the undoubtedly capitalist nations. If we take into account the difficulties that Germany had to overcome in preparation for war, compared to France and Britain with their immensely greater material resources, the superiority of Germany's war-making is far more striking even than it seems. As in the case of rapid territorial expansion, the ability to make war well is never a sign of decadence but of its opposite.

By all reliable accounts and by common experience, Nazi Germany inspires in millions of persons a fanatical loyalty. This, too, never accompanies decadence: the subjects of a decadent regime tend to be characterized by indifference, cynicism, or at most a dogged and rather weary devotion to duty.

A further striking outward sign is the fact that the outstanding political, military, and economic leaders of Germany are much younger, averaging probably a generation younger, than the leaders of France and Britain. To carry on the new war, England and France had to rest on the old men who had been leaders in the first world war and were none too young even then. In Germany, there are new men and, comparatively, young men. This difference symbolizes well the fact that the social systems of England and France at the outset of the second world war were remnants of the past, Germany's a start toward the future.

Finally, there is the notorious Nazi "Fifth Column." The term "Fifth Column" is used so loosely, meaning often no more than those whom a speaker or writer disagrees with, that its full significance is lost sight of. All modern nations have spies and paid agents in other nations, including enemy nations. These do not constitute a Fifth Column in the distinctive sense of the term. The Nazi Fifth Column is made up of persons within other nations who are more loyal to Nazi Germany, or to the general conception of life of which Nazism is one embodiment, than they are to the nation of which they are residents and perhaps citizens, and to its conception of life. This is why genuine Fifth Columns (whether Nazi or Stalinist) cannot be wiped out. Wiping them out is not a question of catching spies and intelligence agents at work; it would have to include changing innermost feelings, loyalties, ideologies; and the propaganda based on capitalist ideologies is no longer strong enough to do this fully. Hitler, like Stalin, can always count on a Fifth Column in every nation. Such a phenomenon is intelligible only if Hitler and Stalin both represent a social-revolutionary force, a force which cuts across and through the boundaries of capitalist-nationalism. So long as capitalism was established as the world system with all nations part of it, any considerable development of a Fifth Column was impossible. The rise of the Fifth Column marks the breakdown of capitalist-nationalism, of the capitalist nation as the ultimate political entity.

This *prima facie* evidence is sufficient to refute the opinion that Nazi Germany is a type of capitalism and to show that it is on the contrary an early stage of a new type of society. This evidence corresponds also with the underlying longer-term facts. The managerial developments did not begin in Germany with Hitler. Rather is Hitler's rise to power a phase of the basic managerial developments and a political expression of the fact that during these last eight years Germany has been turning the corner from the down-road of decadent capitalism, with managerial intrusions, to the up-road of early managerial society, with capitalist remnants.

We find in Germany to an ever-increasing degree those structural changes which we have discovered to be characteristic of the shift from capitalism to managerial society. In the economic sphere, there is a steady reduction, in all senses, of the area of private enterprise, and a correlative increase of state intervention. There was a brief period, immediately following the Nazi accession to state power, when the trend seemed to be in the opposite direction, when even a few enterprises which had been under state operation in the Weimar Republic were handed back to private capitalists. But this quickly reversed. The state intervention in the economy occurs in numerous directions. Outright state ownership and operation, advancing in all fields, are particularly ascendant in the extensive areas of new enterprise opened up during the Nazi rule. However, to confine attention to outright ownership and operation with all legal formalities would be deceptive. Virtually all economic enterprise is subject to rigid state control; and it is control which we have seen to be decisive in relation to the instruments of production. Legal forms, even income privileges, are in the end subordinate to *de facto* control.

Even where private owners still exist in Germany, the decisions about "their" property are not in their hands. They do not decide what to make or not to make. They do not establish prices or bargain about wages. They are not at liberty to buy the raw materials they might choose nor to seek the most profitable markets. They cannot, as a rule, decide how to invest or not invest their surplus funds. In short, they are no longer owners, no longer effective capitalists, whatever certificates they may have in their deposit boxes.

The regulation of production in Germany is no longer left to the market. What is to be produced, and how much, is decided, deliberately, by groups of men, by the state boards and bureaus and commissions. It is they that decide whether a new plant shall be built or an old plant retired, how raw materials shall be allotted and orders distributed, what quotas must be fulfilled by various branches of industry, what goods shall be put aside for export, how prices shall be fixed and credit and exchange extended. There is no requirement that these decisions of the bureaus must be based on any profit aim in the capitalist sense. If it is thought expedient, for whatever reason, to produce, for example, an *ersatz* rubber or wool or food, this will be done even if the production entails, from a capitalist point of view, a heavy loss. Similarly, in order to accumulate foreign exchange or to stimulate some political effect in a foreign nation, goods will be exported regardless of loss. A factory may be compelled to shut down, even though it could operate at a high profit. Banks and individuals are forced to invest their funds with no reference to their private and voluntary opinions about "risks" from a profit standpoint. It is literally true to say that the Nazi economy, already, is not a "profit economy."

The workers, on their side, are no longer the "free proletarians" of capitalism. Under Nazism the workers are, indeed, free from unemployment. At the same time they cannot, as individuals or through their own independent organizations, bargain for wages or change jobs at will. They are assigned to their tasks, and their labor conditions are fixed, by the decisions of the state bureaus and commissions. Millions of them are allotted to the vast state enterprises.

The minimum estimate I have seen (for 1939) gives the percentage of national income representing direct state activities as

50%. With the reduction in the area of private enterprise and the increase of state enterprise, goes also a corresponding reduction in the social position of the private capitalists. So far as control over the instruments of production goes, the capitalists are already near the bottom. As to income privilege: a recent estimate by a New York statistician gives as a mere 5% the share of the German national income going to profits and interest. This is a substantial reduction from the 1933 figures, in spite of a huge increase in the total national income, which, under capitalism, would normally be accompanied by a percentage increase in profits. In the United States, profits and interest are 20% of the national income, even excluding all so-called "entrepreneurial profits." Moreover, of the German capitalists' 5%, the greater part is appropriated by the state as taxes and "contributions." The statistics, however—which are, in any case, not reliable—fail to indicate the full meaning. The German capitalists *as capitalists* (not necessarily always as individuals functioning in other capacities), because of their loss of control over the instruments of production—a loss which leads progressively to their loss of legal ownership rights and of income—slip from their position as the ruling class in Germany. They become, more and more, simply tolerated pensioners, rapidly approaching social impotence.

This reduction toward impotence of the capitalists is accompanied by the rise of precisely the class which we found to be at the top in Russia: the managers, together with their bureaucratic and military colleagues. This is the class (in which some individual capitalists have found a place) that even today in Germany holds the largest share of control over the instruments of production, wields the effective power, and already is receiving the lion's share of the privileges. Even in Nazi law, the position of the manager is beginning to be openly recognized. For example, it is the *de facto* manager of a factory who has final say, subject to certain bureaus and state-controlled courts, about labor disputes—that is, has the right of controlling access to the instruments of production, and is backed by the state in that right.

How strange that it has not yet been remarked how seldom we find a manager among the voluntary or forced exiles from Nazi Germany! There are artists and writers among the exiles, ideologists and politicians, unassimilable foes of the new regime, storekeepers and professionals and teachers, and not a few capitalists, both Jews and Christians. But almost never a manager. It is strange that this has not been remarked but not strange that it is the case. For the managers realize that the society which is developing is *their* society.

In short, Germany is today a managerial state in an early stage. *Structurally,* it is less advanced along managerial lines than Russia; it retains as yet more capitalist elements. There is, we might almost say, a dual social structure at present in Germany. The managerial institutions and modes of operation are growing and expanding inside the still-existing cocoon of capitalism, which lingers as a protective coating and at the same time hides the life within. The direction counts; and the direction is toward the dropping of the remaining capitalist elements. But, though structurally less advanced, Germany is without most of those major weaknesses which we noted in the case of Russia. Its industrial and technological foundation is far stronger; the rising managerial class is much larger, better trained, more able. This is why Hitler had no qualms about the Russian Pact; he knew that, in the Pact, Russia was the minor partner.

Many commentators believe that they adequately sum up present-day Germany, including all those features of German society which I have been listing, by saying that "Germany has a war economy." In their dismissal of all problems with the help of this magic reference to a "war economy" there lies a whole series of grave misconceptions.

In the first place, we must realize that *all* economies are war economies. To suppose that a "war economy" is some special and peculiar kind of economy rests on the naïve assumption that war is something special and peculiar in the history of human societies. The truth is that war, up to the present and into the discernible future, is a normal and integral part of all human societies. All social groups—tribes, empires, city-states, nations including all capitalist nations—have made war constantly. The majority of the time (and this holds for all the capitalist nations) they have actually been at war, actually fighting some other group. When not fighting, they have been recovering from a previous fight and simultaneously getting ready for the next one. Our moral beliefs are such as to make us like to think that war is an "exceptional" type of event; the facts are that it is not. To say this is not to praise war or consider it a "good thing" but only to tell the truth.

It is ridiculous to say that Nazi Germany has a war economy and England and France do not, or did not. It was simply that Nazi Germany had a better, a more effective, war economy than her rivals; taking comparative material resources into account, a much better war economy. England and France won the first world war, and arranged the world in the way that they thought best suited their war aims. Before that war had ended, they began preparing for the second world war. No one noticed England sinking its fleet, razing its ocean bases, or France dropping universal conscription or building workers' houses instead of the Maginot line.

In the second place, it is not true that all "war economies" are alike. Calling a given economy a "war economy" tells us nothing. Societies prepare for and make war after the manner of such societies as they are. In wartime, perhaps, the social relations are drawn somewhat tighter; they are not fundamentally altered. A feudal society doesn't cease being feudal when it makes war—as the ruling class of feudal society did all the time, since it had hardly anything else to do. A capitalist nation doesn't cease being capitalist when it starts war; it fights its capitalist wars capitalistically. It is not even true that a democratic nation ceases to be democratic when it fights: Did England and the United States stop being democracies during the many wars they fought in the nineteenth century? They were capitalist democracies, and they fought as capitalist democracies.

If it is objected that "modern war is different," is "total war" and must be fought by "totalitarian methods"; then the answer is: Yes, modern war is indeed different, and the reason for this difference is that modern war is ceasing to be capitalist war. The first world war was the last great war of capitalist society. Already in that war, though to a less extent than is now remembered, the belligerent states found it necessary to modify their institutions sharply in order to carry on the war. The second world war is the first great war of managerial society. In this war the capitalist institutions no longer have a chance of winning. In order to win the war, these institutions must be transformed. This does not mean changing just "for the duration." It is war that decides the survival of social systems as well as of nations. The fact that the way to win wars is changing is only a phase of the larger fact that society as a whole is changing.

Third, we must observe that "war economies" are not only *war* economies. War is an integral part of social development in history as it happens; and therefore much more than just fighting comes as a consequence of, or in connection with, war measures. It may be an absurd and shocking waste that roads are built, transportation and communication expanded, more goods sold, inventions stimulated, houses constructed, in connection with preparing and fighting a war; but, as things are, this may be and often is the case. What we call things depends upon the interests we predominantly have with reference to them. If, in the light of our present chief interests and fears, we call the Nazi economy a "war economy," we might equally well, from other points of view, call it a "full-employment economy" or a "housing economy" that has built nearly 2,000,000 workers' houses or the "auto-speedway economy" or the "airplane economy." During the five years from 1933 (when Hitler took power) to 1938, German armament production increased 300%; but the production and distribution of the basic goods, such as food and clothing, upon which the real standard of living rests increased also, by a full third.[8]

Finally, it must be observed that, if one type of economic structure enables one nation to fight a war better than it can be fought with other types of economy, then all nations within the sphere of operations of the given nation—which today means the whole world—must adopt that type of economy. This may be regrettable, but it obviously follows. If fighting with guns is more effective than fighting with bows and arrows, and if economy A can produce lots of guns and economy B only bows and arrows, then the nation with economy A is sure to conquer the nation with economy B unless the latter nation adopts the A type of economy. If the managerial structure of economy is superior—as it clearly is—to the capitalist structure for war purposes, then for that reason alone, even if there were not, as there are, many other reasons, capitalist economy would have to give way, on a world scale, to managerial economy.

The *pattern* of the German way to managerial society is, in notable respects, different from the pattern of the Russian way. This difference in pattern is one of the chief of those factors which have obscured the identity in historical direction between the developments in the two countries. We saw that the Russian solution of the managerial triple problem goes roughly in the following order: (1) speedy elimination of the capitalists at home, together with the staving off of the capitalists abroad;

[8] One source for these figures is the Dec. 6, 1940 issue of the authoritative *United States News*. According to the *United States News*, the analysis of Nazi economic methods containing these figures was prepared for the study and use of the defense administration.

(2) the more gradual and drawn-out curbing of the masses under the managerial institutions; (3) the contests to come with rival sectors of the managers. The basic German pattern reverses the first two stages, which yields: (1) the fairly rapid curbing of the masses, in order to prevent a repetition of the Russian pattern and to forestall a break-through toward a free, classless society; together with the alignment of the masses under a managerial ideology and to an increasing extent under managerial institutions; (2) the more gradual reduction of the home capitalists to impotence, combined with direct onslaught against the capitalists abroad and the institutional bulwarks of world capitalism; (3) the contests to come with rival sectors of the managers.

The pattern of the German way thus permits the utilization of the capitalists in the curbing of the masses along managerial lines (the first stage), and then the utilization of the pressure of the masses for the reduction of the capitalists (the second stage). The managerial "curbing of the masses" does not mean only a physical terror directed against the masses. Physical terror is, in the long run, secondary to the job of winning the minds and feelings of the masses to a set of attitudes the consequences of which are the abandonment of both capitalism and the fight for socialism, and the acceptance of the managers and the institutions of managerial society. It was just here that the capitalists helped prepare for their own later ruin. Their support of the Nazis did block a repetition of the pattern of "the Russian way" in Germany: the masses were "curbed"; but the curbing was accomplished along lines that in the end are incompatible with the maintenance of capitalist rule and prepare only for the victory of the managers.

This apparently was suspected by the German capitalists, as indicated in the last paragraph of the quotation which I have cited above. Nevertheless, the action of the capitalists, or a section of them, in making what seemed to be an alliance with Nazism was probably justified under the circumstances. The only alternative was the Russian way. That would have meant drastic and rapid elimination. The Nazi way gave the capitalists a breathing space, was at least slower in tempo from their point of view. Bad as the chance was, it was at least better than the alternative. As it turns out, the chance was not good enough. The German way is slower—even now, after eight years, the German capitalists are not finished; but it is merely a slower death as against a quick one.

One other, and this a real, advantage accrued to the capitalists, not as a class but as individuals, from the German way. It gave some of them more opportunity, as individuals, to fuse themselves into the new order, to become managers as some feudal lords became capitalists. Thus, as individuals, they are able to survive the disappearance of their class, to take, in fact, their place in the new ruling class. This is exactly what the more vigorous and technically best trained of the German capitalists have been doing.

The pattern of the German way, like the Russian pattern, is capable of approximate repetition elsewhere. It was natural for Germany, holding, of all the great nations, the poorest cards in the capitalist deck, to be the first of the great nations to turn vigorously toward the new social structure; just as it was natural for France, England, and the United States, with the most favorable capitalist hands, to resist the turn most bitterly—why should they want to take the risk of a new deck when they are doing at least better than anyone else with the old? Germany, unlike Russia, had an advanced industry and technology, an advanced culture, and a large and trained body of managers. It is perhaps these factors that dictated the difference between the German pattern and the Russian.

The Nazi assumption of power, as we saw, swung Germany from the decadent stages of capitalism with increasing managerial intrusions into the initial stages of managerial society, with (at first, considerable) capitalist leftovers. Internally, Germany still remains in an early stage. However, it was impossible to complete the internal revolution without at once going over to the more grandiose external tasks of the managerial future. Excluding Russia from consideration here, Nazism gave Germany, we might say, a head start over the other great powers in getting ready for the managerial world system. As we noticed, the natural focus of one of the future super-states is the area of advanced industry in Europe. The German boundaries already, in 1933, included a big share of this area. The first great external political task was the extension of Germany's strategic base to cover, directly or indirectly, the entire European area of advanced industry, which automatically meant *de facto* authority over Europe as a whole.

In 1935, the extension began, with the victory in the Saar plebiscite. From that time on it has gone steadily smashing outward. The Nazi success, year after year, can only be explained by the ever-increasing weakness of the capitalist structure of society. Germany still retained much of capitalism, it is true; but her strength in relation to the other powers was derived, not from the capitalist elements in German society, which she shared with France and England, but from the managerial elements wherein she differed from them.

The first series of extensions of the base were achieved peacefully. The Saar, Austria, Czechoslovakia, Memel were incorporated. Unquestionably the Nazis were glad to avoid war. What had they to lose from the peaceful extensions? The Nazis would have gone on by peace; so long as the aims were reached, peace, or only minor fighting, was preferable. Finally, in 1939, capitalist France and England realized that the continuation of the process meant their death and that the process was going to continue. They had tried all means to avoid war, to hide from themselves what was happening. But Munich was of no more use than threats. Desperately, if any war was ever entered upon desperately, they took the field. The Nazis would still have been willing to win without fighting—why not?—or to fight only the easy Polish war. They thought, no doubt, that the announcement of the Soviet Pact might head off major war. And, after conquering Poland, Hitler again tried for a deal. But the issue for England and France was now plainly national and social survival, and they took the plunge. Germany had, of course, to accept the challenge.

The first part of the second world war, up to the fall of France in June, 1940, was in reality the continuation of the strategic extension begun in 1935. This phase, the consolidation of the European base, was completed with France's surrender. It is completed irreversibly and can no longer be undone whatever the outcome of the succeeding phases of the war, which are really other wars. This consolidation, fundamental to the world politics of managerial society, is not going to be dissolved, not even if the present German regime is utterly defeated. In fact, no one expects it to be, not even the English statesmen. The day of a Europe carved into a score of sovereign states is over; if the states remain, they will be little more than administrative units in a larger collectivity. Any attempt to redivide Europe would collapse, not in the twenty years it took the Versailles system to collapse, but in twenty months.

With the completion of the first phase of the war, Germany was naturally willing to have the war end. Again, why not? With the Continental base consolidated, England by itself would be economically and socially helpless, and would have to gravitate into the general European orbit. Therefore, after France's surrender, Hitler again offered peace and throughout the summer of 1940 was clearly trying for a deal with England harder than he was trying to conquer her by military means.

From the time of *Mein Kampf* onward, Hitler has recognized that a deal between Germany and England would be much more advantageous to the European super-state of the future than to have England conquered by Germany. With a deal, in which England would necessarily be subordinate, the tendency would be for the British Empire to keep attached to the European central area. In the course of the military conquest of England, most of the Empire tends to drop off to the spheres of the United States and the Asiatic central area. But the English capitalists weighed the costs and decided to keep on fighting.

Thus the second phase of the war, really a second war, goes on as I write. In this phase, with most of the strategic European base consolidated, the effect is to wreck capitalists and capitalist institutions abroad—in the first instance, the British Empire, greatest and most typical capitalist institution. Interestingly enough, this phase thus begins before the task of reducing the German home capitalists to impotence is finished. Such over-lappings are common in history.

The general outcome of the second war is also assured. It is assured because it does not depend upon a military victory by Germany, which is in any case likely. The hopelessness of the position of the British capitalists has been shown from the beginning of the second world war by the fact that they have absolutely no peace plans ("war aims"). During the first year and a half of the war, their spokesmen did not even pretend to be able to formulate war aims. If they finally make some sort of statement, it will be empty of all meaningful content. They cannot have war aims (peace plans) because there is no possible solution on a capitalist basis. England, no matter with what non-European allies, cannot conceivably hope to conquer the European Continent; and could no longer run the Continent if she could conquer. Revolutions on the Continent, even if they should get rid of the Hitler regime, cannot benefit England. Nor could they repartition Europe into independent, fully sovereign states. The same general result would follow them as a Hitler military victory: the consolidation of the European strategic base, with England compelled to integrate into it. Military ups and downs, mass revolts, can alter the time schedule for this general outcome, can mean more or less chaos in the intervening period, but there is no prospect of its being essentially changed.

But the consolidation of the European central area does not end the world political process. There remain the contests with the other sections of the managers—with Russia as we have already seen, and the struggles among the European, the Asiatic, and the American centers for their respective shares in the rest of the world. Though the perspective of these wars stretches into the future, their first actions are already beginning, overlapping the second phase of the second world war. By the end of 1940 it was clear that the focus of the war was shifting, that the result of the European struggle was in fundamentals decided, and that a new, third, phase was beginning wherein the mighty opponents of the future—the three political structures based on the three central areas—were undertaking their first trials of strength. The voice of Chamberlain, Churchill, Bevin, and England was giving place to that of Roosevelt and the United States. These wars of the developing super-states will not end with the end of this war. Their result, we have noted, is sure to be inconclusive, since none of the three central areas can firmly conquer any of the others. But they will be fought nonetheless, and in them the disposition of the rest of the world will be decided, and redecided.

In a war such as started in September, 1939, we may plainly observe the social-revolutionary effect of the war process. Considering the war from the point of view of Germany, this revolutionary effect is threefold. In the first place, the Nazi armies carry the new and revolutionary ideas and institutions into the lands they conquer. Sometimes this is done by the direct imposition of these ideas and institutions upon the conquered peoples. But it also operates by contagion, or as a semivoluntary consequence of military defeat, as in France. Second, the opposing nations discover that they can compete in war with Germany only by going over more and more, not merely to the same military means that Germany uses, but to the same type of institutions and ideas that characterize German society. This somewhat ironic relation holds: the surest way, the only way, to defeat Germany would be for the opposing nations to go over, not merely to institutions and ideas similar to those of Germany, but still further along the managerial road than Germany has yet gone. For, just as the strength of the German war-making machine is derived from her managerial, noncapitalist elements, (combined with her advanced productive plant), so are her weaknesses in war-making the result chiefly of the remaining capitalist elements.

Third, the war process speeds up the revolution inside Germany itself. In general, wars speed the tempo of the social tendencies which are present, but more leisurely, in peacetime. In the case of Germany now this is plainly apparent: the war-making means the still-greater extension of the state throughout the economy; the still-faster cutting off of the arena of private enterprise; the still-further reduction to impotence of the already fatally undermined private capitalists; the still-deeper reliance upon the managers and their bureaucratic and military colleagues as the only ones who can run the state; the still-sharper penetration of the managerial ideologies. The direction is well marked by the increasing "radicalization" of Hitler's speeches as the war continues.

The developments which have already taken place and those which may be confidently predicted for the near future exclude a reversal of the social direction which has been established in Germany. Germany, and with it the rest of Europe, are leaving capitalism behind, and moving toward the managerial structure of society. They are not going to shift back again. Capitalism is not going to be restored, but on the contrary what is left of capitalism is going to be eliminated. British and American capitalists may dream of a docile new Weimar Republic or of a friendly German monarchy or of a Europe pulverized into an even greater number of even smaller states than were left under Versailles. But the dream is absurd on the face of it. It couldn't work even in the 1920's. How infinitely less a chance is there for it to work in the '40's!

The German capitalists also, no doubt, dream of a restored capitalism in Germany. If Germany is definitively victorious in the war, they presumably hope for a restored "liberty," with unchecked rule, power and privileges once again securely in their hands. Even some of the Nazi politicians, perhaps even Hitler himself, have some such perspective as this. But it is too late; too much has happened. The servants have outgrown the masters. The institutions and the ideologies have been too profoundly altered. The managers and their allies know that they can wield the power, have been wielding it—why should they give it up? And the masses would not permit the reversal of direction. The road back to capitalism would mean, as the masses would see it, going back to the unemployment, the humiliations, the confusions, the moral and social pointlessness of 1932. However hard the lot of the masses under Nazism, they can see hope only further along the road that has been taken, not in a return. If the Hitler regime will not continue on this road, will not complete the reduction of the capitalists to impotence and the elimination of the leftovers of capitalism, then it will give way to a new regime, a regime differing from Hitler's not by being capitalist but by being a more matured representative of the managerial future.

Two events of recent years, secondary in themselves, have been striking symbols of the fact that the social revolution in Germany cannot be reversed. The first was the retirement of Schacht from the front rank; the second, the exile of Thyssen. Schacht was not a big capitalist in his own right. He was a trained and expert representative of the capitalists. For the first years of Nazism, he continued as a capitalist representative, trying no doubt to guide events along the lines envisaged by the capitalists in the quotation I have given earlier in this chapter. The new regime welcomed him and used him. Then the revolution went beyond Schacht. Perhaps he, like the purged Russians, would have been willing to fuse himself into the managerial order. But, also like the Russian trials and executions, his virtual retirement was a ritualistic act in recognition of the dying of the old regime. Thyssen, on his side, was one of the biggest capitalists and prior to 1933 the leading supporter of the Nazis from among the big capitalists. The exile of Thyssen, and his subsequent renunciation of Nazism, signifies the recognition by German capitalism of the error in their original hope that Nazism could be the savior of German capitalism, their understanding that Nazism is merely a variant pattern in the liquidation of capitalism.

None of this means, of course, that the revolution will be stabilized on the present Nazi lines. Present-day Nazism is, as all our previous discussion will have shown, a primitive stage of the managerial development of society. With the consolidation of the managerial social structure on a world scale, Nazism will fade into hardly recognizable forms. But the direction is established. Nor is the "Germany" of today the final type of the state of the future. What will emerge, as we have seen, will be a super-state based upon the European area of advanced industry. The Germany of 1933 and of now is the nuclear first stage in the development of that super-state.

XVI

THE FUTURE OF
THE UNITED STATES

DURING THE past year or more, the doctrine of "isolationism" has been swinging out of public favor in the United States, and the isolationist politicians have become almost a laughingstock when they are not denounced as Fifth Columnists. As so often happens, however, sentiment has been changing for the wrong reasons.

The usual argument is conducted over what might be called *military* isolationism, over the problem whether the United States can be successfully invaded by a foreign power. So far as the military dispute goes, the isolationists are in all probability correct. It is not a question of a few sporadic bombing or submarine raids, or even brief armed forays into a few sections of the country—any foreign nation with enough nerve could accomplish these. But the definite conquest of continental United States by a foreign armed force is excluded for the discernible future. The oceans remain adequate barriers: whoever began to have doubts should have had them quieted by witnessing what trouble twenty miles of Channel caused the most powerful military machine in the history of the world.

Nor can the idea of stage-by-stage conquest, from bases first established in South America, be taken any more seriously. Suppose a section of a foreign army did occupy a base in Brazil, for example. It could be inconvenient, true enough. However, a modern army doesn't fight with coffee beans and tropical plants. The only areas which can supply the needs of a modern army are the three central areas of advanced industry, in Europe, Asia, and the United States. The managers are indeed skillful, but they are not magicians enough to turn Brazil into a rival area of advanced industry in a month or a year or a decade.

The fundamental problem of isolationism is hardly touched on by either side in the public dispute. This is the question not of military but of *social* isolationism. In connection with the social problem, most of the anti-isolationists share the opinions of their isolationist opponents: and both are one hundred per cent wrong. From a military standpoint, the continental United States remains, by and large, isolated from any serious threat from the rest of the world. From a social standpoint, the United States is linked unbreakably with all the rest of the modern world. Its ability to keep going depends upon its relations to the rest of the world. The same general social forces are at work in the United States as in the rest of the world. Geographical isolation and the incomparable material advantages which the United States has had in the past delay slightly the development of these social forces; but they are operating here as surely as everywhere else.

If we review what has been happening in the United States during the past ten or fifteen years, we find the same long-term factors that we have noticed in the case of the other great powers: the factors, namely, that are involved in the dissolution of capitalist society and the growth of the managerial structure of society. The United States, certainly, has not escaped mass unemployment nor permanent agricultural depression nor colossally growing debt nor idle capital funds nor the inability to utilize technological possibilities. If the reduction in the area of private enterprise in the total economy is as yet behind that in Russia and Germany, the tendency and direction are no less unmistakable. As in other nations, the reduction is twofold in character: an ever-greater percentage of enterprise is conducted outright by the state, and to an ever-firmer extent the rest of enterprise is subject to state controls.

In the United States, very conspicuously, the great private capitalists have been withdrawing from direct contact with production, traveling from direct supervision of the instruments of production to finance to occasional directors' meetings to almost complete economic retirement. By this course, they give up, more and more, the *de facto* control of the instruments of production, upon which social rule in the end rests. Correlatively, more and more of the control over production, both within the arena of private enterprise and in the state, goes into the hands of the managers.

In the United States, as plainly as everywhere else, the capitalist ideologies lose their power to move the masses. And in the United States the political-structural changes proceed in managerial directions with most evident and rapid speed.

This is not all. Already in the United States, the tendency away from capitalism and toward managerial society has received a specific native ideological and institutional expression. This expression, suited to an earlier stage in the process than that reached in Russia or Germany, is the "New Deal," which we have surveyed in some of its ideological aspects.

We must be careful not to identify the New Deal and New Dealism with Franklin Roosevelt and his acts. Roosevelt is a brilliant and demagogic popular politician, who did not in the least create, but merely rides when it fits his purposes, the New Deal. The New Deal sprang from the inner structural drives of modern society, the forces that are operating to end capitalism and begin a new type of social organization, the same forces which at later stages and under different local circumstances produced the revolutions in Russia and Germany. The firmest representatives of the New Deal are not Roosevelt or the other conspicuous "New Deal politicians," but the younger group of administrators, experts, technicians, bureaucrats who have been finding places throughout the state apparatus: not merely those who specialize in political technique, in writing up laws with concealed "jokers," in handing Roosevelt a dramatic new idea, but also those who are doing the actual running of the extending government enterprises: in short, managers. These men include some of the clearest-headed of all managers to be found in any country. They are confident and aggressive. Though many of them have some background in Marxism, they have no faith in the masses of such a sort as to lead them to believe in the ideal of a free, classless society. At the same time they are, sometimes openly, scornful of capitalists and capitalist ideas. They are ready to work with anyone and are not so squeamish as to insist that their words should coincide with their actions and aims. They believe that they can run things, and they like to run things.

It is important to insist that Roosevelt is not the New Deal in order to understand unambiguously that the direction represented by the New Deal is in no way dependent upon Roosevelt. In the general development, his presence or absence does not make 10% difference.

With the advent of the New Deal, the rate of those changes, to which we have so often referred and some of which I have just listed, quickened. State intervention really got going. The percentage of the national income accounted for by direct governmental enterprises doubled in five years. A substantial percentage of the population became directly or indirectly dependent upon the state for livelihood. State controls of a hundred kinds extended throughout the economy. Agriculture became wholly dependent upon state subsidy and control. Export and import regulations increased, moving toward the monopoly state control of foreign trade characteristic of the managerial state. Private control over capital funds was curtailed by acts governing the issuance of and trading in securities, and the structure of holding companies. Money left its "free" metallic base to become "managed currency" under the direction of the state. In utter disregard of capitalist-conceived budgetary principles, the state permitted itself annual deficits of billions of dollars and used the national debt as an instrument of managerial social policy. Tax bills were designed to secure social and political ends, rather than income. The state, through various agencies, became by far the greatest banking establishment. In general, measure after measure curtailed capitalist private property rights and thereby weakened the relative social power of the capitalists. In the United States the same shift occurred which had begun earlier on a world scale. The expansion of capitalist relations in the total economy was replaced by a continuous and growing contraction. The percentage of the economy subject to capitalist relations, whether measured in terms of outright ownership and operation or of degree of control, began to decrease at an ever more rapid rate.

The managers, in the governmental apparatus and in private enterprise, flourished while the capitalists lamented among themselves about "that man." Congress, with occasional petty rebellions, sank lower and lower as sovereignty shifted from the parliament toward the bureaus and agencies. One after another, the executive bureaus took into their hands the attributes and functions of sovereignty; the bureaus became the *de facto* "lawmakers." By 1940, it was plain that Congress no longer possessed even the war-making power, the crux of sovereignty. The Constitutional provision could not stand against the structural changes in modern society and in the nature of modern war: the decisions about war and peace had left the control of the parliament. Time after time this last fact was flung publicly in the face of Congress—by the holdup of the *Bremen,* the freezing of foreign balances in accordance with policies never submitted to Congress, the dispatch of confidential personal emissaries in the place of regular diplomatic officials, the release of military supplies and secrets to belligerent powers, outstandingly by the executive trade of destroyers for naval bases and by the provisions of the "lend-lease" plan (and by all that these two acts implied). The parliament had so far lost even its confidence that it did not dare protest.

The New Deal is not Stalinism and not Nazism. It is not even a direct American analogue of them, for the New Deal is far more primitive with respect to managerial development, and capitalism is not yet over in the United States. But no candid observer, friend or enemy of the New Deal, can deny that in terms of economic, social, political, ideological changes from traditional capitalism, the New Deal moves in the same *direction* as Stalinism and Nazism. The New Deal is a phase of the transition process from capitalism to managerial society.

There has been a mystery about the New Deal which has often puzzled and dismayed old-fashioned liberals, like Oswald Garrison Villard, who have on the whole enthusiastically supported it. The New Deal, as against the "Tories," the Republicans and the "right wing" of the Democratic party, has certainly seemed to be the "liberal," the "progressive" side. Nevertheless, on a number of important and symptomatic issues, it was the Tories and Republicans who were lined up against the New Deal in defense of what was historically without doubt the "liberal" point of view. Such was the relationship, for example, in connection with the Supreme Court "packing" proposal, where the New Deal position was unquestionably directed against liberal and democratic institutions. So also in the case of the original executive reorganization plan, which was a heavy blow against parliamentary democracy; and again in connection with the attitude of New Dealers like Ickes and Roosevelt himself toward the press, or the whole question of a third term. So, indeed, in the case of many other of the New Deal measures, if their true significance had been realized. On these issues, it was the Republicans and Tories who were, apparently, defending liberty. Many of the Villard type of liberal found themselves compelled to desert for the moment the New Deal standard, and to line up with the Tories.

How is this mystery, this paradox, to be explained? It is usually dismissed without much thought. The New Deal "attempts to encroach on liberty" are held to be well-meant but dangerous mistakes. The Tory defense of liberty is passed off as mere sham and camouflage. However, mistakes and shams and paradoxes of this sort do not happen in serious politics.

Here, also, it is the job of a correct theory to get rid of mysteries; and from the point of view of the theory of the managerial revolution the paradoxes of the New Deal easily dissolve. The fact of the matter is that the New Deal's liberalism and progressivism are *not* liberalism and progressivism in the historical meaning of these terms; not, that is to say, *capitalist* liberalism and progressivism. Its progressivism, if we wish to call it that, consists of the steps it takes toward managerial society. Some of these steps have a surface resemblance to those traditionally advocated by capitalist liberalism. It was through this surface resemblance that the New Deal was able to take the genuine liberals, who are perpetually confused about the meaning of politics, into camp. But many of the New Deal steps are just the contrary of capitalist liberalism; and the historical direction of the New Deal as a whole runs entirely counter to the ideals and aims of liberalism. Some of the older generation of liberals, who are more principled and less adaptable than the younger crowd, finally woke up to this in 1940, and, like Villard himself, quite logically supported Willkie in the Presidential campaign.

There is nothing sham or hypocritical about the Republican-Tory defense of "liberty." The liberty in question means, in reality, *capitalist* liberty. Historically and today the Republican party is the authentic representative of capitalist liberty and capitalist progressivism. These it is trying to defend, without success, against the New Deal onslaught. The Republican party, let us remember, was born in the social crisis that culminated in the Civil War. It is not the Republicans but the world that has changed.

The New Deal has simultaneously been undermining capitalist institutions (and thus the social position of the capitalists), making easier the rise of the managers, and curbing the masses along lines adapted to the managerial future. How can this be denied when one abandons high-flown theories and looks at what has happened during the New Deal years? Can anyone pretend that during the New Deal years the capitalists and capitalist institutions have become socially stronger, the managers (including especially the managers in government) thrust into the background, the masses made more enthusiastic about capitalist institutions and ideologies? The very contention would be absurd.

The New Deal has curbed the masses along lines adapted to the managerial future, in the first place ideologically, by using a propaganda that weakens confidence in the basic ideas and slogans supporting capitalist institutions, and popularizing ideas and slogans suited for the transition to the managerial structure. And the New Deal has further curbed the masses by tying the popular organizations closer and closer to the state. This development is characteristic of the managerial revolution in all nations. It is strikingly illustrated in the United States by the history of the labor movement during the New Deal period.

The older section of the mass labor movement, the A. F. of L., has traditionally, in keeping with the "limited state" principle of capitalism, been careful to preserve a large measure of trade-union autonomy, to avoid close tie-ups with the state apparatus, to rely on independent bargaining power just as private capitalists strive to keep independent status on the market. This policy was continued unchanged by the A. F. of L. during the first five or six years of the New Deal. The C. I. O. was a product of the New Deal period. For several years, it was, on the one hand, favored, almost sponsored, by the government; and, on the other, it moved always toward integration with the state. Everyone knows the intimate relations that were in force between the C. I. O. and the National Labor Relations Board. The C. I. O. formed Labor's Non-Partisan League as a political arm, and the League was, in effect, part of the New Deal political movement. The C. I. O. functioned prominently and openly in the

1936 presidential campaign, and in numerous state campaigns. More recently the New Deal government has been restoring a more general balance by withdrawing special favors from the C. I. O. in order to bring the labor movement as a whole, including the A. F. of L., into closer relations with the state apparatus. The A. F. of L., as a result, is abandoning its traditional stand-off policy. Moreover, the history of the New Deal relations with farmers' and consumers' organizations parallels the labor movement tendencies. The examples of Russia and Germany have already taught us that the early forms of managerial society require fusion of the popular organizations with the state. The bureaucrats in charge of the popular mass organizations, in fact, take their places among the managers. This tendency, like the other managerial tendencies, is conspicuous in the New Deal.

We must not, furthermore, neglect the significance of the capitalist opposition to the New Deal. After the first two years, when hardly anyone saw clearly what was happening, the capitalists have been overwhelmingly opposed to the New Deal. In the 1936 elections, probably three-quarters or more of the bona fide capitalists were against Roosevelt. In 1940 the figure must have been above 90%, and there was not even a handful of big capitalists supporting Roosevelt. Orthodox Marxists are very hard put to it to explain this simple and undoubted fact. They are compelled by their theory to say that Roosevelt and the New Deal represent capitalism and the capitalist class. Why, then, are almost all capitalists against, apoplectically against, Roosevelt and the New Deal? This, apparently, must be partly hypocrisy and partly because the capitalists "do not understand their own interests." What a pitiful way out of a theoretical difficulty! And what a weak insult to the capitalists, who number among themselves not a few very intelligent persons!

A correct theory cannot toss aside so revealing a piece of evidence as the almost united capitalist opposition to the New Deal. The simplest explanation which can cover the facts is here, as always, the best. This explanation is merely that the capitalists oppose the New Deal because they realize, without being wholly clear about the full problem, the truth: that the New Deal is in direction and tendency anticapitalist.

The capitalists, unfortunately for themselves, do not, however, have any program of their own to offer in place of the New Deal. They can only, as Landon did for them in 1936 and Willkie in 1940, repeat the traditional capitalist symbolic ritual of "liberty," "free enterprise," "the American way," "opportunity," "individual initiative." They repeat it sincerely, as their fathers repeated it before them. But the ritual has lost its meaning and its mass appeal. In order to reach any sort of audience, the capitalist spokesmen must accompany it by protestations that they accept most of the New Deal "reforms"—they have nothing indeed with which to counter them—but dislike its "methods." Such a dislike does not constitute a convincing program, as Landon and Willkie discovered.

The 1940 presidential election—which may well have been the last regular presidential election in the history of this country, or, at most, the next to last—was a symbolic landmark, a guarantee of the course of the future. The united capitalist efforts and resources, united as never before in United States history, could not elect their man. Those who represented, however incompletely and primitively, the managerial world current, carried the field easily and confidently. It was amusing to read the complaints of the hysterical New Deal type of liberal hanger-on that the Willkie backers were "evading the Hatch Act," spending $20,000,000 or $30,000,000 on the campaign and using the services of the "biggest advertising agencies." They forgot, somehow, that the New Dealers had at their disposal every day more money than the largest sum they estimated for the entire Republican campaign; that they had all the other resources, direct and indirect, of the mighty state power; and that the New Deal propagandists were modeling their techniques on the methods of the European managerial politicians, not relying on the outworn rules for selling soap or perfume. The Willkie backers, in truth, as Willkie's own conduct on election night so eloquently witnessed, never knew what hit them. They did not understand what it meant to be up against, not a country squire from Dutchess County, but the rising tide of a world social revolution.

* * *

The beginning of the second world war, the first formative war of managerial society, found the United States unprepared to fill the role which opened up for her in the new historical era. Everyone knows that the United States was not adequately prepared in a military sense. Many are beginning to suspect, what is much more important, that the United States is not socially prepared, does not have a social structure able to cope with the tasks of the future. Wars, however, have the general habit of speeding up the rate of social change. When society is, as at present, already in a process of major transition—that is, in a period when the rate of social change is unusually rapid—the effect of war is especially dynamic. That this is the case with the second world war, no one will deny.

The natural perspective which confronts the United States follows from the world political problem that we have discussed. Within its own continental boundaries, the United States includes one of the three central areas of advanced industry. The United States thus constitutes naturally the nucleus of one of the great super-states of the future. From her continental base, the United States is called on to make a bid for maximum world power as against the super-states to be based on the other two central areas. For her to try to make this bid is hardly a matter of choice, since survival in the coming world system can only be accomplished by the expansive attempt. For the United States to try to draw back into a national shell bounded by the forty-eight states would be fairly rapid political suicide. Suicides are committed by nations as well as by individuals. But there is not the slightest reason to suppose that the United States will accept suicide. On the contrary, it is sure that she will make her bid.

The general problem for the United States is very much the same as Germany's, only on the whole considerably easier. First, there is the consolidation of the main strategic base. In Europe this consolidation meant smashing the Continental political system. In the Americas, most of the base is already included within the boundaries of the United States. Consolidation therefore reduces itself primarily to internal measures, to strengthening internal "unity" and co-ordinated efficiency.

Next comes the protective extension of the base with the aim of making it invulnerable for defense and convenient for attack. This, in current terms, is the policy of "modified hemisphere defense," to draw a ring around all of North America and northern South America. The second stage is already well advanced. It was prepared for by the series of Pan-American conferences and agreements and by what is propagandistically referred to as the "Good Neighbor Policy." It has gone forward through such measures as the establishment of air lines throughout Latin America, the visits of warships and war planes, the projection of the Pan-American Highway, the strengthening of the Panama Canal, reciprocal military agreements with Latin-American nations, the defense alliance with Canada which in effect subordinates Canada's sovereignty to the United States, and the deal with Britain which secured outlying bases in the Atlantic. Naturally, this stage will not stop with these moves. It will issue in a situation comparable to what Hitler aims at in most of Europe: the *de facto* elimination of independent sovereignty in all nations and colonies of the area except the United States, and thus the creation of a single interrelated territory so far as *de facto* political sovereignty goes. There is every reason to suppose that this stage will be successfully accomplished.

The third and grandiose stage, which, though it has already begun for the United States, will extend many decades into the future, and for which the first two stages are preparation, is the bid for the maximum of world power against the claims of the European and Asiatic central areas. The United States is forced to begin this third stage before the preparatory first two stages are finished.

The first great plan in the third stage is for the United States to become what might be called the "receiver" for the disintegrating British Empire. (We are not, of course, interested in the propagandistic terms that are used in current references to this action.) The attempt is to swing the orientation of the Empire from its historical dependence on Europe to dependence on and subordination to the American central area. Success in the case of the English Dominion (Canada) and possessions located in the Americas is already at hand—in fact, Canada really swung into the United States orbit some years ago. There are obstacles to the plan, however, in the case of the more distant parts of the Empire. Many of these fall more readily into the orbit of the Asiatic or European areas than into the American; and it is to be therefore doubted that the plan can be wholly carried through.

We see here, again, why Hitler has always preferred a deal with England to conquering her completely. A deal with England gives the best legal as well as military groundwork for keeping the vast Empire territories attached to the European central area, whereas in the process of the annihilation of England, the Empire tends to swing toward the American area.

Along with the United States' receivership plan for the British Empire go still broader aims in connection with the rest of South America, the Far East (including conspicuously the Far Eastern colonies of formerly sovereign European states) and in fact the whole world. The struggle which has begun is the world struggle of the super-states of the future. This struggle, as I have remarked, is bound to be inconclusive. No one of the three central areas is able to conquer definitively the other central areas, and therefore no one state power can in fact rule the world. This will not, however, prevent the struggle from taking place. And, besides, there *will* be periodically decided just how much of the world will fall within the spheres of each of the super-states. I have outlined in Chapters XII and XV the general forms of the wars and conflicts that may be expected.

This, then, is the course set for the United States. It, too, is not a question of personal speculation: the United States has already embarked on this course, and is plainly going to persist in it with whatever deviations and interruptions. Roosevelt's speeches, from the time of the Dayton, Ohio, "hemisphere talk" during the campaign, express the perspective more and more openly. This perspective for the United States follows from the general perspective of world politics in managerial society. But the perspective is for *managerial* society, presupposing managerial social organization for the chief participants. And the United States is not yet a managerial state.

The capitalist social structure cannot hold its own in these scheduled conflicts. This we have seen in many ways, but we may review here certain evidences that are even now clear in relation to the United States and the specific problems which the United States faces.

In the first place, capitalism cannot hold its own economically against managerial economic organization. This has been shown, in fact and by analysis, in connection with South America. The capitalist institutions, still prevailing in the United States, have proved themselves unable to handle the economic side of the South American problem. It is not *profitable,* in the capitalist sense, to integrate South America into a super-state dominated by the United States; and yet extension into such a super-state is a necessity for the political survival of the United States. Almost all able economists in this country are lately agreed that capitalist institutions, "private initiative," will not hold up against the controlled managerial methods in an economic battle over South America. The South American problem is no different from the problem of the rest of the world.

Nor can arming (not merely the building of armaments, but their co-ordinated use) be adequately done under capitalist institutions. Adequate arming—that is, adequate, for the tasks imposed, against rival arming—also is no longer *profitable* to capitalism. This, as I have noted, has been shown by the examples of France and England, who were not able to arm adequately—though they certainly realized what was at stake—under their capitalist institutions. It is being discovered by the United States during the course of the experiences of the second world war. The armament program just doesn't seem to get going properly.

It would be very superficial to attribute the trouble to the evil will of capitalists who own the armament industries or to trade unions or to the incompetence of officials. It is not ill will or incompetence, though these also, as under any system, are often present, but the institutions of capitalism that make the obstacles —owners who must have an adequate profit in order to expand and keep going, autonomous and independent trade-unions with the right to strike, price changes under the influence of market conditions, capital funds at the disposal of private individuals, a governmental structure too limited in scope and too little co-ordinated. In the debates over "excess profits" and "amortization allowances," over plans to "conscript" industry and to establish compulsory priorities and price controls, over the propriety of strikes in armament plants, there spreads the growing shadow of this fundamental problem; nor will that shadow be withdrawn. This does not mean that capitalist institutions are not still capable of very considerable armament efforts; enough, no doubt, to forestall for some years the resolution of the problem in the United States. But the efforts will prove, before so very long and perhaps most bitterly for many, not enough.

Third, capitalist institutions and the ideologies affiliated with them are no longer capable of arousing adequately the popular morale, a by-no-means secondary part of the task for the future. This I have already commented on, and discussed in relation to the failure of voluntary military enlistment, as well as to the passivity with which conscription is accepted. It is further stressed by the inability of capitalism, in this case United States capitalism, to get rid of the Fifth Column. The Fifth Column can be got rid of, not by any conceivable number of G-men, but only when the ideologies and methods that call it into being can be challenged by at least equally effective ideologies and methods.

From these considerations we may conclude once again that the United States will shift more and more, and more and more rapidly, toward the managerial social structure. This is not a startling conclusion. It does not mean any shift from the historical direction of the past decade but, on the contrary, merely a deepening of the tendency already established. Thus the initial world struggle, begun openly in September, 1939, will gradually merge into the world conflict among the rival sections of the managers.

It might seem that certain events of the past year argue against this analysis. Roosevelt, it might be argued, has been granting "concessions" to capitalists in order to help "national defense" along. Granted that the New Deal is managerial in tendency, do not these concessions show that the effect of the war is to bring a reversal back toward the strengthening of capitalism?

It is true that some concessions to capitalists have been made—though we should remember that there have been other concession periods in the New Deal history (as there have been in Nazi history), and that, in any case, Roosevelt is not identical with the New Deal. It may even be true that these might bring about a temporary relative strengthening of the social position of the capitalists and capitalist institutions, though Willkie, as spokesman for the capitalists, scarcely seemed to think so. But the further effects of the war preparations, the wars, and the between-war interludes that are coming guarantee that the concessions will prove illusory. Modern total war is not profitable for capitalism, and consequently capitalism cannot adequately fight it. This was really proved by the first world war, which was unprofitable, as has often been shown, for the victors as well as for the vanquished. This was not the case with the earlier wars of capitalism, which were almost always profitable for the victors and often for the losers as well. Indeed, the unprofitableness of the first world war was an important demonstration of the fact that it was the last great war of capitalism.

As a matter of fact, there are cruel catches in any concessions which might seem to have been made to the capitalists. Perhaps, though the stock market is not very optimistic, they permit larger profits. We have seen, however, that *de facto* control over the instruments of production, rather than a privileged share in the national income, is decisive in the long run. The constant effect of the war measures, even of the apparent concessions, is to decrease the control exercised by private capitalist owners. The weight of control is shifted toward the managers, in and out of government, along with their bureaucratic and military colleagues. In the first world war, armament production was run as a private preserve of the capitalists. As the Senate munitions inquiries proved, billions of dollars were siphoned off into capitalist pockets through the autonomous War Industries Board, headed by the finance-capitalist, Bernard Baruch. Even the name of the new agency—the Office of Production Management—is symptomatic. It is headed by William Knudsen, who, though closely affiliated through his past with the capitalists and no doubt in his own mind a firm believer in capitalism, is nevertheless by training and experience a production man, a manager. Moreover, the OPM, unlike the War Resources Board, is firmly anchored within the state apparatus.

In all probability, the unions will be prohibited, either by statute or agreement, from strikes in armament industries—which can be interpreted to mean nearly all important industries. Though such a prohibition will doubtless be welcomed at first by the private capitalists, it will not mean that the unions will be left to the unchecked mercy of the capitalists. The managers will have other plans for the control of the unions, as of the industries. In general, the concessions will in the end turn to dust in the capitalist mouths. The further development of the war preparations, the economic world conflicts, and the wars, will prove in practice that success in none of them can be won along capitalist lines. When that proof is plain enough, the country will go over to definitive managerial structure.

It will be seen that I take herein for granted that the United States will be in the war. This, also, is not much of a speculation. By earlier standards of the meaning of war and peace, the United States has been in the second world war almost from its start. As I write, the United States armed forces are not being killed; but for this as yet the strategy of the present war has no need. Factories making belligerent airplanes in New York or New Jersey or California are as much a part of the total war machine as those located in Coventry or Southampton or Manchester. Warships and planes in preventive patrol of the western Atlantic or the Far East are part of the warring fleets, even if the immediate circumstances of the war dictate that they shall not be fired on.

The line between war and peace in the contemporary world is not so formally drawn as it used to be. From the point of view of historical development, and in terms of social effects upon this as upon other nations, the United States is in the second world war. Indeed, by the end of 1940 it was correct to say that the United States had become one of the two major belligerent powers in the world conflict. Even though England was carrying the brunt of one side of the actual fighting, it was clear that her role had become, as it was bound to become, secondary to that of the United States. If this stage of the war continues without an interruption through a peace arrangement between England and Germany, it is plain that the United States will join the war in all respects during 1941. An interruption, however, would change only the time schedule, for the world political problems remain. In that case, formal war participated in by the United States, the opening stages of the battle of the three central areas, will begin in a comparatively few years.

* *
*

The *pattern* of the United States way to managerial society is, from all evidence so far, closer to the German than to the Russian pattern. This is to be expected from the closer similarity in general social circumstances: the United States, like Germany, has an extensive and advanced industry and technology, a culture which though probably not as advanced as the German is far above the Russian, and a large, able, and trained group of managers already existing.

There are, however, as is also to be expected, differences between the United States pattern and the German. For one thing, the solution of the first two parts of the managerial problem—the reduction of the capitalists to impotence and the curbing of the masses along managerial lines—has up to now developed more gradually in this country than in Germany. This slower pace has been no doubt due to the more favored position, from almost every point of view, that the United States has enjoyed under the capitalist world system. But a far more important difference lies in the relation of the war to the decisive crisis that swings the nations from capitalist dissolution definitely into the managerial road—the crisis which the United States has not yet reached. Germany made the break six years before the second world war began. It is in the midst of war itself that the United States crisis develops. The United States way is the war way. In order to take its place in the new era of world politics now opening up, in the new type of economic conflict and the wars that are an integral part of the new era, the United States will be compelled to go over to the managerial structure. Thus the United States must meet all three parts of the managerial problem—the reduction of the capitalists, the curbing of the masses, and the competition with the other sections of the managers—more or less at once, instead of by the rather clearly separated stages that we noticed in the Russian and German ways.

Already, in the case of the United States, just as with the rest of the world, we may conclude that the direction toward managerial society is irreversible. Capitalism, in the United States as elsewhere, fights a losing battle. Every apparent victory the capitalists win leaves them only weaker, for their base is being constantly sapped. The next few years, war and near-war years, will thrust them always further back. A peaceful interlude, during which they might hope to regain their full rights and privileges, will find too much changed in the major institutions and relations of society to permit a return.

Even if a return were institutionally possible, neither the managers nor the masses would permit it. Why should the managers and their bureaucratic-military allies accept a return that would thrust them back into the servant quarters? They are servants who are learning to speak with the voice of the master. And, as in Germany, a return would present itself to the minds of the masses as the road back toward everlasting mass unemployment and bread lines, social meaninglessness, a lack of ideological perspectives. Therefore, however harsh the lot of the masses, they will choose to solve their problem by further advance along the managerial road, not by a return. If the governmental regime then existing attempts the return, that regime will be overthrown, and another, welded to the managerial structure, will be put in its place.

There remains a further and, humanly, most important question. In the case of the United States, will a revolutionary mass movement, and the terror and purges that accompany such movements, be part of the managerial development as they have been (and will be) in Russia and Germany? Historical precedent and an analysis of present conditions do not make possible an assured answer. There have been instances of social revolutions carried through without revolutionary mass movements and without a major terror: in particular, when these revolutions, as will be the case for the United States in the present world revolution, are socially similar to what has already been carried through, with the aid of mass movements and terror, in other localities. Some sort of mass movement is undoubtedly required in the United States. The experience of the New Deal suggests, however, that it may be possible to create such a movement officially, we might say—from above, from the government itself; in fact, such a movement already exists, at least in primitive form, within the New Deal forces. The development of such a movement need not be at all the same as that of those movements which grow up apart from and opposed to the government and "law and order." Given such a course, and granted reasonable good will and sufficient clarity about what is happening in the world, it is even possible that the United States could accomplish the transition to managerial society in a comparatively democratic fashion.

Nevertheless, though this now seems possible, it is the less likely variant. There is not much clarity, and there is so much for social groups to lose, and to win. The capitalists are to lose all, or nearly all. The masses, during the course of the transition, will lose the hopes of a free, classless society which the circumstances of revolutionary transition will stimulate in them. There will be much struggle for places in the new ruling class. Revolutionary mass movements, terror, purges, are usual phases of a major social transition. Societies do not seem willing merely to change the old. At some stage they seem to wish to smash it, at least symbolically. It is more likely than not that these more strenuous features, also, will be included in the United States way.

XVII

OBJECTIONS

I AM WELL aware that the conclusions reached in this book will be displeasing to most of those who read it. Nevertheless, denunciation of the book, or of its author, will have no bearing upon the truth of these conclusions, if they are true. Denunciation may persuade people not to *believe* what the book says. But truth is a function, not of belief, but of evidence.

The aim of propaganda is to persuade people to accept certain ideas or feelings or attitudes. The aim of science is to discover the truth about the world. The propagandistic aim is usually best served by being thoroughly one-sided, by presenting only what is favorable to your case and suppressing all that might weaken it and bolster your opponent. As Hitler remarks in one of his shrewd chapters on propaganda, you don't sell your brand of soap by pointing out that a rival brand is really just as good.

In the case of any hypothesis which is under consideration, science, in contrast to propaganda, is always anxious to present all the evidence, for and against. The scientific aim is just as well served by proving a hypothesis false as by proving it true. This book, though faulty in execution, is scientific in its aim. I have no personal wish to prove the theory of the managerial revolution true. On the contrary, my personal interests, material as well as moral, and my hopes are in conflict with the conclusions of this theory.

If there is evidence against the theory of the managerial revolution, I wish to take it into account as fully as the evidence for it. I have, during the course of the book, tried to include a discussion of negative evidence in appropriate contexts. I wish to return to it in this final chapter. I do not pretend to be at all complete in listing possible objections, since that would be outside my present scope. In this book I have had to restrict myself primarily to the formulation of the theory of the managerial revolution; a comparison between it and rival theories; a general outline of its meaning and content and the evidence for it; and a somewhat more specific application of it to the problems of world politics, of Russia, Germany, and the United States.

There is a peculiar difficulty in giving due weight to the evidence against the theory. This arises from the fact that, so far as I know, the theory of the managerial revolution has never up to now been systematically formulated. Consequently, no one has yet had an opportunity to disprove it, if it can be disproved. I have been compelled to assemble negative evidence as well as positive. However, there have been presented, though somewhat roughly and incompletely, many of the elements of the theory as well as recognizably similar theories using the term "bureaucratic" rather than "managerial" revolution. And these theories of a bureaucratic revolution have been argued against. I shall make further reference to the arguments in what follows.

In estimating the weight of the evidence against the theory of the managerial revolution, we must keep in mind an obvious principle of scientific method. To disprove the theory, it is not enough to show that it is not 100% certain, that difficulties confront it, and certain evidence seems to be against it. It must be further shown that it is *less* certain than alternative theories covering the same subject matter, that there are in its case *more* difficulties, *more* negative evidence than in the case of at least some one alternate theory. No theory about what actually happens and will happen is ever "certain." It can never, whether in the field of physics or history or anything else, be anything except more or less probable on the evidence. If a given theory is more probable than any alternative theories on the same subject, then that is all that can be required; and, from a scientific point of view, we must accept it. The theory of the separate creation of biological species is not made scientifically acceptable by showing, as it can be shown, that there are serious difficulties with the biological theory of evolution. The theory of evolution is more probable than the theory of specific creation in spite of the difficulties. The theory of the managerial revolution will not be disproved merely by showing, as it can be shown, that difficulties confront it; it will have also to be shown that fewer difficulties confront some alternative hypothesis—in particular, either the theory of the permanence of capitalism or the theory of the proletarian socialist revolution, for variants of one or another of these include all the alternatives which have, so far, been seriously put forward.

It is possible to object to the *formulation* of the theory of the managerial revolution. Objections of this kind are to be expected on opposite grounds: from some, that it is too vague; from others, that it is too precise.

The theory is too vaguely formulated, it may be said, because it doesn't include any exact "mathematical laws," any precise dates, any rules for calculating stock prices next Tuesday. Now there is no doubt that the theory is vague, in this sense, compared to theories in the physical sciences. This vagueness, however, is a comment not so much on this theory as on the relatively undeveloped stage at which sociological science today rests in general. With the exception of a few very limited ranges of their subject matter, the sociological and historical sciences have not yet reached even the level that the physical sciences held in ancient Greece. When we find elaborate mathematical laws in books about the general development of history and societies, we can be sure either that the authors are fooling themselves or that the alleged laws are false or empty. As Aristotle long ago wisely mentioned, it is a mark not of intelligence but of ignorance and pedantry to expect more accuracy in a field than the field is capable of.

The theory of the managerial revolution is vague but not too vague to be significant. The test for the empirical significance of a statement is whether that statement and the deductions that may be drawn from it make any difference, any observable difference, as compared with other statements dealing with the same subject matter and the deductions that may be drawn from them. Most metaphysical and religious statements, such as "all things are ideas" or "God created the world," are not empirically significant because it doesn't make any observable difference whether or not they are true. Most general theories of world history, like causal theories holding that destiny or God or economic relations or what not are "responsible" for everything that happens historically, are not significant, because, again, it doesn't make any observable difference whether or not they are true. But Boyle's Law of Gases is significant, because observable differences in the behavior of gases under varying pressures and volumes may be expected logically to follow from its truth or falsity.

If we compare the theory of the managerial revolution with the theory of the permanence of capitalism or the theory of the socialist revolution, then it is plain that all three theories are significant: that is, it is plain that it makes an enormous amount of observable difference which of the three is true. The world that we will shortly live in will be a very observably different place if the theory of the managerial revolution is true rather than the others. Altogether different expectations and predictions, in most spheres of social life, follow from the three different theories.

The theory of the managerial revolution is, indeed, more precise than this book suggests. Here it was necessary, because of the novelty and complexity of the subject, to present what is little more than a general outline. And month-by-month predictions do not have much point anyway in a book, where many months intervene between the writing and publication. It is, however, possible and easy to make specific probable predictions on the basis of the theory, more specific than the many predictions I have included, and to test the theory further with their help.

Objections on the ground that the theory is too precise will probably be more frequent than those based on its vagueness. Many people seem to be offended by definite statements about what is going to happen in human history; it is felt to be a kind of sacrilege. They say: Nobody really knows what is going to happen. They prefer to think that it is "all accident" or "God's will." This attitude is partly a reflection of the primitiveness of sociological sciences to which I have referred. It is true that these sciences are not very helpful guides. But the attitude has an even deeper root: people, for the most part, do not want to know what is going to happen; and, above all, the ruling groups in society find it advantageous to keep knowledge about what is going to happen in society from developing and extending.

If politicians say before election that they are not going to lead the country into war and then go to war after election, it is obviously more advantageous to them to have people regard this as an unfortunate accident, or punishment, than to have it realized, when the pre-election promise is given, that, in spite of the words, going into war is a predictable consequence of what is being done. Naturally a capitalist does not want it believed that mass unemployment is a predictable consequence of the maintenance of capitalist institutions under present-day circumstances. Unemployment, also, is to be considered an "accident" or "exception." Nor do the managerial ideologues wish to have it publicly pointed out in advance that their proposals will bring, not peace and plenty and freedom, but a new form of class rule and exploitation.

Nevertheless, the general methods of the social sciences can be no different from those of the other sciences, and the same type of results can be obtained. We try to arrange our data in an orderly manner; and, on the basis of past experience, we make probable predictions about the future. If we don't yet know society as we know the solar system, we yet do know, if we want to, something about it; and, as in the other sciences, we can know at least some things, with some degree of probability, *before* they happen. Because it lets us know what is probably going to happen before it happens—that, after all, is why scientific knowledge is worth having.

I conclude, therefore, that the formulation of the theory of the managerial revolution is adequate. I recognize, however, that the formulation can be greatly improved and clarified, and I hope that others more skilled than I in these matters will so improve and clarify it.

The more important objections are those that may be made not to the formulation of the theory but to what it says, to its content. Two of these have been advanced in criticisms of the similar theory of the bureaucratic revolution. This latter theory, insofar as it has been stated, agrees with the theory presented by this book in holding that it is false that capitalism is going to continue and false that socialism (in the sense of a free, classless, international society) is going to replace capitalism; the theory agrees also with much of our account of the structural features of the new society now developing, especially in the case of the economic institutions—the differences in the account of the political structure, which are considerable, need not concern us. But the theory of the bureaucratic revolution maintains that the ruling social class in the new society, the class with power and privilege, will be, exclusively, the "bureaucrats": that is, the politicians in the narrower sense, those who carry out the "nonproductive" functions of political administration, diplomacy, policing, and fighting.

A sharp criticism has been made of this view on the ground that the bureaucrats are not capable of constituting themselves an effective and stable ruling class in society. Social rule, it is argued,

depends on *de facto* control of the instruments of production—
the means whereby society lives; and such control can be held
only by some group which plays a direct and integral role in
production. The bureaucrats have no such role. They can achieve
a temporary semblance of dominance in society only under
exceptional and brief circumstances of social confusion, when
they are able to utilize for their own purposes the conflicts
among other classes in society which do have a direct role in
production. The bureaucrats, it might be said, balance for a while
on a kind of social tightrope between the major social classes.
In such a way the bureaucracy under Napoleon III of France
gained a brief independence and dominance by playing French
capitalists and peasants and workers off against each other. So,
in our own day, have the bureaucracies in Russia and Germany
been able to do, for a brief while: in the former case, jockeying
between the Russian workers and peasants, in the latter, between
the German capitalists and workers. But, so the criticism runs,
such a state of affairs cannot last. The weight will have to fall,
sooner rather than later, to one of the great social classes directly
functioning in social production. When it does, the bureaucracy
will have to swing with it and lose all measure of social independence.

This criticism, upon examination, may be seen to be weak
even in relation to the theory of the bureaucratic revolution,
and without any validity in relation to the theory of the managerial revolution.

The criticism is largely based upon a widespread misunderstanding of contemporary "bureaucracies" which amounts to a
confusion between them and the bureaucracies of a few generations ago. In the old days, it could be plausibly stated, as it was,
that the functions of the political bureaucrats were "nonproductive" (Veblen included them in the "leisure class")—though the
view even then was only partly true, since production as men
actually carry it on includes diplomacy and war and political
administration and policing. The state, then, as we have so often

insisted, was strictly limited in its sphere of activities; production was, for the overwhelming part, carried forward outside the state sphere. Under such circumstances, the bureaucracy could not have been, and was not, the ruling social class, in spite of superficial appearances. The ruling class was the capitalists, who controlled production. The bureaucracy, by and large, represented the capitalists and, on the political field, acted in their interests.

The contemporary bureaucracies, above all in those states which have moved furthest toward the new social structure, are functionally a quite different group from the old bureaucracies. The new bureaucrats are not merely concerned in production; they are directing, in all nations already, the biggest enterprises; and, through various types of control, they have their hands in almost all enterprises. Moreover, as we saw, even the bureaucrats still primarily occupied with "government" in the narrower sense are applying to their tasks the techniques and methods taken over from modern industry and science and invention. It is a ridiculous caricature to think of the modern bureaucrat—as many still think of him—in terms of the fussy, briefcase-carrying incompetent whom we read about in nineteenth-century novels. This caricature lies back of the criticism that the bureaucracy is incapable of becoming a ruling class.

When we correct the "bureaucratic theory" by the "managerial theory's" demonstration that it is not the bureaucracy, conceived in any narrow sense, but the managing group which is becoming the ruling class in society, the criticism falls wholly. The managers are certainly concerned directly in production: indeed, the development of modern industry places them in the *key* positions of production even *before* the transition to managerial society takes place. Before the managerial structure is consolidated, the managers function throughout enterprise, both private and governmental. With the consolidation of the managerial structure, which includes the state monopoly of all important enterprise, the position of the managers is assured. To a large extent, as we saw, the managers and the bureaucrats fuse into a single

class with a united interest. Far from being incapable of constituting a ruling class, the managers, by the very conditions
of modern technology and contemporary institutional evolution,
would have a hard time avoiding rule. Just as the struggle of
the capitalists against the feudal lords was largely won before
the open stages of the struggle began, so too is the struggle of
the managers already fairly well decided in the initial period
of the transition, before men realize explicitly that the struggle
has started.

It is perhaps worth remarking that there is an interesting piece
of psychological evidence for the assured social position of the
managers. The managers—these administrators, experts, directing
engineers, production executives, propaganda specialists, technocrats—are the only social group among almost all of whose
members we find an attitude of self-confidence. Bankers, capitalist owners, liberal politicians, workers, farmers, shopkeepers—
all these display, in public and private, doubts and fears and
worries and gloom. But no one who comes into contact with
managers will fail to have noticed a very considerable assurance
in their whole bearing. They know they are indispensable in
modern society. Whether or not they have thought it out, they
grasp the fact that they have nothing to fear from the immense
social changes speeding forward over the whole world. When
they begin to think, they get ready to welcome those changes,
and often to help them along.

A second criticism which has been directed, chiefly by Marxists, against the "bureaucratic theory," runs as follows: The
"solution" of the major problems confronting modern society
"requires" the elimination of capitalist private property in the
instruments of production. This the bureaucrats (for which we
may read "managers") are able to carry out. But elimination
of private property is not enough. If society is not to be destroyed,
national states must also be eliminated, and world political unity
established. This the bureaucrats (managers) are unable to do.
On the contrary, they gain power with the help of a nationalism

even more extreme than capitalist nationalism, and thus lay the basis for an unending series of wars.

It may be noticed that this criticism, if valid, would not in the least, as the Marxists imagine, go to show that socialism is coming. It would only indicate that complete chaos, the destruction of all organized social life, is coming.

However, the criticism is not valid. In the first place, the nationalist ideologies of the managers are misunderstood. The nationalism is a device for social consolidation, the effectiveness of which has been well proved by experience. It is, however, a device of great flexibility, and one which can be modified as need arises. It is, as Germany and Russia and Japan have certainly proved, not at all incompatible with the breaking down of existing national boundaries. Germany, consolidating initially to the tune of "the German fatherland" and "the German folk," easily extends this to "Europe and Europeans" or to "the Aryan race" or to "workers" or anything else that proves convenient. Extreme Japanese nationalism dovetails neatly with a pan-Eastern ideology and practice. The present rise of extreme United States nationalism is not exclusive: it fits itself in readily with the "hemisphere policy," and it will have no trouble getting outside of the hemisphere.

Second, the managers *can* "solve" the problem of *capitalist* nationalism, are, in fact, busily engaged in solving it. Capitalist nationalism means a comparatively large number of independent, sovereign national states. The managerial structure is moving to break this political system forever, and to substitute for it a small number of great sovereign areas: the "super-states," as I have called them.

It is true that this managerial "solution" is not according to the Marxist formula and that it will not yield a unified single world state. It is true also that it will lay the basis for many wars, just as wars are part of the process of arriving at it. But there is no one or nothing, except ideal formulas, that "requires" the "logical solution" of one world state and no more war.

History is not a theorem of geometry or a game of chess, both of which proceed according to ideal rules that we impose upon them. There is no evidence that men adopt those historical solutions which seem "logical" to a calm mind of good will; and there is plenty of evidence that men fight wars and will continue to fight them. The capitalist-nationalist political system has, during the past generation, become unworkable and is on its way out. The new world political system based on a small number of super-states will still leave problems—more, perhaps, than a unified single world-state; but it will be enough of a "solution" for society to keep going. Nor is there any sufficient reason to believe that these problems of the managerial world system, including the managerial wars, will "destroy civilization." It is almost inconceivable even what it could mean for civilization—that is, some form of complexly organized society—to be literally destroyed. Once again: what is being destroyed is *our* civilization, not civilization.

A different kind of criticism of the theory of the managerial revolution has, and will, run as follows: You conclude that society is changing to a new structure of class rule, exploitation, wars, and, for some time at least, tyranny. But you neglect what most people want, what they feel and hope for, what they will do. Why should they put up with such a perspective? If they want peace and plenty and freedom, they will sweep aside your managers and managerial institutions and anything and everyone else that stand in their way.

I would be the last to deny the historical importance of what people want and feel and hope for. I have not the slightest sympathy with any theory of historical "mechanism" or "determinism" which pretends that human wishes and thoughts and wills have nothing to do with the historical process: it is, it seems to me, perfectly obvious that human wishes and decisions and hopes are an integral causal part of the historical process.

But a correct historical theory also takes into account what people are probably going to wish and hope and decide. Human wishes and decisions are themselves part of the world of actual events; and, as with other events, on the basis of the experience of them in the past we infer what they will be like in the future. When, on the basis of experience, I know a man's character, I can have a fairly good idea, in advance, of what he will probably say and want and do under varying circumstances; even more fully in the case of social groups can we know with some probability beforehand what they will do, granted such and such a situation. Everyone knows just about what a football crowd at a big game will eat, drink, feel, shout, and hope; and grounds-keepers and hot-dog salesmen plan successfully on the basis of such foreknowledge.

If most people did indeed want peace, plenty, and freedom from all forms of exploitation and tyranny; and *if* (what is just as necessary, though less often remarked) they also *knew* the means whereby these were to be got; and *if* they were willing and courageous and strong and intelligent and self-sacrificing enough to bring about those means to those ends; *then* no doubt the world would achieve a society organized in such a way as to realize peace, plenty, and freedom. But there is not any evidence at all from past or present history that all three (and all three would be required) of these conditions will be met. On the contrary, the evidence of the analogies from the past and the circumstances of the present is that people will act and wish and hope and decide in ways that will aid in the managerial revolution, in the carrying through of the social transition which will end in the consolidation of managerial society.

This last criticism, about the "human factor," reduces to a more general fallacy: When we deal with the problems of history we usually misread them in terms of what we hope instead of understanding them as the evidence dictates. And I suspect that most objections to the theory of the managerial revolution will be found to rest on hopes, not on evidence.

Clarity about what is happening in the world has been blocked in recent times by unexamined acceptance of one or the other of the two assumptions which we have so often noticed: the very naïve assumption that capitalism is the only possible form of human social organization because it is somehow a part of eternal human nature; or the more common assumption that in modern times capitalism and socialism are the only possible alternative forms of social organization. Not only do these assumptions prevent us from knowing what the future is to bring; they compel us, more and more during the past two decades, to distort and twist our understanding of what is happening before our eyes.

The second of these assumptions, merely by being stated, disposes of the first. The theory of the managerial revolution, as soon as it is formulated, disposes of both so far as *assumption* goes. Instead of assumptions, we are left with three theories, hypotheses about the future: that capitalism will continue; that capitalism will change into socialism; that capitalism will change into managerial society. The problem is, then, which of these three theories is the most probable on the evidence? That will be the theory which we must believe, if we wish to be rational, quite apart from what, if anything, we may decide to do about it. On the evidence so far available, I see little doubt that the theory of the managerial revolution is the most probable.

There will be those who will find in this a renewed proof of what they will call the essential tragedy of the human situation. But I do not see with what meaning the human situation as a whole can be called tragic, or comic. Tragedy and comedy occur only *within* the human situation. There is no background against which to judge the human situation as a whole. It is merely what it happens to be.

Lightning Source UK Ltd.
Milton Keynes UK
UKOW05n0029200317

297040UK00004B/19/P

9 780837 156781